## BY SQUADRON LEADER CLIVE ROWLEY MBE RAF (RETD), FORMER OFFICER COMMANDING THE RAF BATTLE OF BRITAIN MEMORIAL FLIGHT

**T**he Second World War witnessed a titanic struggle for control of the air in a global arena. In the end, Allied air power proved to be decisive. It brought the economy which sustained the enemy's war efforts to virtual collapse, it denied the enemy freedom of movement, it provided direct air support to troops on the ground and it helped to turn the tide overwhelmingly in the favour of the Allied ground forces in all the various theatres of the war.

The Royal Air Force fought in every major theatre of the war, from Europe to the Far East, and contributed hugely to the final victory. The RAF fights entirely with machines. For the RAF, its aircraft and the technology that supports its operations were, and are, at its core. When Britain declared war against Germany on September 3, 1939, the RAF fielded approximately 1000 fighter aircraft, with almost 150 of those being obsolete biplanes.

At the end of the war in 1945 the RAF had over 9000 aircraft on charge, of which almost half were fighter types. These fighter aircraft were used in many varied roles additional to the air-to-air/air defence/air superiority functions that most people expect. They were also used for ground-attack, close air support, fighter reconnaissance and many other specialist and disparate tasks.

Not only did the Second World War create an aircraft industry that could turn out thousands upon thousands of aircraft, it also acted as a catalyst for technological leaps in aircraft design and performance which re-cast the nature of air warfare. The improvements in aircraft capabilities and performance, not least with the fighter aircraft of the time, advanced at a rate which is difficult to comprehend today and which has never been matched since. Although final victory in the Second World War could never have been achieved without the human element – the men and women who designed and built the aircraft, and then maintained, repaired and flew them – the aircraft themselves were vital.

In this bookazine, renowned aviation artist Chris Sandham-Bailey profiles many of those RAF fighter aircraft, from various theatres of the war, which were the cutting-edge hardware of the day. Chris's beautiful, detailed artwork is much in demand for aviation magazines, not least those published by the Battle of Britain Memorial Flight. His meticulous research and attention to detail lead to aircraft profiles of incredible accuracy and authenticity, as this publication bears out.

During the 11 years in which I was privileged to fly the historic fighters of the RAF Battle of Britain Memorial Flight I was able to experience what it is like to fly Hurricanes and Spitfires of Second World War vintage, some of them with amazing wartime pedigrees. Surely every pilot's and enthusiast's dream! I was able to revel in the delightful handling of the Spitfires and the rugged toughness of the Hurricanes, and I was allowed to glimpse what it was like for those who did this 'for real' in far more dangerous circumstances than I faced. I am left with an indelible impression of the brilliance of the aircraft designs, a passion for the aircraft themselves and most of all a deep respect for those who operated and flew them.

Colour images of wartime RAF aircraft are rare. I hope that you will enjoy seeing them in full colour in Chris's profiles and that, as you revel in the details, you will remember those who used these machines of war to defend our freedom, many of whom paid the ultimate price.

*Clive Rowley*

# RAF WWII FIGHTERS CONTENTS

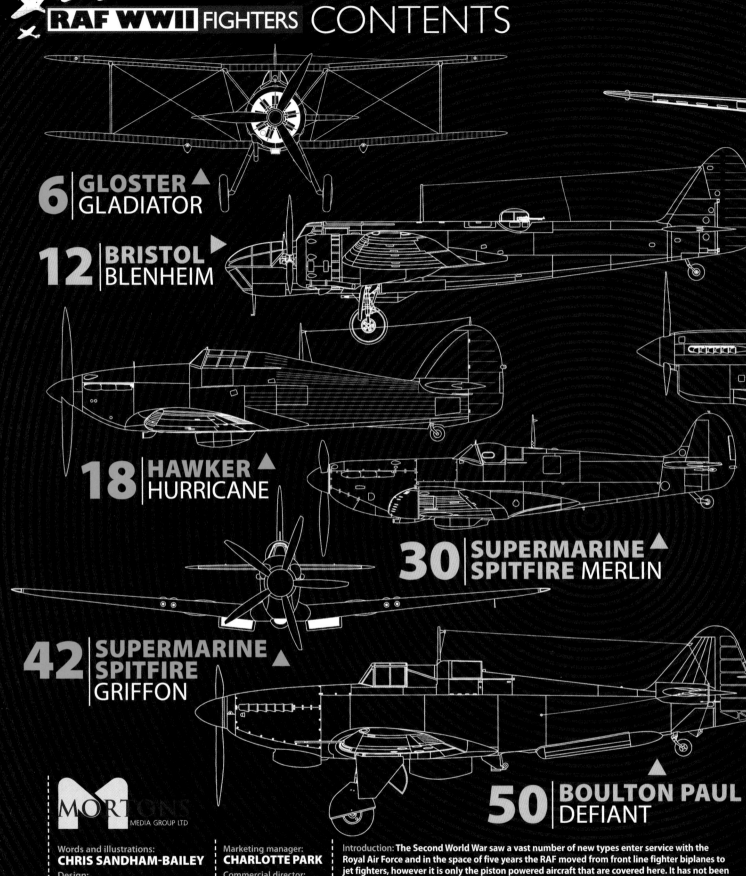

**6** GLOSTER ▲ GLADIATOR

**12** BRISTOL ▶ BLENHEIM

**18** HAWKER ▲ HURRICANE

**30** SUPERMARINE ▲ SPITFIRE MERLIN

**42** SUPERMARINE ▲ SPITFIRE GRIFFON

**50** BOULTON PAUL ▲ DEFIANT

**MORTONS** MEDIA GROUP LTD

Words and illustrations:
**CHRIS SANDHAM-BAILEY**

Design:
**GARETH WILLIAMS**

Publishing director:
**DAN SAVAGE**

Publisher:
**STEVE O'HARA**

Reprographics:
**JONATHAN SCHOFIELD & PAUL FINCHAM**

Production editor:
**DAN SHARP**

Marketing manager:
**CHARLOTTE PARK**

Commercial director:
**NIGEL HOLE**

Published by:
**MORTONS MEDIA GROUP LTD, MEDIA CENTRE, MORTON WAY, HORNCASTLE, LINCOLNSHIRE LN9 6JR.**

Tel. **01507 529529**

Introduction: **The Second World War saw a vast number of new types enter service with the Royal Air Force and in the space of five years the RAF moved from front line fighter biplanes to jet fighters, however it is only the piston powered aircraft that are covered here. It has not been possible to cover in detail any of the aircraft featured; books covering the Spitfire alone run into the thousands and the number of squadrons using some of the types was vast. Where possible, RAF squadrons are represented but some other Commonwealth squadrons which operated under the RAF have been included. Instead of covering any topic in detail this publication is intended to provide a broad overview of each type giving a brief history and a range of variants and markings.**

Thanks: **James Bentley, Ronnie Olsthoorn, Marc Teclenborg, John Smith, Barry Wallond, The People's Mosquito, Clive Rowley and the BBMF, Dan Sharp and Heather.**

Printed by: **William Gibbons and Sons, Wolverhampton**

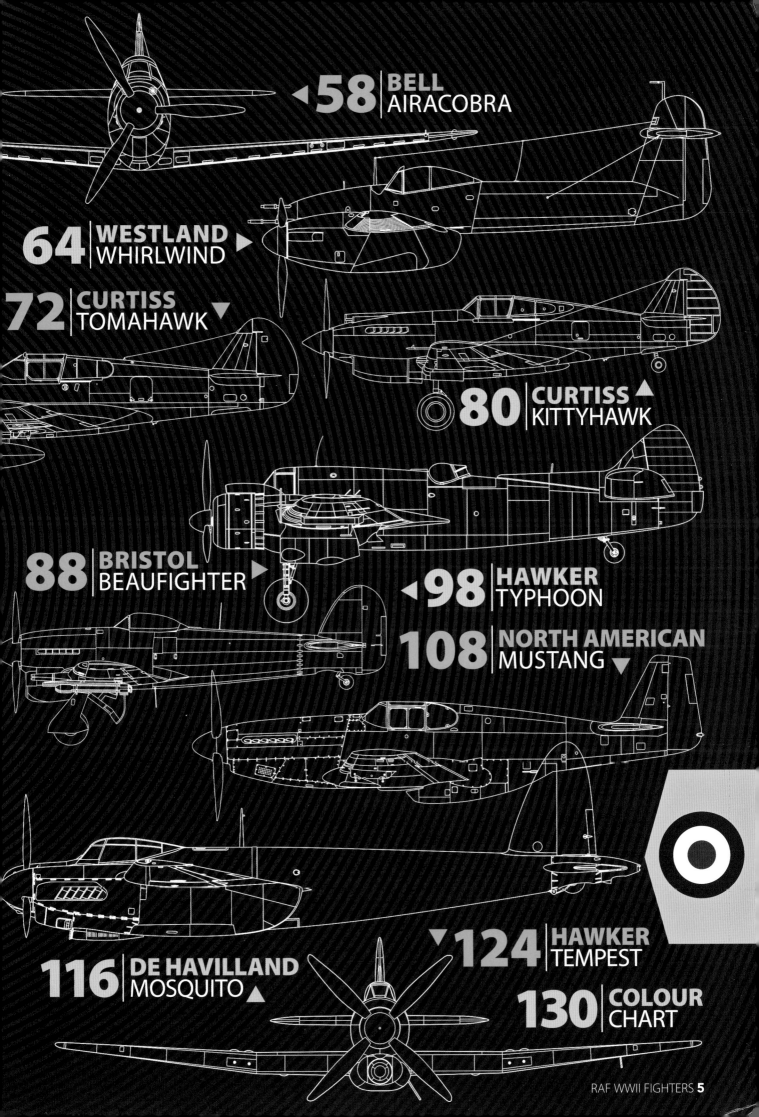

◄ **58** | BELL
AIRACOBRA

**64** | WESTLAND ►
WHIRLWIND

**72** | CURTISS ▼
TOMAHAWK

**80** | CURTISS ▲
KITTYHAWK

**88** | BRISTOL ►
BEAUFIGHTER

◄ **98** | HAWKER
TYPHOON

**108** | NORTH AMERICAN
MUSTANG ▼

**116** | DE HAVILLAND
MOSQUITO ▲

▼ **124** | HAWKER
TEMPEST

**130** | COLOUR
CHART

# GLOSTER
## GLADIATOR

When the Gladiator was first conceived it was at the cutting edge of aviation, although the potential of monoplanes was already becoming apparent and these would very quickly make the Gladiator obsolete.

**1936-1944**

**T**he Gladiator entered service during a period of air pageants when tight precise formation flying was a highly respected skill (on occasions multiple aircraft were tied together for the duration of the display) but such was the need for aircraft when war came that it was forced to compete against advanced monoplanes until suitable replacements could be produced and delivered to units.

The biplane was pressed into service in the Middle East and Mediterranean for the first two years of the war, the three Sea Gladiators of Malta becoming legends in their own time when defending the island.

During the interwar years the Gloster Aircraft Company had continued to supply the RAF with a range of biplanes such as the Gamecock, Goshawk and Gauntlet. The main advantage these had over earlier fighters was their metal structure, a concept that the company's chief designer Henry Folland had been keen to promote. The open cockpit fighters performed well but there was a constant need for faster aircraft that could intercept fast bombers, prompting the Air Ministry to issue Specification F7/30 in 1930. This called for a fighter with a maximum speed of 250mph at 15,000ft, a landing speed of 50mph and fitted with four guns. Several companies including Bristol, Hawker and Supermarine expressed an interest, however Gloster was not initially among them due to Gauntlet production taking up much of the company's resources. Revisions to the Gauntlet design by Folland led to an aircraft that could be a suitable contender for F7/30. The Bristol Mercury engine was retained but the wings were refined to strengthen them, the undercarriage was altered so it no longer required supporting struts or wire bracing, a large cooler was also

role and fitted with the Mercury IV it first flew on September 12, 1934, with F/Lt Sayer in control. Upgrading to the Mercury VI produced a top speed of 242mph, still short of the required 250mph but it was adequate. The following April the prototype received the serial K5200 and was sent to A&AEE for evaluation.

Folland continued work on the design and introduced a sliding closed-canopy cockpit. The Mercury was yet again upgraded to the IX and on July 1 the S.S.37 officially became the Gladiator. As events continued to move towards war on the continent, the Air Ministry became more clearly aware of the pressing need to rearm the RAF and placed an initial order for 23 examples in July, followed by another order for 120 in September to equip 14 squadrons, with deliveries commencing in 1936.

72 Squadron based at RAF Tangmere was the first to receive the Gladiator in February 1937 having just been re-formed. It is interesting to note that by the time it entered service the biplane was already obsolete, the Hurricane having flown in late 1935 and the Spitfire in May 1936. These were still a long way from front line service though so the Gladiator would fill the role until then.

## GLOSTER GLADIATOR MK.II N5682 HP-K 247 SQUADRON

247 Sqn, based at RAF Roborough, was the only unit to operate the Gladiator during the Battle of Britain. Flown by Sqn Ldr Peter O'Brien. The squadron replaced its Gladiators with Hurricanes in December 1940.

fitted to the outside of the starboard fuselage. The Gauntlet had two guns fitted in the fuselage so the two extra guns were mounted in pods fitted under the lower wings.

Despite being a late contender it was a timely entry as none of the other entries were able to meet the requirements; the Westland F7/30 only managed a top speed of 146mph and both Hawker and Supermarine had begun focusing on their new advanced monoplane designs. The latter two would not be ready until 1937 at the earliest and an interim solution was still required.

The Gloster S.S.37 was chosen to fill this stopgap

A few weeks after 72 Squadron, 3 Squadron took delivery of their first three Gladiators, followed by 80 Squadron who would continue to operate the Gladiator until March 1941, a move to the Middle East shortly after receiving the Gladiators being a major factor in their continued use. Deliveries continued during the next two years and eight squadrons were eventually equipped with Gladiators, with some aircraft being sent on to other squadrons. A total of 38 RAF squadrons eventually used the aircraft, this does not include the 23 Fleet Air Arm squadrons or the Met and training flights which also used Gladiators in a variety of roles.

As the number of Gladiator squadrons increased it was becoming clear that the aircraft could still be improved. A yet more powerful version of the

DURING THE PHONEY WAR THEY SAW LITTLE ACTION ALTHOUGH UK-BASED SQUADRONS DID INTERCEPT LUFTWAFFE AIRCRAFT DURING THE WINTER

Mercury was available – the VIIIA – which was the first to have a manual boost option and provided a new top speed of 257mph. The instrumentation in the cockpit was upgraded and the Vokes filter was added to those operating in the hotter climates. Trials by A&AEE using K7922 with both the two-bladed wooden Watts propeller and three-bladed metal Fairey-Reed propeller were undertaken, once in service the three-bladed prop was primarily used on the Mk.II but during service they were interchangeable.

With the outbreak of hostilities, the British Expeditionary Force was sent to bolster French defences and Air Chief Marshall Hugh Dowding was reluctant to risk any of the new Spitfires, foreseeing a need to keep them in reserve for the defence of Britain should France fall, but the Gladiators were considered expendable so 607 and 615 Squadrons joined the BEF at Merville on November 15, 1939. During the Phoney War they saw little action although UK-based squadrons did intercept Luftwaffe aircraft during the winter, 263 and 152 Squadrons both engaging the enemy.

To further stretch resources, 263 Squadron was sent to Norway in response to the German invasion on April 18, 1940. Flying from Filton to Scapa Flow, they were based on HMS *Glorious* which departed two days later. Upon arrival they operated from a frozen lake and were later joined by 18 more Mk.IIs to make up for the losses sustained. During the retreat 10 of the pilots landed their Gladiators along with the Hurricanes of 46 Squadron back on HMS *Glorious* following a final patrol on June 7. The next day the carrier and her escorts were sunk by the *Scharnhorst* and *Gneisenau*.

In the May of 1940 the two squadrons based in France were involved in heavy action during the Blitzkrieg and withdrawal of British forces. On May 10, 607 Squadron claimed seven before breakfast. Some Gladiators were lost in combat but a sizable number were destroyed on the ground when Vitry-En-Artois was bombed. The survivors were then destroyed by the British themselves to stop them falling into the hands of the enemy.

Only one Gladiator squadron participated in the Battle of Britain: 247 Squadron was re-formed on August 1, 1940, at Roborough, Devon, with the purpose of providing fighter cover for the Naval ports of Plymouth and Falmouth. With most of the

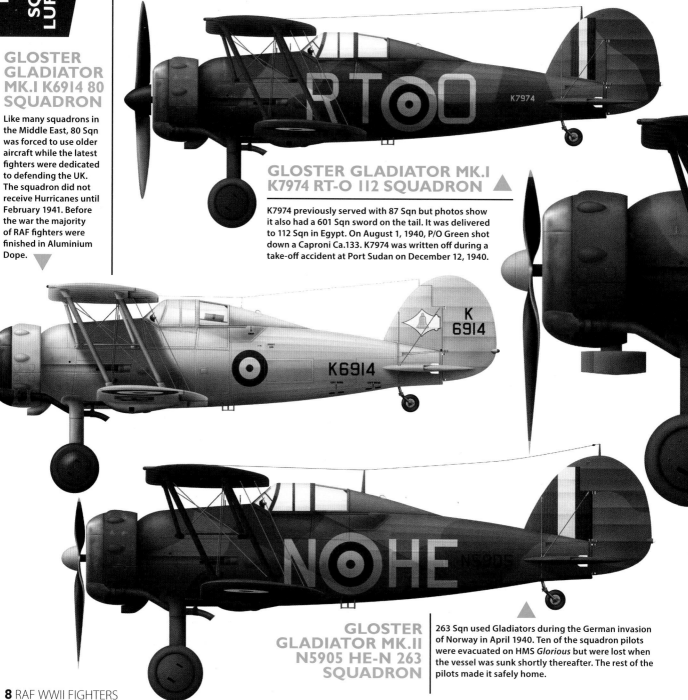

## GLOSTER GLADIATOR MK.I K6914 80 SQUADRON

Like many squadrons in the Middle East, 80 Sqn was forced to use older aircraft while the latest fighters were dedicated to defending the UK. The squadron did not receive Hurricanes until February 1941. Before the war the majority of RAF fighters were finished in Aluminium Dope.

## GLOSTER GLADIATOR MK.I K7974 RT-O 112 SQUADRON ▲

K7974 previously served with 87 Sqn but photos show it also had a 601 Sqn sword on the tail. It was delivered to 112 Sqn in Egypt. On August 1, 1940, P/O Green shot down a Caproni Ca.133. K7974 was written off during a take-off accident at Port Sudan on December 12, 1940.

## GLOSTER GLADIATOR MK.II N5905 HE-N 263 SQUADRON

263 Sqn used Gladiators during the German invasion of Norway in April 1940. Ten of the squadron pilots were evacuated on HMS *Glorious* but were lost when the vessel was sunk shortly thereafter. The rest of the pilots made it safely home.

| VARIANT | LENGTH | SPAN | HEIGHT | ENGINE |
|---------|--------|------|--------|--------|
| MK.I | 27FT 5IN / 8.36M | 32FT 3IN / 9.83M | 11FT 9IN / 3.58M | BRISTOL MERCURY IX |
| MK.II | 27FT 5IN / 8.36M | 32FT 3IN / 9.83M | 11FT 9IN / 3.58M | BRISTOL MERCURY VIIIA |

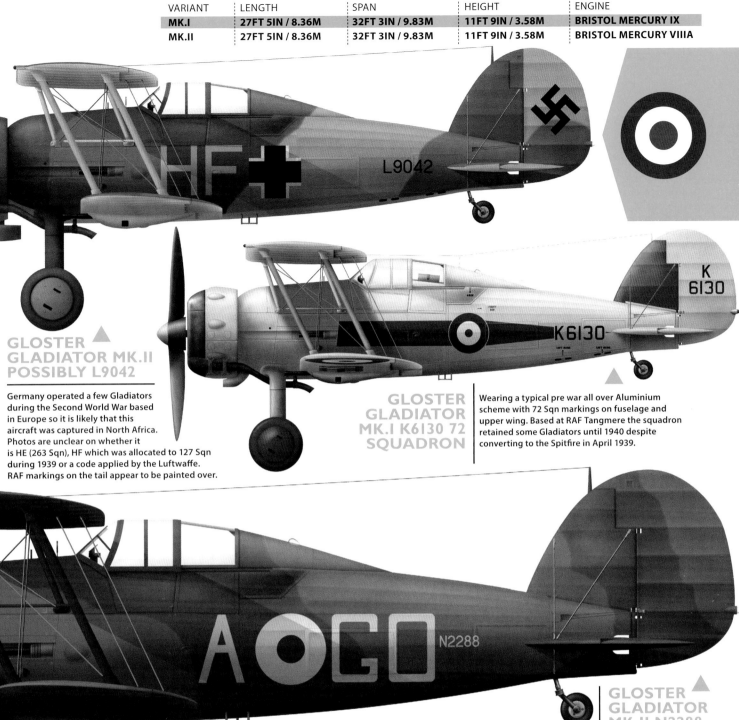

## GLOSTER GLADIATOR MK.II POSSIBLY L9042

Germany operated a few Gladiators during the Second World War based in Europe so it is likely that this aircraft was captured in North Africa. Photos are unclear on whether it is HE (263 Sqn), HF which was allocated to 127 Sqn during 1939 or a code applied by the Luftwaffe. RAF markings on the tail appear to be painted over.

## GLOSTER GLADIATOR MK.I K6130 72 SQUADRON

Wearing a typical pre war all over Aluminium scheme with 72 Sqn markings on fuselage and upper wing. Based at RAF Tangmere the squadron retained some Gladiators until 1940 despite converting to the Spitfire in April 1939.

## GLOSTER GLADIATOR MK.II N2288 GO-A 94 SQUADRON

An unusual scheme that was applied in the field to N2288, this included a temporary revision of the roundel. When Aden was attacked by Italian bombers on June 13, 1940, the squadron Gladiators successfully repelled them.

action focusing on the south-east, the Gladiators saw little action. Due to the speed and climb rate of the Gladiator they had minimal success, instead relying on locally based Hurricane squadrons to make the interceptions. The unit's conversion to Hurricanes on Christmas Eve 1940 ended the use of biplane fighters in British skies.

The majority of the action that Gladiator squadrons were involved in was in the Mediterranean and Middle East, 30 and 80 Squadrons operating in Egypt from 1938. The following year, in Aden, 94 Squadron re-formed with a mix of Gladiator Mk.Is and Sea Gladiators. Having dealt with local tribal tensions, 33 Squadron was first involved in combat against Italian Fiat CR.32s and Caproni Ca.310s only four days after Italy joined the war on June 10, 1940.

During the encounter two of the CR.32s were destroyed. Just before

80 Squadron was relieved by 112 Squadron in Libya, a young pilot fresh from training, Roald Dahl, set out to join them. However, he crashed between the two front lines and did not join the squadron until they were flying Hurricanes in Greece. As the new aircraft filtered through from the factories in Great Britain the Gladiators all ended up with 112 Squadron before being retired.

This however was not the last combat for RAF Gladiators. A British force was hastily dispatched to quash a revolt in Iraq backed by pro-Axis forces in 1941. The force included 94 Squadron who had appropriated Gladiators that were then in storage along with those already at the Habbaniya base, just west of Baghdad, the revolt finally ending on May 30, 1941. 127 Squadron was involved in combat against Vichy French Dewoitine D.520s and for a

brief period 6 Squadron flew the Gladiator while waiting for their Hurricanes to be refurbished in Libya.

The Gladiator proved to be a reliable and rugged aircraft that was the culmination of the fighter biplane, a configuration that only 30 years earlier was an unproven concept but it was just a little too late and was eclipsed by the monoplanes which were to dominate the war. Ironically, they too would be made obsolete within a decade by the introduction of another Gloster design, the Meteor, the first RAF jet. A total of 747 Gladiators were built and served with 14 nations all together. It may have already been obsolete by the outbreak of the war but a Gladiator in the hands of a skilled pilot still performed well and it earned a respectable reputation, rather fitting for the last biplane to serve with the RAF. ☉

# GLOSTER
# GLADIATOR

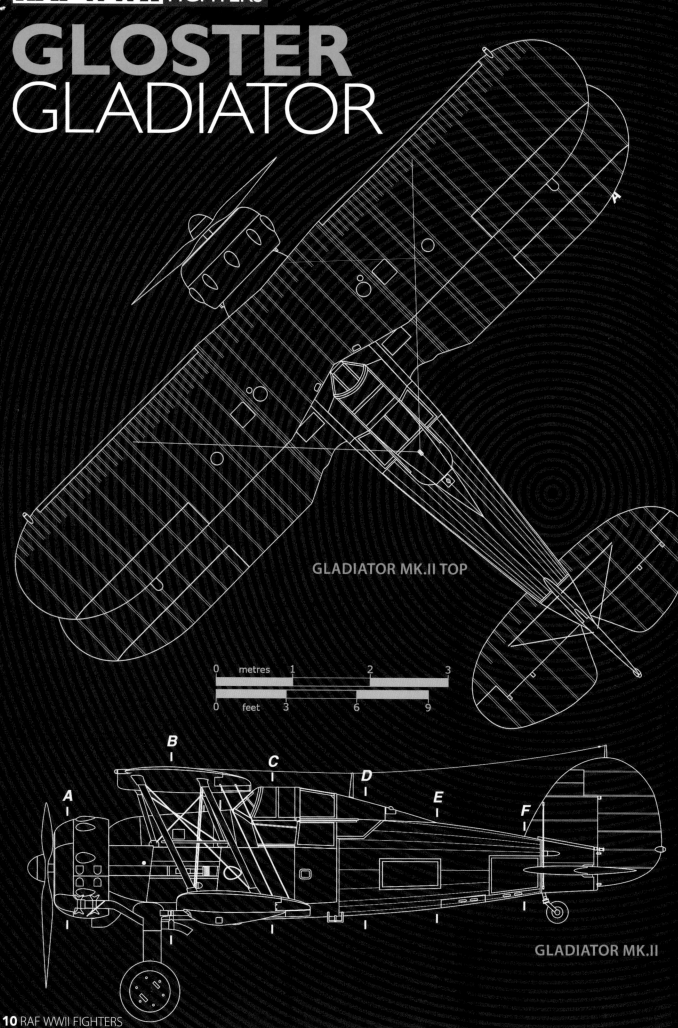

GLADIATOR MK.II TOP

| 0 | metres | 1 | 2 | 3 |
|---|--------|---|---|---|

| 0 | feet | 3 | 6 | 9 |
|---|------|---|---|---|

GLADIATOR MK.II

GLADIATOR MK.II FRONT

UNDERCARRIAGE
SCRAP VIEW

GLADIATOR MK.II UNDERSIDE

A          B          C          D          E

Ahead of its time when it entered service in the late 1930s, the Blenheim bomber was faster than most fighters – making its own conversion into a fighter all but inevitable. As the war began it was quickly outperformed by new enemy fighters but later found a new role as a night fighter.

# BRISTOL
## BLENHEIM

The Bristol Blenheim began life as a private venture by the Bristol company to create a twin engine civilian monoplane which would have higher cruising and top speeds than contemporary rivals. The Type 142 was designed by the chief engineer at Bristol, Frank Barnwell, who began sketching rough ideas in early 1933. Despite the board's reluctance to engage in private ventures Barnwell continued with his project until it crystallized into the Type 135.

The aircraft would have the capacity for two crew and six passengers, retractable undercarriage and stressed skin. These were radical ideas when aircraft flying at the time still had fabric covers, fixed undercarriage and were predominantly biplanes. It would be powered by two of the company's own Bristol Aquila nine-cylinder sleeve valve radial engines.

The designs would have ended up in storage and forgotten if it had not been for the intervention of Lord Rothermere, owner of the *Daily Mail* and aviation enthusiast. Learning of the Type 135 from the *Bristol Evening World* editor Robert T Lewis, Rothermere decided that the specifications loosely fitted with his own requirement for a commercial passenger plane with a range of 1000 miles and a top speed of 250mph.

A single aircraft that was closely based on the Type 135 was commissioned for £18,500, half up front and half upon completion. It received a new designation, the Type 142, and was later named 'Britain First' by Rothermere. In a change to the Type 135, the Bristol Mercury was selected. This resulted in a company decision to also develop the Type 143 which would not have as high a top speed but would be more economical. The fuselage would be slightly larger than that of the Type 142 and would accommodate eight passengers. To keep things simple, 70% of the parts were used in both aircraft.

One benefit of the decision to go with the Mercury was that Bristol could keep all development in-house. The decline in engine manufacturers during the interwar years resulted in Bristol and Rolls-Royce being the only major constructors left. Other aircraft design companies were in the position of having to rely on external suppliers, which on occasion caused delays to the completion of aircraft.

The Type 142 flew for the first time on April 12, 1935, with Bristol chief test pilot Cyril Uwins at the controls.

Incidentally, he held this role for 29 years from 1918 until 1947! The first flight was with four-bladed fixed pitch propellers, but these were soon changed. Uwins was very positive about the Type 142 after the flight as it had exceeded expectations.

With Hitler's announcement that he intended to form the Luftwaffe in March 1935, the Air Ministry had no choice but to respond and look at expansion of the RAF. The Type 142's performance was impressive enough for both the Finnish and British governments to consider a military version. It had exceeded 300mph, an astounding feat considering that the top speed of the RAF's latest fighter, the Gloster Gauntlet, was only 230mph. Therefore an order for 150 Type 142Ms was placed in August 1935. This was followed by a provisional order for a further 450 with the intention that they would all be bombers.

The first pre-production Blenheim, K7033, was completed albeit with a dummy turret in June 1936 and initially flew unpainted with just the serial on the wings, fuselage and rudder along with the roundel. As flight trials began there was a significant incident which almost delayed the project by many months; Uwins was making the final approach during the second flight of K7033 in deteriorating weather conditions and selected flaps down – only for the starboard flap to remain in position. The port flap would then not retract, forcing Uwins to land that way in a cross

wind with no margin for error. Having corrected this potentially fatal issue the trials continued and K7033 was soon joined by K7034, increasing the rate of progress. The trials revealed that only minor alterations were required such as angling the exhausts outwards, fitting cooling gills to the engine cowlings and stopping draughts caused by the forward glazing. Hubs were fitted to the spinner and despite the aesthetic improvement they made no discernible difference to the performance.

Following the German remilitarisation of the Rhineland in March 1936, it was becoming increasingly evident to the British government that rearmament would be required. Bristol received a further order for 434 aircraft, soon followed by another order for 134.

As 1937 began, so too did full scale Blenheim production at Bristol's Filton factory and a total of 330 were delivered during that year. To fully cope with the demand, shadow factories were set up and run by companies such as Fairey and A V Roe Ltd. Certainly, the latter's Roy Chadwick would have had access to the Blenheim's construction methods, especially the all-metal stressed skin

which would have no doubt influenced his work on the Manchester and later Lancaster designs.

K7033 was delivered to the Aeroplane and Armament Experimental Establishment in October 1936 but it was not until March 4, 1937, when K7035, the first all metal monoplane with retractable undercarriage was delivered to 114 Squadron of the RAF. K7035 was special in that it had been fitted with dual controls. As deliveries to the squadron continued, they replaced their Hawker Audax biplanes with the new cutting edge bomber.

Over the next few months, five more squadrons received the Blenheim. During this period squadrons undertook their own conversion and training so it was perhaps inevitable that there was a high attrition rate during the early days. Pilots who had been familiar with the more forgiving handling characteristics of the Hawker Audax or Hind were now flying faster in a twin engine monoplane with retractable undercarriage.

During exercises undertaken in 1937, the fighter aircraft of the time found it hard to intercept the Blenheim due to the then-top speed of 277mph at 20,000ft whereas the Hawker Demon could only manage 182mph at 13,000ft. It was therefore safe for the Air Ministry to assume that German bombers would be of comparable performance. The Spitfire and Hurricane were not yet ready to enter service and the Munich Crisis in September 1938 forced the British government to accept the reality that war with Germany was likely imminent

and that an interim solution was required.

The short term solution was to convert the Blenheim into a fighter. It was a relatively straightforward to add an externally mounted gun pack under the bomb bay, utilising a steel structure within the bomb bay to secure it. Within the pack were four fixed forward-firing Browning .303 machine guns, the 500 rounds of ammunition per gun being conveniently stored in the bomb bay. L1424 was used as the trials aircraft and the modification proved satisfactory with only minor

BRISTOL BLENHEIM MK.IF L1336 WR-E 248 SQUADRON

The squadron was re-formed as a night fighter squadron after war broke out and was supplied with the Blenheim Mk.IF in December 1939. These were replaced with IVFs the following February. Squadron aircraft initially had a mix of White and Night undersides but were originally all black undersides.

WR●E L1336

alterations to the initial design required. Heating was introduced to avoid the guns freezing at high altitude and the ammunition feed was made more efficient.

The Blenheim factories had no resources to spare with construction of the aircraft at capacity so the gun packs were built by Southern Railways in Ashford, Kent, and later mated with the aircraft. To save weight it was proposed that the rear turret be removed but due to the poor rear visibility of the Blenheim a rear observer would still be required. Tradition dictated that a rear observer be armed so the turret was to remain for the time being. So the only external difference between the Mk.I and the Mk.IF was the inclusion of the gun pack.

During December 1938 23 Sqn, based at RAF Wittering, replaced their Hawker Demons with the Mk.IF. At the same time 25 Sqn, which operated as a night fighter unit, replaced their Gloster Gladiators with the Mk.IF at RAF Hawkinge. 29 Sqn at RAF Debden and 64 Sqn

at RAF Church Fenton also replaced their aging Demons. The following month the auxiliary squadrons; 600, 601 and 604 all at RAF Hendon, received the fighter.

While exercises in the late 1930s had proven the superiority of the Blenheim over the biplane fighters of the RAF, it was soon apparent that in combat the Blenheim would not be able to compete with the Spitfire or Hurricane. Both had higher top speeds, tighter turning circles and superior handling. These characteristics were not quite so essential in the night fighter role so by the outbreak of war the Blenheim was relegated to this role, there being no dedicated night fighter units until this appointment. The bomber variant however undertook a far more active role during the early stages of the war.

The Mk.I may have been a vastly superior aeroplane compared to those it was replacing but even before the outbreak of war deficiencies became clear during standard flying and exercises. The issue that was to have the biggest

impact on the look of the Blenheim was the cramped conditions in which the navigator had to work. The solution was to extend the nose and create more room. However, early modifications reduced the forward visibility of the pilot especially when taxiing on the ground. Revisions were carried out on trial aircraft with the eventual offset scalloped nose being chosen. This provided sufficient space for the navigator to fulfil his role on one side but the dip also gave the pilot a clear line of sight. Range was extended with 94 gallon tanks being fitted in the outer wing, increasing the Blenheim's total capacity to 468 gallons. More power was required too, so the Mercury VIIIs were replaced by the Mercury XV with an output of 920 horsepower. The extra 80hp was gained by a combination of engineering and allowing them to run with 100 octane fuel. It took some time to create the new jigs but by March 1939 the first Blenheim Mk.IVs were arriving at the frontline squadrons.

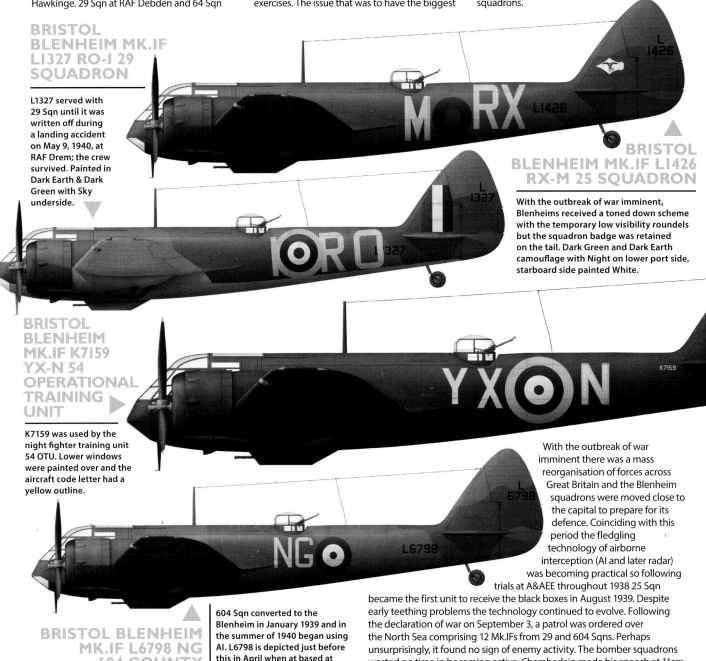

**BRISTOL BLENHEIM MK.IF L1327 RO-I 29 SQUADRON**

L1327 served with 29 Sqn until it was written off during a landing accident on May 9, 1940, at RAF Drem; the crew survived. Painted in Dark Earth & Dark Green with Sky underside.

**BRISTOL BLENHEIM MK.IF L1426 RX-M 25 SQUADRON**

With the outbreak of war imminent, Blenheims received a toned down scheme with the temporary low visibility roundels but the squadron badge was retained on the tail. Dark Green and Dark Earth camouflage with Night on lower port side, starboard side painted White.

**BRISTOL BLENHEIM MK.IF K7159 YX-N 54 OPERATIONAL TRAINING UNIT**

K7159 was used by the night fighter training unit 54 OTU. Lower windows were painted over and the aircraft code letter had a yellow outline.

**BRISTOL BLENHEIM MK.IF L6798 NG 604 COUNTY OF MIDDLESEX SQUADRON**

604 Sqn converted to the Blenheim in January 1939 and in the summer of 1940 began using AI. L6798 is depicted just before this in April when at based at RAF Northolt. No individual code letters or the fin flash were applied at this time.

With the outbreak of war imminent there was a mass reorganisation of forces across Great Britain and the Blenheim squadrons were moved close to the capital to prepare for its defence. Coinciding with this period the fledgling technology of airborne interception (AI and later radar) was becoming practical so following trials at A&AEE throughout 1938 25 Sqn became the first unit to receive the black boxes in August 1939. Despite early teething problems the technology continued to evolve. Following the declaration of war on September 3, a patrol was ordered over the North Sea comprising 12 Mk.IFs from 29 and 604 Sqns. Perhaps unsurprisingly, it found no sign of enemy activity. The bomber squadrons wasted no time in becoming active. Chamberlain made his speech at 11am and by 12.03pm 139 Sqn had sent off N6215, a Mk.IV, to locate the German navy's forces north of Wilhelmshaven. And just over three hours later

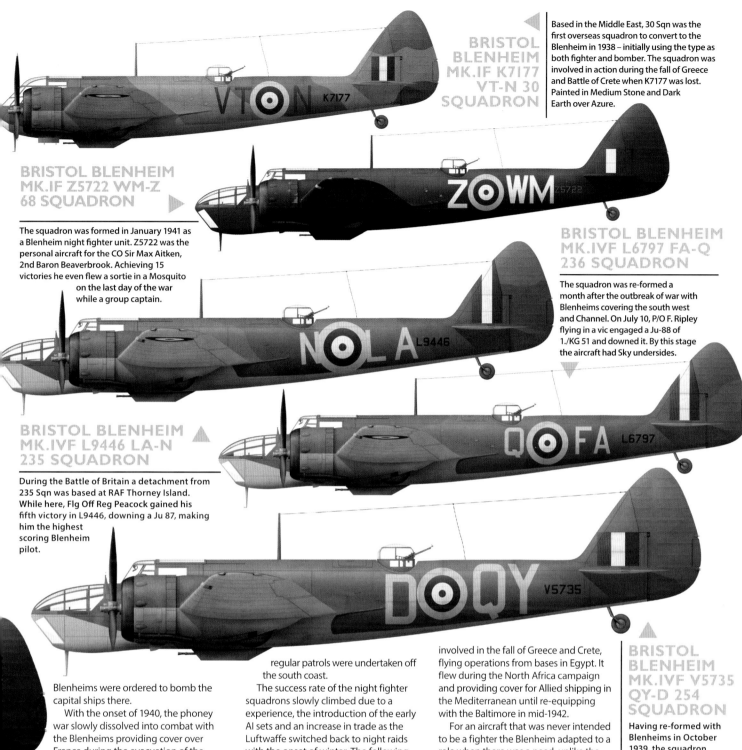

Based in the Middle East, 30 Sqn was the first overseas squadron to convert to the Blenheim in 1938 – initially using the type as both fighter and bomber. The squadron was involved in action during the fall of Greece and Battle of Crete when K7177 was lost. Painted in Medium Stone and Dark Earth over Azure.

## BRISTOL BLENHEIM MK.IF Z5722 WM-Z 68 SQUADRON

The squadron was formed in January 1941 as a Blenheim night fighter unit. Z5722 was the personal aircraft for the CO Sir Max Aitken, 2nd Baron Beaverbrook. Achieving 15 victories he even flew a sortie in a Mosquito on the last day of the war while a group captain.

## BRISTOL BLENHEIM MK.IVF L6797 FA-Q 236 SQUADRON

The squadron was re-formed a month after the outbreak of war with Blenheims covering the south west and Channel. On July 10, P/O F. Ripley flying in a vic engaged a Ju-88 of 1./KG 51 and downed it. By this stage the aircraft had Sky undersides.

## BRISTOL BLENHEIM MK.IVF L9446 LA-N 235 SQUADRON

During the Battle of Britain a detachment from 235 Sqn was based at RAF Thorney Island. While here, Flg Off Reg Peacock gained his fifth victory in L9446, downing a Ju 87, making him the highest scoring Blenheim pilot.

## BRISTOL BLENHEIM MK.IVF V5735 QY-D 254 SQUADRON

Having re-formed with Blenheims in October 1939, the squadron was transferred to Coastal Command and was based in Scotland and Northern Ireland providing fighter cover to convoy patrols. Aircraft were initially standard RAF colours but repainted in Dark Slate Grey and Extra Dark Sea Grey over Sky.

Blenheims were ordered to bomb the capital ships there.

With the onset of 1940, the phoney war slowly dissolved into combat with the Blenheims providing cover over France during the evacuation of the British Expeditionary Force. Deliveries of both the Mk.IF and Mk.IVF continued during the early months of the war until there were 19 Blenheim squadrons within Fighter Command. The Mk.IVF conversion was identical to that applied to the Mk.IF with the gun pack being mounted under the bomb bay.

The Luftwaffe conducted its first major raid on Britain on June 18, 1940, with more than 70 He 111s involved. By this stage the Blenheim fighter squadrons were classed as night fighter units so 23 and 29 Squadrons were tasked with intercepting the raiders. Seven claims were made but only five were lost that night. Not only did they act as defensive night fighters but regular patrols were undertaken off the south coast.

The success rate of the night fighter squadrons slowly climbed due to a experience, the introduction of the early AI sets and an increase in trade as the Luftwaffe switched back to night raids with the onset of winter. The following spring the Blenheims were replaced with the Bristol Beaufighter which was more suitable for the night fighter role but far less forgiving as an aircraft.

Despite being retired in the UK, the fighters continued in service in the Middle East where many older types ended up. The only squadron to operate the fighter version when Italy declared war on June 10, 1940, was 203 Squadron which was based in Aden and they were involved in raids on Italian airfields the following day.

203 Squadron also used Blenheims to help quell a revolt in Iraq in May 1941 when, backed by Germany, Iraqi generals attempted a coup. The squadron was involved in the fall of Greece and Crete, flying operations from bases in Egypt. It flew during the North Africa campaign and providing cover for Allied shipping in the Mediterranean until re-equipping with the Baltimore in mid-1942.

For an aircraft that was never intended to be a fighter the Blenheim adapted to a role when there was a need, unlike the single seat fighters it was suited to the role of night fighter when a second crew member was required for the fledgling AI sets. The pace of progression meant it was soon outclassed and obsolete. It continued as a bomber for many years and development issues with both the Taurus and Hercules engines which were destined for successors to the Blenheim meant that it continued to serve for longer than originally anticipated in a range of secondary roles.

The aircraft served with 16 nations and more than 4000 were built but as a fighter it was only ever intended to be a stopgap until something better could be introduced. ⊙

| VARIANT | LENGTH | SPAN | HEIGHT | ENGINE |
|---|---|---|---|---|
| MK.I | 39FT 8IN / 12.09M | 56FT 4IN / 17.17M | 12FT 9IN / 3.89M | 2 X MERCURY VIII |
| MK.IF | 39FT 8IN / 12.09M | 56FT 4IN / 17.17M | 12FT 9IN / 3.89M | 2 X MERCURY VIII |
| MK.IV | 42FT 9IN / 13.03M | 56FT 4IN / 17.17M | 12FT 9IN / 3.89M | 2 X MERCURY XV |
| MK.IVF | 42FT 9IN / 13.03M | 56FT 4IN / 17.17M | 12FT 9IN / 3.89M | 2 X MERCURY XV |
| MK.V | 44FT / 13.14M | 56FT 4IN / 17.17M | 12FT 10IN / 3.91M | 2 X MERCURY XXX |

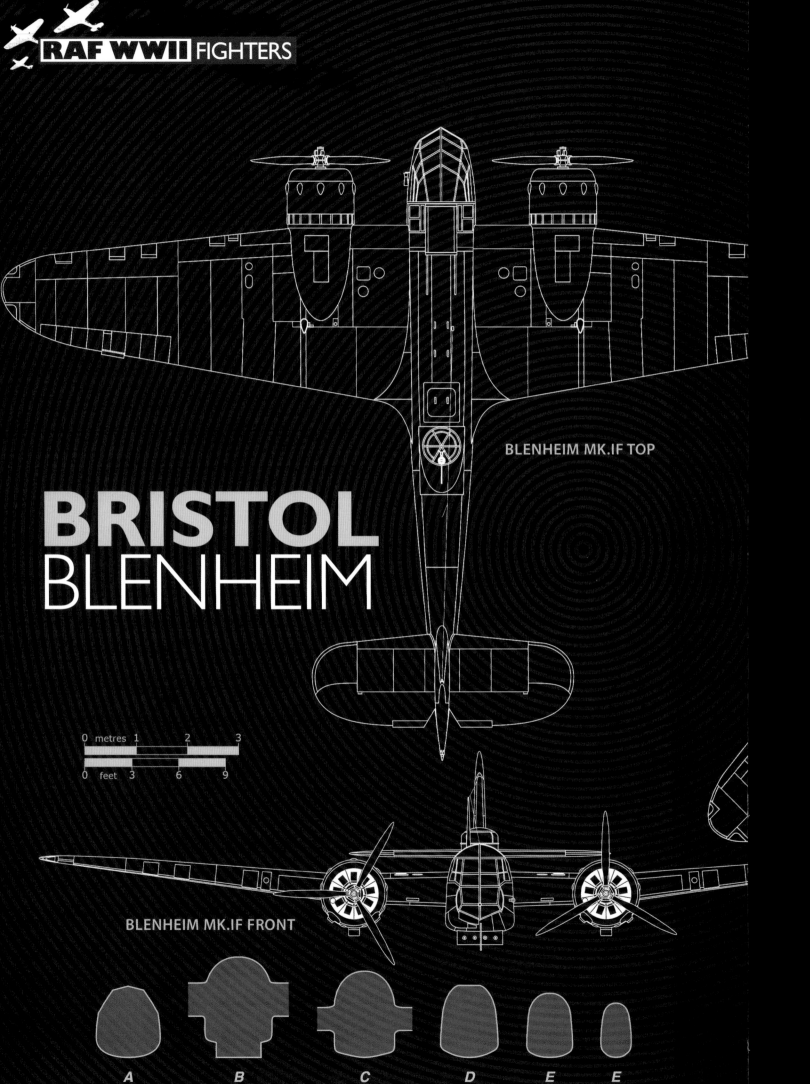

BLENHEIM MK.IF TOP

BRISTOL
BLENHEIM

0 metres 1 2 3
0 feet 3 6 9

BLENHEIM MK.IF FRONT

A    B    C    D    E    E

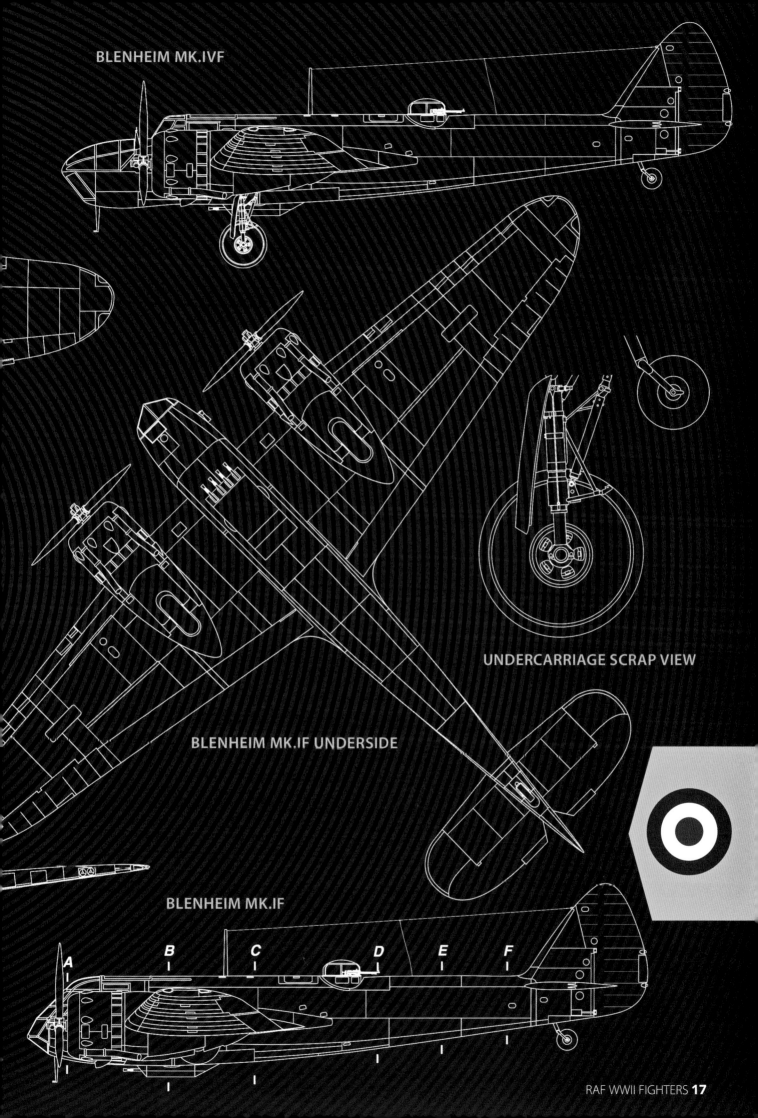

BLENHEIM MK.IVF

BLENHEIM MK.IF UNDERSIDE

UNDERCARRIAGE SCRAP VIEW

BLENHEIM MK.IF

A    B    C    D    E    F

# HAWKER
## HURRICANE

**1937-1947**

**Many of the new late-1930s monoplanes such as the Bf 109 and the Spitfire were entirely new designs but the Hurricane perhaps best represents the evolutionary step between the rugged frames found in biplanes and the more aerodynamic designs that were to dominate the war years.**

**U**nlike the Hurricane's peers, which were new designs, the Hurricane was only one stage in the evolution of the Hawker design that can be traced back to the Hawker Hart and culminated with the Hawker Sea Fury. The Hurricane was a safe design that was based on well known technology so while it may not have been as advanced as the Spitfire it was reliable and had a reputation for taking heavy damage but still getting the pilot home safely. Having played a vital role during the Battle of Britain it went on to serve in all theatres throughout the war and in a range of secondary roles.

During the early 1930s, the Hawker Fury formed the backbone of fighter defence for the RAF and at the time was a formidable aircraft.

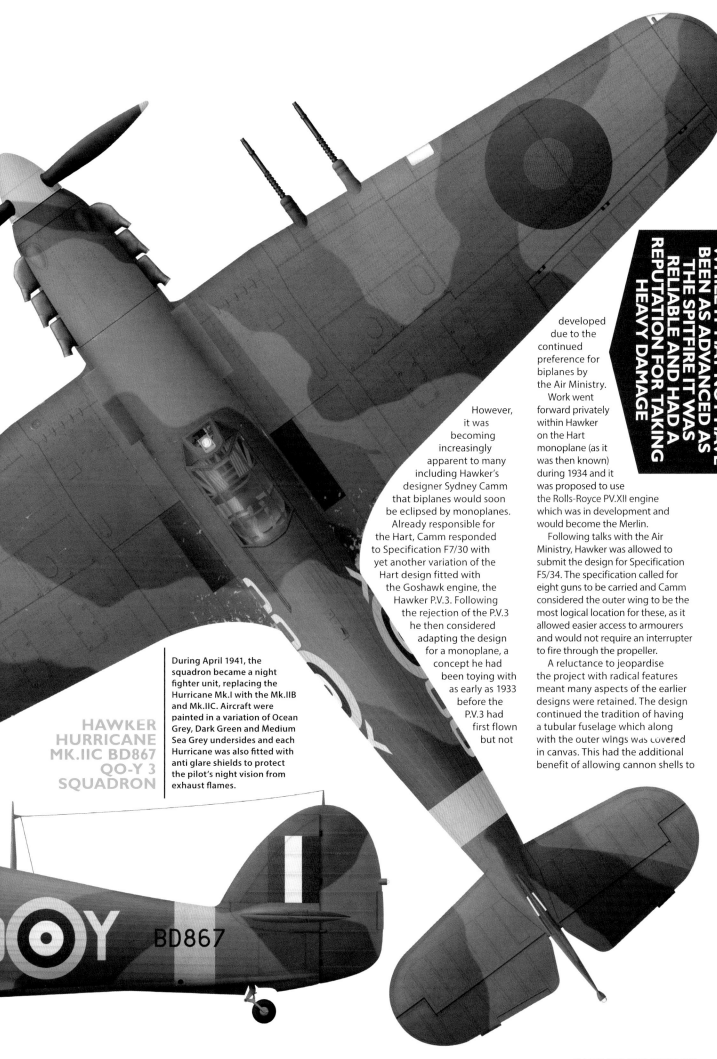

However, it was becoming increasingly apparent to many including Hawker's designer Sydney Camm that biplanes would soon be eclipsed by monoplanes. Already responsible for the Hart, Camm responded to Specification F7/30 with yet another variation of the Hart design fitted with the Goshawk engine, the Hawker P.V.3. Following the rejection of the P.V.3 he then considered adapting the design for a monoplane, a concept he had been toying with as early as 1933 before the P.V.3 had first flown but not

developed due to the continued preference for biplanes by the Air Ministry. Work went forward privately within Hawker on the Hart monoplane (as it was then known) during 1934 and it was proposed to use the Rolls-Royce PV.XII engine which was in development and would become the Merlin.

Following talks with the Air Ministry, Hawker was allowed to submit the design for Specification F5/34. The specification called for eight guns to be carried and Camm considered the outer wing to be the most logical location for these, as it allowed easier access to armourers and would not require an interrupter to fire through the propeller.

A reluctance to jeopardise the project with radical features meant many aspects of the earlier designs were retained. The design continued the tradition of having a tubular fuselage which along with the outer wings was covered in canvas. This had the additional benefit of allowing cannon shells to

**HAWKER HURRICANE MK.IIC BD867 QO-Y 3 SQUADRON**

During April 1941, the squadron became a night fighter unit, replacing the Hurricane Mk.I with the Mk.IIB and Mk.IIC. Aircraft were painted in a variation of Ocean Grey, Dark Green and Medium Sea Grey undersides and each Hurricane was also fitted with anti glare shields to protect the pilot's night vision from exhaust flames.

BD867

**HAWKER HURRICANE MK.I P2647 TP-X 73 SQUADRON**

While in France as part of the BEF P2647 was involved in a ground collision with another aircraft and heavily damaged. Despite the tail and canopy being destroyed it was rebuilt and returned to action. Painted in Dark Earth and Dark Green with Night underside.

**HAWKER HURRICANE MK.I P3395 JX-B I SQUADRON**

The personal aircraft of the ace Sgt Plt Arthur Clowes who was heavily involved in the Battle of Britain. It has a yellow band on the nose and a wasp on both sides of the nose. The Wasp and code have since been worn by a Harrier and Typhoon.

**HAWKER HURRICANE MK.I P2673 VY-E 85 SQUADRON**

Having claimed three destroyed and one damaged during the Battle of Britain, Sgt J. H. M. Ellis was flying L1915 VY-B when he was damaged and made it back to England before baling out. Three days later, in P2673, he was shot down by a Bf 109 near Kenley on September 1, 1940. His remains were not identified until 1992.

pass through unimpeded and the repairs were very simple. The Air Ministry was concerned about the strength of the wings with all the guns firing, so in line with other designs the wings were soon replaced with all metal wings.

Along with the single wing there were two other significant differences the new design introduced: The first was the addition of a retractable undercarriage; unlike its contemporaries the Bf 109 and Spitfire, the Hurricane's retracted inwards, creating a wide wheelbase and making it much more stable during taxiing and avoiding the accidents on rough terrain

that the Spitfire and Bf 109 suffered. The second was the closed cockpit which improved the aerodynamics while no longer exposing the pilot to the elements. Despite these benefits there would be a litany of complaints from fighter pilots as they transitioned from the open cockpits they had been long used to.

Work on the prototype, K5083, was completed in October 1935 and the aircraft was transported from the factory at Canbury Park Road, Kingston, a short distance to Brooklands for final assembly and on November 6 the maiden flight, with company chief test pilot Flt Lt P. W.

S. 'George' Bulman at the controls. As the prototype was fitted with the latest and then-untested Merlin C the first few flights were restricted to basic manoeuvres and it was only after four months that the aircraft was delivered to the RAF at Martlesham Heath for service trials.

The Hurricane was impressive compared to the fighters then in service. At 16,200ft, K5083 produced a top speed of 315mph, 85mph faster than the Gloster Gauntlet and 133mph faster than the Hawker Demon.

Work on both the aircraft and the engine continued and the following June the Air Ministry placed an order

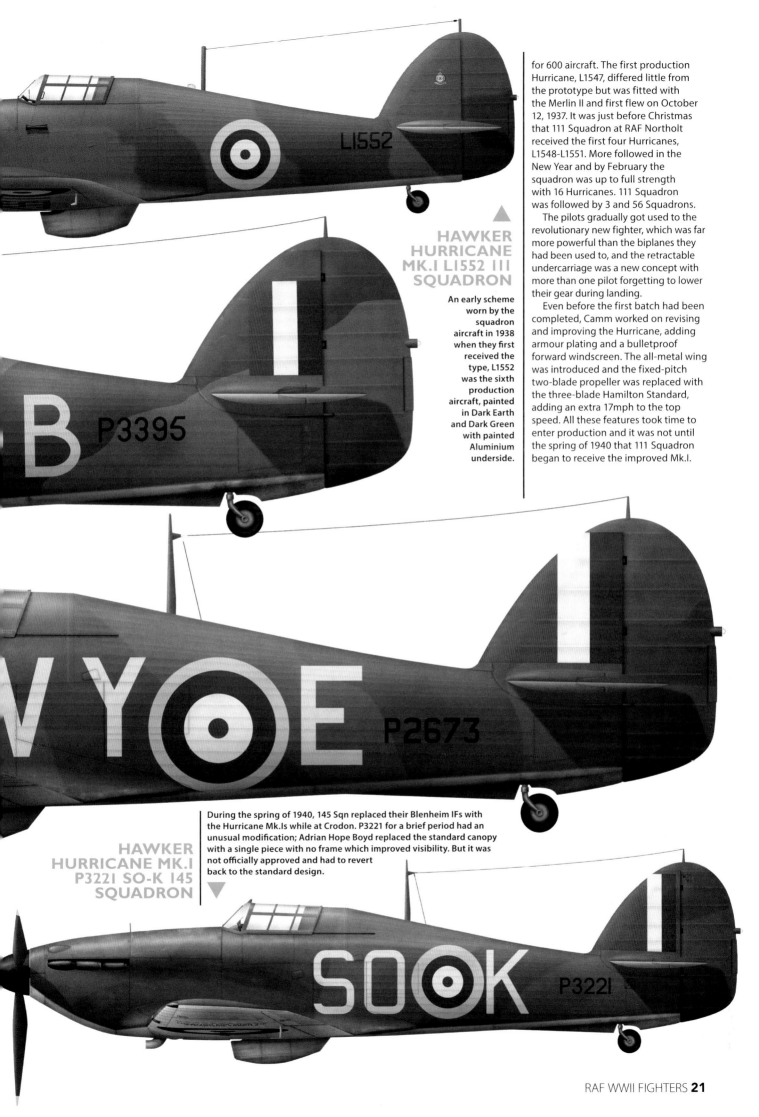

for 600 aircraft. The first production Hurricane, L1547, differed little from the prototype but was fitted with the Merlin II and first flew on October 12, 1937. It was just before Christmas that 111 Squadron at RAF Northolt received the first four Hurricanes, L1548-L1551. More followed in the New Year and by February the squadron was up to full strength with 16 Hurricanes. 111 Squadron was followed by 3 and 56 Squadrons.

The pilots gradually got used to the revolutionary new fighter, which was far more powerful than the biplanes they had been used to, and the retractable undercarriage was a new concept with more than one pilot forgetting to lower their gear during landing.

Even before the first batch had been completed, Camm worked on revising and improving the Hurricane, adding armour plating and a bulletproof forward windscreen. The all-metal wing was introduced and the fixed-pitch two-blade propeller was replaced with the three-blade Hamilton Standard, adding an extra 17mph to the top speed. All these features took time to enter production and it was not until the spring of 1940 that 111 Squadron began to receive the improved Mk.I.

**HAWKER HURRICANE MK.I L1552 111 SQUADRON**

An early scheme worn by the squadron aircraft in 1938 when they first received the type, L1552 was the sixth production aircraft, painted in Dark Earth and Dark Green with painted Aluminium underside.

During the spring of 1940, 145 Sqn replaced their Blenheim IFs with the Hurricane Mk.Is while at Crodon. P3221 for a brief period had an unusual modification; Adrian Hope Boyd replaced the standard canopy with a single piece with no frame which improved visibility. But it was not officially approved and had to revert back to the standard design.

**HAWKER HURRICANE MK.I P3221 SO-K 145 SQUADRON**

## HAWKER HURRICANE MK.I P3113 AK-!!! 213 SQUADRON

P3113 was the personal aeroplane of the squadron CO Sqn Ldr D. S. MacDonald and the exclamation marks represented kills. On September 15, 1940, it was being flown by Sgt R. T. Llwellyn when he was attacked by a Bf 110 and forced to bail out.

The first Hurricanes to be lost during the war were the victims of friendly fire during what became known as the Battle of Barking Creek.

On September 6, 1939, an unidentified aircraft was picked up. With tensions running high, 151 Squadron scrambled their Hurricanes, followed shortly after by two reserves flown by Pilot Officers Montague Hulton-Harrop and Frank Rose. Three Spitfire squadrons were also scrambled and those of 74 Squadron intercepted and downed the two Hurricanes although Rose survived.

It was not until the following month when 46 and 72 Squadrons intercepted nine He 115B seaplanes on October 21, damaging one and destroying three in the process. Prior to this during the Phoney War 1, 73, 85 and 87 Squadrons were sent to France to support the British Expeditionary Force, 1 Squadron moving to Octevill near Le Havre on September 7. Dowding was reluctant to commit his forces, accurately predicting that once France had fallen he would need every available fighter and pilot to defend Great Britain, although more fighter and bomber squadrons were posted to France before it fell.

As the evacuation took place all available aircraft returned to England to prepare for the coming Battle of Britain. Although slightly overshadowed by the

## HAWKER HURRICANE MK.I P2961 LE-A 242 SQUADRON

Commanded by Douglas Bader, 242 Sqn had a reputation all of its own but William McKnight stood out. Before he was lost on a sweep on January 12, 1941, he had made 17 claims. As well as the squadron art of Hitler being kicked, McKnight also added his own personal art on the side of P2961.

**ALTHOUGH SLIGHTLY OVERSHADOWED BY THE SPITFIRE, IT WAS DURING THE SUMMER OF 1940 THAT THE HURRICANE REALLY PROVED ITS WORTH.**

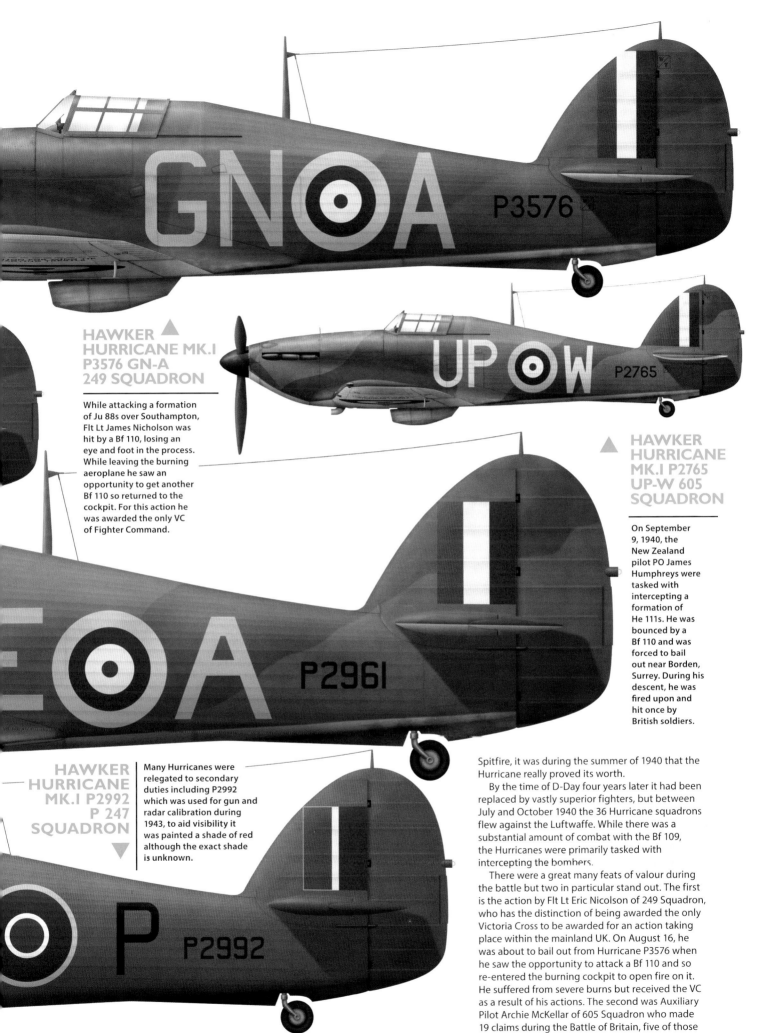

### HAWKER HURRICANE MK.I P3576 GN-A 249 SQUADRON

While attacking a formation of Ju 88s over Southampton, Flt Lt James Nicholson was hit by a Bf 110, losing an eye and foot in the process. While leaving the burning aeroplane he saw an opportunity to get another Bf 110 so returned to the cockpit. For this action he was awarded the only VC of Fighter Command.

### HAWKER HURRICANE MK.I P2765 UP-W 605 SQUADRON

On September 9, 1940, the New Zealand pilot PO James Humphreys were tasked with intercepting a formation of He 111s. He was bounced by a Bf 110 and was forced to bail out near Borden, Surrey. During his descent, he was fired upon and hit once by British soldiers.

### HAWKER HURRICANE MK.I P2992 P 247 SQUADRON

Many Hurricanes were relegated to secondary duties including P2992 which was used for gun and radar calibration during 1943, to aid visibility it was painted a shade of red although the exact shade is unknown.

Spitfire, it was during the summer of 1940 that the Hurricane really proved its worth.

By the time of D-Day four years later it had been replaced by vastly superior fighters, but between July and October 1940 the 36 Hurricane squadrons flew against the Luftwaffe. While there was a substantial amount of combat with the Bf 109, the Hurricanes were primarily tasked with intercepting the bombers.

There were a great many feats of valour during the battle but two in particular stand out. The first is the action by Flt Lt Eric Nicolson of 249 Squadron, who has the distinction of being awarded the only Victoria Cross to be awarded for an action taking place within the mainland UK. On August 16, he was about to bail out from Hurricane P3576 when he saw the opportunity to attack a Bf 110 and so re-entered the burning cockpit to open fire on it. He suffered from severe burns but received the VC as a result of his actions. The second was Auxiliary Pilot Archie McKellar of 605 Squadron who made 19 claims during the Battle of Britain, five of those on October 7, his total when he was killed on November 1 was 21.

With the onset of winter and decline in daylight raids the Hurricane was, along with Blenheims and Defiants, tasked with night defence. Although the improved Mk.IIB and cannon armed Mk.IIC did produce results, a single aircraft flying alone at night trying to follow instructions from control who were in turn tracking enemy aircraft via radar did not get spectacularly high results. Plus the introduction of radar necessitated a second crew member.

This was not the end of the Hurricane's nocturnal activities however, as they went on to fly night intruder missions over Europe from 1942. The MK.IIA differed little from the Mk.I but was powered by the Merlin III, providing a top speed of 330mph at

## HAWKER HURRICANE MK.IIB TROP Z5628 YB-L 17 SQUADRON

Z5628 served with 17 Sqn in the Far East where they were primarily tasked with defending Burma. Z5628 had originally been shipped to Taoradi, ferried to Egypt and then, with the fall of Rangoon imminent, taken on to Burma.

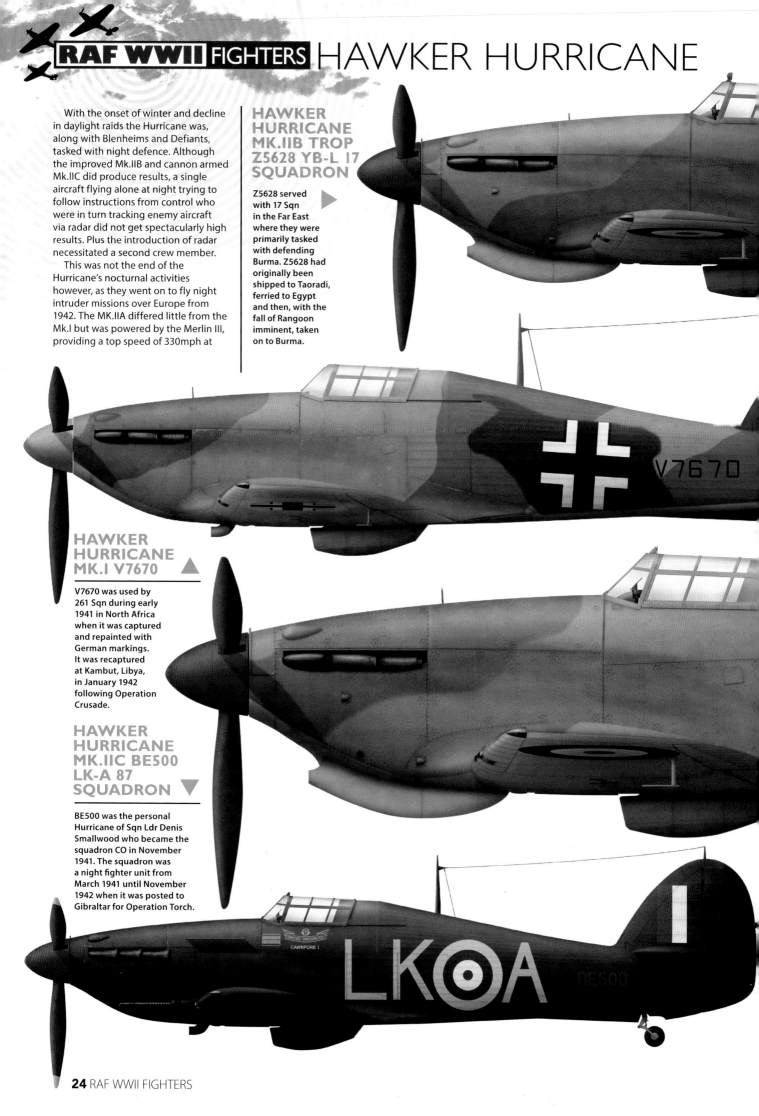

## HAWKER HURRICANE MK.I V7670 ▲

V7670 was used by 261 Sqn during early 1941 in North Africa when it was captured and repainted with German markings. It was recaptured at Kambut, Libya, in January 1942 following Operation Crusade.

## HAWKER HURRICANE MK.IIC BE500 LK-A 87 SQUADRON ▼

BE500 was the personal Hurricane of Sqn Ldr Denis Smallwood who became the squadron CO in November 1941. The squadron was a night fighter unit from March 1941 until November 1942 when it was posted to Gibraltar for Operation Torch.

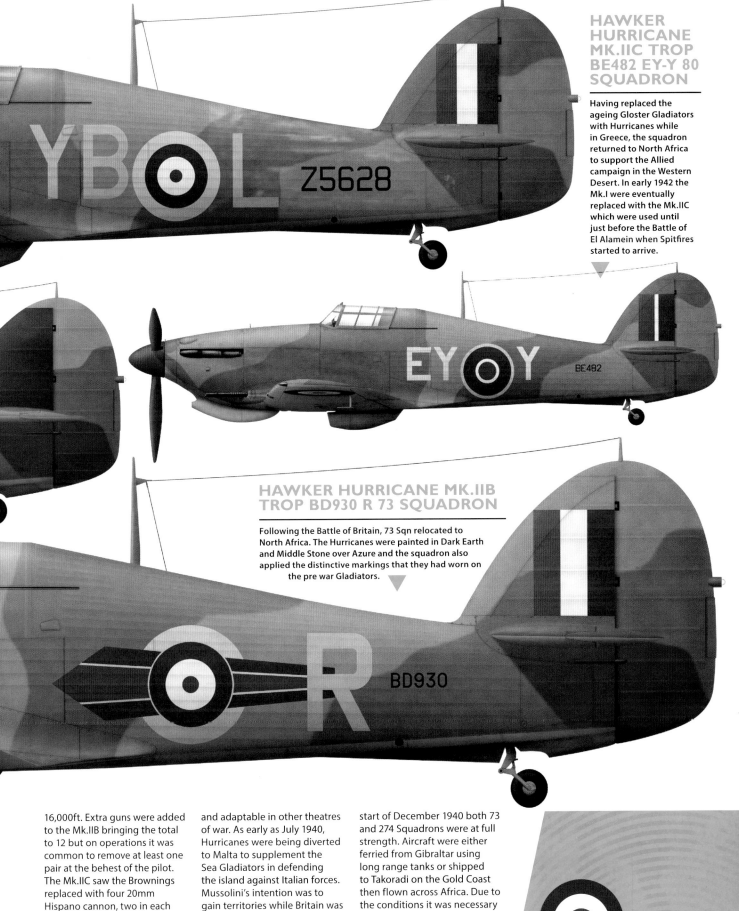

Having replaced the ageing Gloster Gladiators with Hurricanes while in Greece, the squadron returned to North Africa to support the Allied campaign in the Western Desert. In early 1942 the Mk.I were eventually replaced with the Mk.IIC which were used until just before the Battle of El Alamein when Spitfires started to arrive.

## HAWKER HURRICANE MK.IIB TROP BD930 R 73 SQUADRON

Following the Battle of Britain, 73 Sqn relocated to North Africa. The Hurricanes were painted in Dark Earth and Middle Stone over Azure and the squadron also applied the distinctive markings that they had worn on the pre war Gladiators.

16,000ft. Extra guns were added to the Mk.IIB bringing the total to 12 but on operations it was common to remove at least one pair at the behest of the pilot. The Mk.IIC saw the Brownings replaced with four 20mm Hispano cannon, two in each wing. Despite being less guns the destructive power of the cannon was a big improvement and all subsequent Hawker fighters were also equipped with them.

The Hurricane may have been replaced by superior aircraft on the home front but Camm's design was to prove rugged and adaptable in other theatres of war. As early as July 1940, Hurricanes were being diverted to Malta to supplement the Sea Gladiators in defending the island against Italian forces. Mussolini's intention was to gain territories while Britain was preoccupied with the expected invasion. Despite high losses, Hurricanes continued to bolster the island's defences until sufficient Spitfires could be spared and sent to Malta.

One theatre where the Hurricane excelled was North Africa, with the aircraft initially being sent to Egypt and by the start of December 1940 both 73 and 274 Squadrons were at full strength. Aircraft were either ferried from Gibraltar using long range tanks or shipped to Takoradi on the Gold Coast then flown across Africa. Due to the conditions it was necessary to fit Vokes Filters, which were suitable for the desert conditions. The Hurricanes were soon outclassed by Regia Aeronautia and Luftwaffe fighters and began being phased out with the arrival of P-40 Tomahawks. To prolong the life of the Hurricane the Mk.IID was introduced as a tank

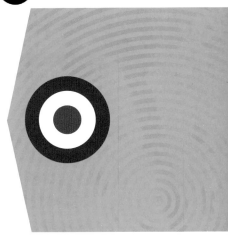

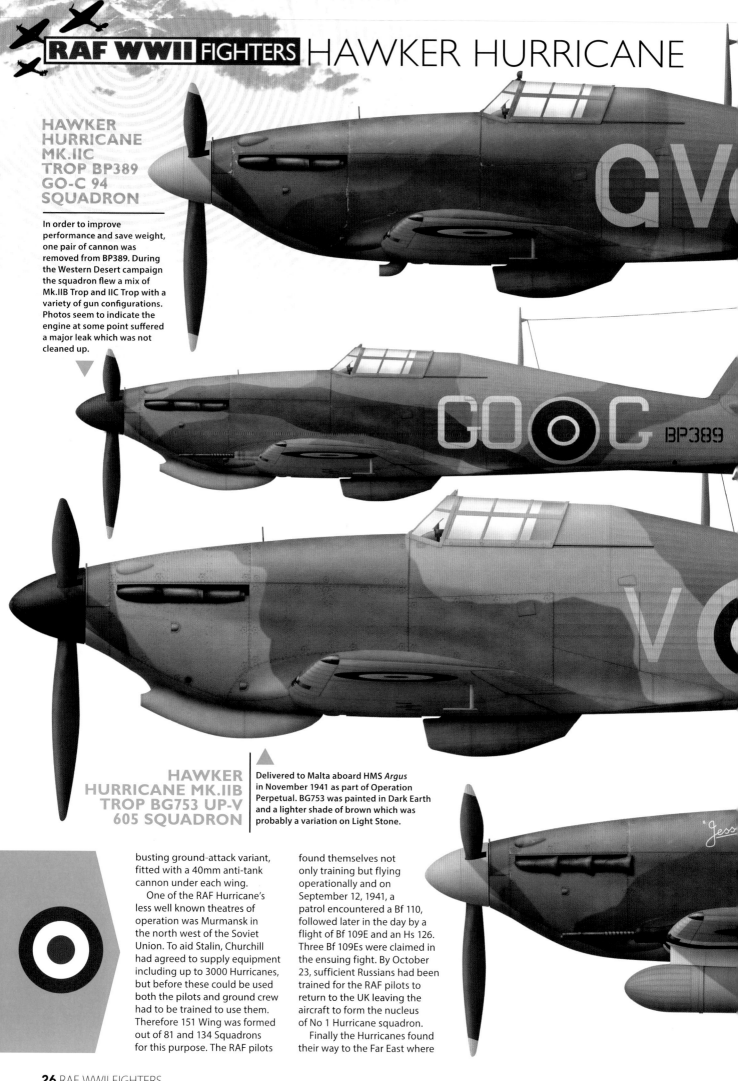

## HAWKER HURRICANE MK.IIC TROP BP389 GO-C 94 SQUADRON

In order to improve performance and save weight, one pair of cannon was removed from BP389. During the Western Desert campaign the squadron flew a mix of Mk.IIB Trop and IIC Trop with a variety of gun configurations. Photos seem to indicate the engine at some point suffered a major leak which was not cleaned up.

## HAWKER HURRICANE MK.IIB TROP BG753 UP-V 605 SQUADRON

Delivered to Malta aboard HMS *Argus* in November 1941 as part of Operation Perpetual. BG753 was painted in Dark Earth and a lighter shade of brown which was probably a variation on Light Stone.

busting ground-attack variant, fitted with a 40mm anti-tank cannon under each wing.

One of the RAF Hurricane's less well known theatres of operation was Murmansk in the north west of the Soviet Union. To aid Stalin, Churchill had agreed to supply equipment including up to 3000 Hurricanes, but before these could be used both the pilots and ground crew had to be trained to use them. Therefore 151 Wing was formed out of 81 and 134 Squadrons for this purpose. The RAF pilots

found themselves not only training but flying operationally and on September 12, 1941, a patrol encountered a Bf 110, followed later in the day by a flight of Bf 109E and an Hs 126. Three Bf 109Es were claimed in the ensuing fight. By October 23, sufficient Russians had been trained for the RAF pilots to return to the UK leaving the aircraft to form the nucleus of No 1 Hurricane squadron.

Finally the Hurricanes found their way to the Far East where

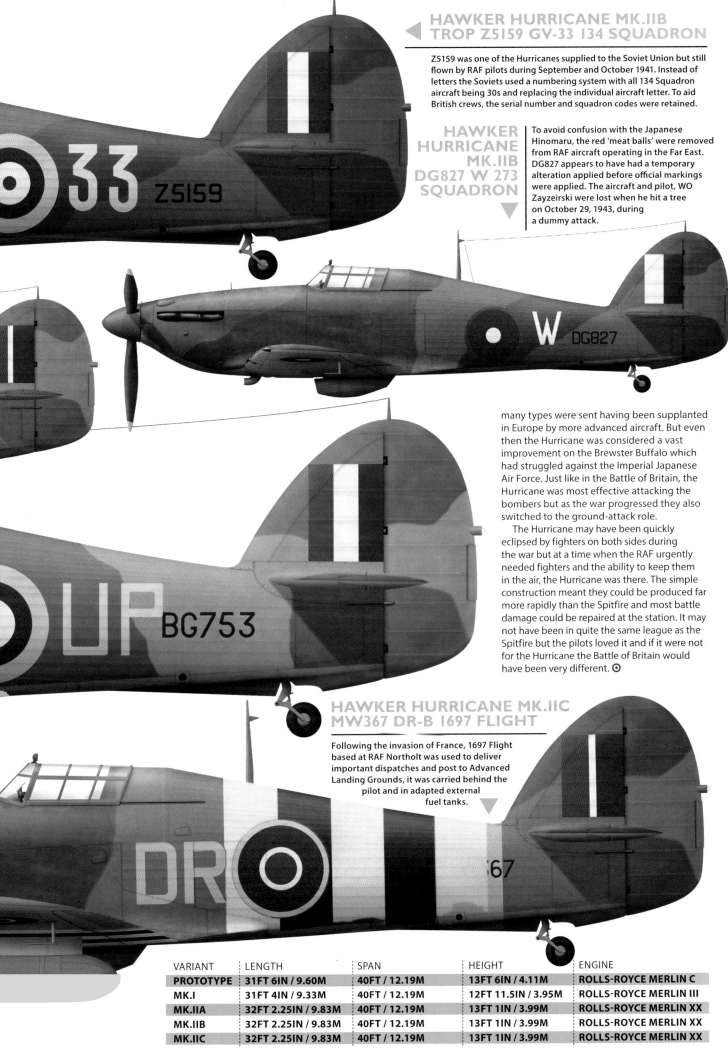

## HAWKER HURRICANE MK.IIB TROP Z5159 GV-33 134 SQUADRON

Z5159 was one of the Hurricanes supplied to the Soviet Union but still flown by RAF pilots during September and October 1941. Instead of letters the Soviets used a numbering system with all 134 Squadron aircraft being 30s and replacing the individual aircraft letter. To aid British crews, the serial number and squadron codes were retained.

## HAWKER HURRICANE MK.IIB DG827 W 273 SQUADRON

To avoid confusion with the Japanese Hinomaru, the red 'meat balls' were removed from RAF aircraft operating in the Far East. DG827 appears to have had a temporary alteration applied before official markings were applied. The aircraft and pilot, WO Zayzeirski were lost when he hit a tree on October 29, 1943, during a dummy attack.

many types were sent having been supplanted in Europe by more advanced aircraft. But even then the Hurricane was considered a vast improvement on the Brewster Buffalo which had struggled against the Imperial Japanese Air Force. Just like in the Battle of Britain, the Hurricane was most effective attacking the bombers but as the war progressed they also switched to the ground-attack role.

The Hurricane may have been quickly eclipsed by fighters on both sides during the war but at a time when the RAF urgently needed fighters and the ability to keep them in the air, the Hurricane was there. The simple construction meant they could be produced far more rapidly than the Spitfire and most battle damage could be repaired at the station. It may not have been in quite the same league as the Spitfire but the pilots loved it and if it were not for the Hurricane the Battle of Britain would have been very different. ⊙

## HAWKER HURRICANE MK.IIC MW367 DR-B 1697 FLIGHT

Following the invasion of France, 1697 Flight based at RAF Northolt was used to deliver important dispatches and post to Advanced Landing Grounds, it was carried behind the pilot and in adapted external fuel tanks.

| VARIANT | LENGTH | SPAN | HEIGHT | ENGINE |
|---|---|---|---|---|
| PROTOTYPE | 31FT 6IN / 9.60M | 40FT / 12.19M | 13FT 6IN / 4.11M | ROLLS-ROYCE MERLIN C |
| MK.I | 31FT 4IN / 9.33M | 40FT / 12.19M | 12FT 11.5IN / 3.95M | ROLLS-ROYCE MERLIN III |
| MK.IIA | 32FT 2.25IN / 9.83M | 40FT / 12.19M | 13FT 1IN / 3.99M | ROLLS-ROYCE MERLIN XX |
| MK.IIB | 32FT 2.25IN / 9.83M | 40FT / 12.19M | 13FT 1IN / 3.99M | ROLLS-ROYCE MERLIN XX |
| MK.IIC | 32FT 2.25IN / 9.83M | 40FT / 12.19M | 13FT 1IN / 3.99M | ROLLS-ROYCE MERLIN XX |

# HAWKER HURRICANE

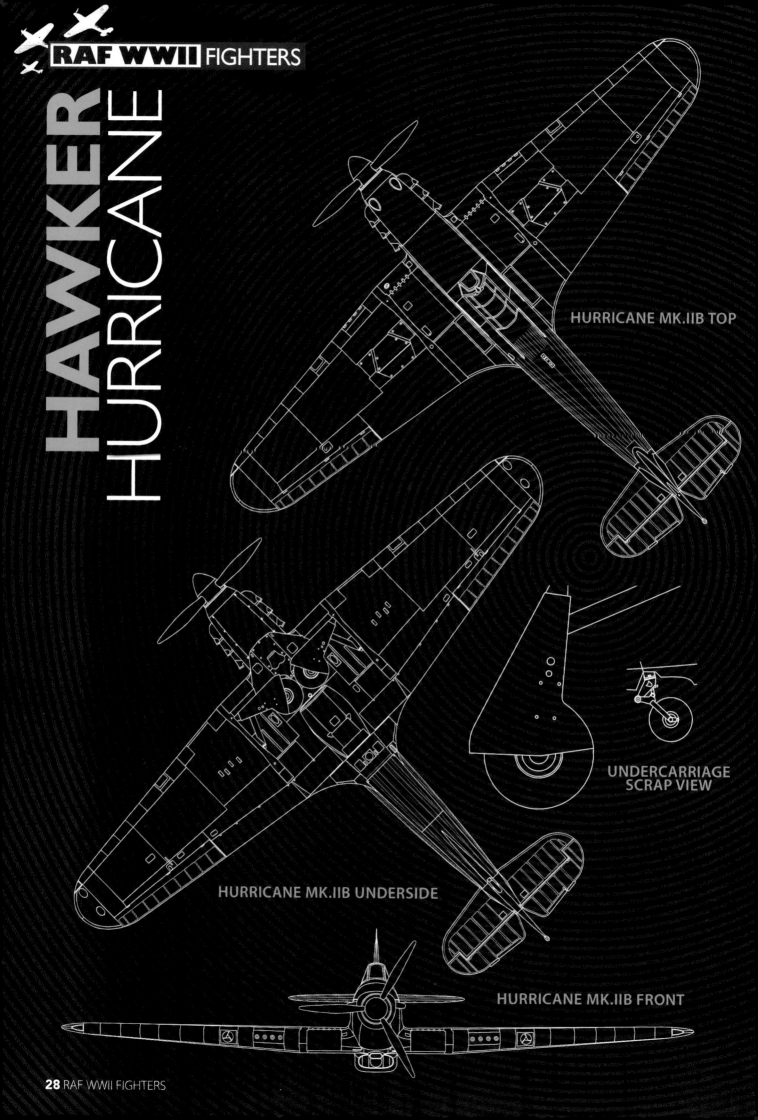

HURRICANE MK.IIB TOP

HURRICANE MK.IIB UNDERSIDE

UNDERCARRIAGE SCRAP VIEW

HURRICANE MK.IIB FRONT

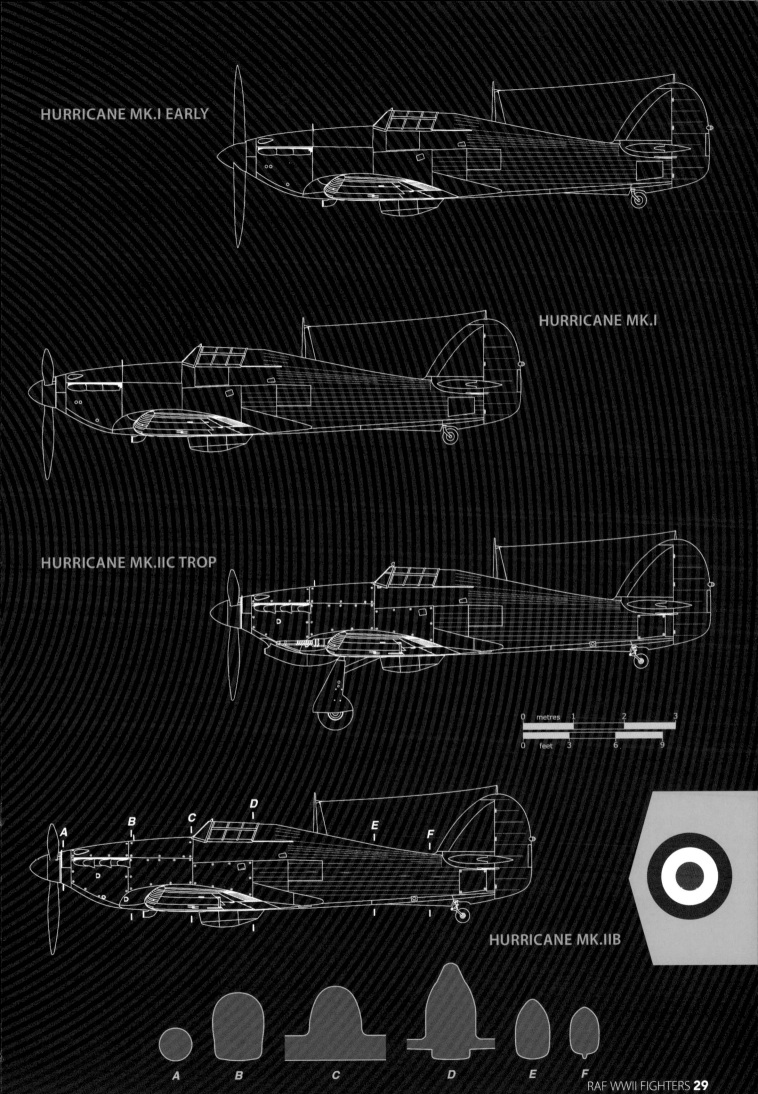

HURRICANE MK.I EARLY

HURRICANE MK.I

HURRICANE MK.IIC TROP

HURRICANE MK.IIB

0  metres  1  2  3
0  feet  3  6  9

A  B  C  D  E  F

If there is one British fighter which stands out and is more likely to be known and recognised than any other it is the Supermarine Spitfire. It has a reputation as a pure thoroughbred and the design was of such quality that it continued to be developed throughout the war and into the jet age (albeit somewhat tenuously).

# SUPERMARINE
# SPITFIRE MERLIN

## 1938-1955

**T**he Spitfire design originated with the chief designer at Supermarine, Reginald J Mitchell, who had joined the company as a draughtsman aged 21 in 1917. Working his way up during the intervening years, Mitchell was responsible for the flying boats which the company entered in the prestigious Schneider Trophy, a series of races aimed at advancing aviation technology utilising floatplanes. Having success with the S.4, S.5 and S.6 the competition was won for the third consecutive time with the S.6B in 1931, it also held the world speed record when it surpassed 407mph.

Even during the comparatively peaceful post war years the British Government was continuing to forge ahead with the development of the British armed forces including the Royal Air Force and in 1930 issued Specification F.7/30 in October 1931 for an all metal fighter capable of exceeding 250mph and armed with four guns that would operate as both a day and night fighter. The only successful result was the Gloster Gladiator but Supermarine did tender and construct the Type 224. It had gull wings and fixed undercarriage enclosed in faired spats. It was beset with problems from the outset but can be considered a vital step in the evolution of the Spitfire.

However, Mitchell was determined to make something of the doomed project so he embarked on a series of major alterations to the Type 224 integrating elements of the S.6B. Changes included streamlining in order to eke out more speed, the cockpit was covered, the main undercarriage was retractable, the narrower and instantly recognisable wing shape was designed, an oxygen system for the pilot was introduced among other things.

The underpowered Rolls-Royce Goshawk engine was replaced with the new Merlin engine (still called the PV-XII at that stage). So far removed from the 224 was the new design that it was re-designated as the Type 300. This new design fell so far outside the remit of Specification F.7/30 that the Air Ministry who were very much interested in the new design felt the need to issue a new specification to accommodate the Type 300, F.37/34 being issued on January 5, 1935. Official test tests indicated that eight guns would be the optimum armament with a two second burst

being sufficient to destroy an enemy aircraft so in light of these findings Specification F.10/35 was issued in the spring. To save time and resources Supermarine was invited to alter the Type 300 to fit the requirements. Concurrently to this, work had progressed on building the airframe and it was completed in early 1936.

On March 5, Joseph 'Mutt' Summers made the maiden flight in K5054 from Eastleigh Aerodrome. Upon landing, he said: "I don't want anything touched." This has since been interpreted as the Spitfire being close to perfection but he most likely meant that he did not want any settings altered before the next test flight. K5054 soon received a paint scheme that is thought to be a blueish grey but the exact shade is not known for certain. By May, the Type 300 was named the Spitfire, a name originally allocated to the Type 224.

It was much better than the Shrew, which had also been briefly considered. Encouraged by the prototype an order was placed for 310 aircraft so work continued on refining K5054 during 1936 and into 1937. Jeffrey Quill took over the role of leading the flight testing of the Spitfire for the company, although much of the testing took place at A&AEE. Radio equipment and aerial were fitted, guns were installed in the wings, the surface area of the rudder was increased and the bubble canopy was fitted to improve visibility. On May 11, 1937, Mitchell passed away due to cancer and Supermarine appointed Joe Smith as chief designer. He was tasked refining the Spitfire and preparing it for service.

The first production Mk.I, K9787, flew on May 14, 1938, and following some handling trials with the A&AEE was sent to 19 Sqn at RAF Duxford. It was not the first though as Quill had already delivered K9789 on August 4. By the end of the year 66 Sqn was also fully equipped with the Spitfire. There were a number of mishaps with the narrow undercarriage causing problems and on occasion pilots forgetting to lower the wheels, understandable when all aircraft had so far been fixed undercarriage. Early night flying also saw a high attrition rate with 38 Spitfires lost between the outbreak of war and the end of the year. Another flaw, this time with the Merlin

**SUPERMARINE SPITFIRE MK.VB BL415 AZ-B 234 (MADRAS PRESIDENCY) SQUADRON**

Flown by Flt Lt Walt 'Johnnie' Johnston. The squadron, based at Deanland ALG, Kent provided air cover to Sword Beach and escort to gliders on D-Day, hit by flak on June 15 BL415 crash landed at B6 Coulombs airfield. Later repaired and struck off charge on July 4, 1946.

**FOLLOWING THE MAIDEN FLIGHT, SUMMERS SAID: "I DON'T WANT ANYTHING TOUCHED."**

engine, was not resolved until 1941. When pitching forward or inducing negative G the carburettor cut out. The eventual solution was found by a team led by Beatrice 'Tilly' Shilling who proposed a smaller diameter hole to restrict flow sufficiently for it to no longer be a problem.

With the build up of forces by the Wermacht, new orders were placed by the Air Ministry but production of the Spitfire was still slow. Therefore, a shadow factory was set up at Castle Bromwich to alleviate the pressure on the Supermarine factory at Southampton. The factory was beset by problems the first 10 Spitfires finally being completed in June 1940. With changes instigated by Lord Beaverbrook the factory did eventually become efficient and produced 12,129 Spitfires of all marks.

By the outbreak of war the RAF had a grand total of seven Spitfire equipped squadrons and they were first involved in action during the regrettable Battle of Barking Creek when 74 Sqn Spitfires under the command of Adolf 'Sailor' Malan mistakenly identified the Hurricanes of 151 Sqn and engaged them, downing two and killing P/O

## SUPERMARINE SPITFIRE K5054

When the prototype first flew it was largely unpainted but it received a light Blue/Grey scheme in time for the first public display at Hendon during the Royal Air Force Pageant on June 27, 1936, later painted in Dark Earth and Dark Green.

## SUPERMARINE SPITFIRE MK.I R6981 KL-B 54 SQUADRON

Flt Lt Al Deere was forced to bail out of R6981 on August 15, 1940, at low level while being chased by the Luftwaffe, he had already had two confirmed kills, a third probable and damaged yet another when his Spitfire was damaged over the channel.

## SUPERMARINE SPITFIRE MK.II P7350 UO-T 266 SQUADRON

As the fourteenth Spitfire to be built at Castle Bromwich it was delivered to 266 Sqn, then at RAF Wittering during the height of the Battle of Britain on September 6. It went on to serve with 603 and 616 Squadrons, later appeared in the Battle of Britain film and is now flown by the BBMF.

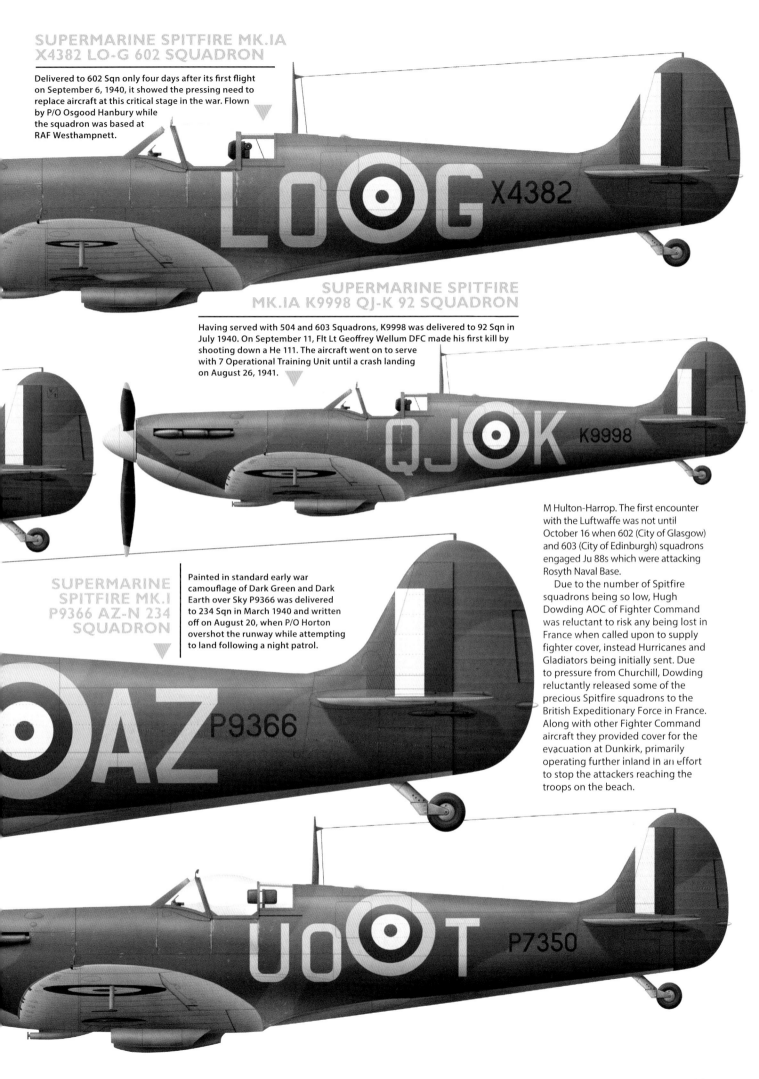

## SUPERMARINE SPITFIRE MK.IA
## X4382 LO-G 602 SQUADRON

Delivered to 602 Sqn only four days after its first flight on September 6, 1940, it showed the pressing need to replace aircraft at this critical stage in the war. Flown by P/O Osgood Hanbury while the squadron was based at RAF Westhampnett.

## SUPERMARINE SPITFIRE
## MK.IA K9998 QJ-K 92 SQUADRON

Having served with 504 and 603 Squadrons, K9998 was delivered to 92 Sqn in July 1940. On September 11, Flt Lt Geoffrey Wellum DFC made his first kill by shooting down a He 111. The aircraft went on to serve with 7 Operational Training Unit until a crash landing on August 26, 1941.

## SUPERMARINE SPITFIRE MK.I P9366 AZ-N 234 SQUADRON

Painted in standard early war camouflage of Dark Green and Dark Earth over Sky P9366 was delivered to 234 Sqn in March 1940 and written off on August 20, when P/O Horton overshot the runway while attempting to land following a night patrol.

M Hulton-Harrop. The first encounter with the Luftwaffe was not until October 16 when 602 (City of Glasgow) and 603 (City of Edinburgh) squadrons engaged Ju 88s which were attacking Rosyth Naval Base.

Due to the number of Spitfire squadrons being so low, Hugh Dowding AOC of Fighter Command was reluctant to risk any being lost in France when called upon to supply fighter cover, instead Hurricanes and Gladiators being initially sent. Due to pressure from Churchill, Dowding reluctantly released some of the precious Spitfire squadrons to the British Expeditionary Force in France. Along with other Fighter Command aircraft they provided cover for the evacuation at Dunkirk, primarily operating further inland in an effort to stop the attackers reaching the troops on the beach.

With the collapse of France an invasion of Great Britain looked imminent and it was perhaps for this moment that the Spitfire and Hurricane were created. After the fall in May there was a few weeks' respite for Fighter Command; small scale raids commencing in early July and continuing for just over a month until the intensity increased. That is not to say that the pilots had a rest as the squadrons based in the south were called into action daily but it was during August and September that pilots were expected to be on standby from before dawn until after dusk during the long summer days. This coincided with the Spitfire Mk.II entering service, the only difference from the Mk.I was the more powerful Merlin XII replacing the Merlin II and III.

Attacks were primarily made on fighter airfields and aircraft factories but the Luftwaffe failed to gain aerial superiority and on September 16 Göring ordered a switch to

## SUPERMARINE SPITFIRE MK.I P9386 QV-K 19 SQUADRON

Flown by Sqn Ldr Brian Lane DFC during the Battle of Britain, on September 7, 1940, he shot down a Bf 110. Lane went on to get six kills. There is some debate about the colour of the spinner but as the aircraft was originally used for Supermarine airspeed trials it was probably yellow.

## SUPERMARINE SPITFIRE MK.VB AB509 MC-J 142 WING

AB509 was the personal mount for Wg Cdr Johnny M Checketts, an ace with 12 victories. He flew AB509 several times on D-Day. The aircraft wears his personal initials along with the markings of the Polish and Canadian units within 142 Wing.

## SUPERMARINE SPITFIRE MK.N3277 AZ-H 234 SQUADRON

During a patrol on August 15, 1940, P/O Richard Hardy's Spitfire received damage and he made a forced landing on the beach near Cherbourg. Hardy was captured, N3277 was restored to flight and tested by the Luftwaffe.

## SUPERMARINE SPITFIRE MK.VB EP120 AE-A 501 SQUADRON

Delivered to 45 MU on May 23, 1942, and sent to 501 Sqn on June 4 where Sqn Ldr Geoffrey Northcott claimed six destroyed. Following damage it returned to the squadron, Wg Cdr Pat Gibbs claiming a Do 217. Following a period as a gate guardian it was restored to flight by the Fighter Collection at Duxford.

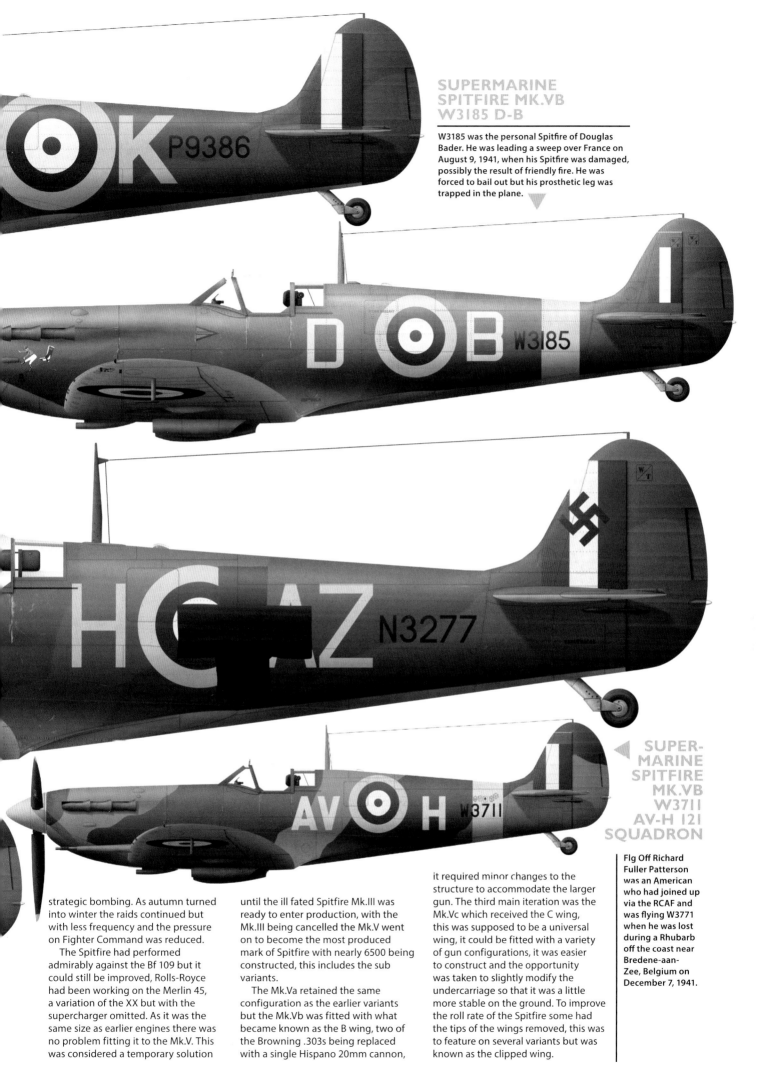

W3185 was the personal Spitfire of Douglas Bader. He was leading a sweep over France on August 9, 1941, when his Spitfire was damaged, possibly the result of friendly fire. He was forced to bail out but his prosthetic leg was trapped in the plane.

P9386

W3185

N3277

AV H W3711

SUPER-
MARINE
SPITFIRE
MK.VB
W3711
AV-H 121
SQUADRON

Flg Off Richard Fuller Patterson was an American who had joined up via the RCAF and was flying W3771 when he was lost during a Rhubarb off the coast near Bredene-aan-Zee, Belgium on December 7, 1941.

strategic bombing. As autumn turned into winter the raids continued but with less frequency and the pressure on Fighter Command was reduced.

The Spitfire had performed admirably against the Bf 109 but it could still be improved, Rolls-Royce had been working on the Merlin 45, a variation of the XX but with the supercharger omitted. As it was the same size as earlier engines there was no problem fitting it to the Mk.V. This was considered a temporary solution

until the ill fated Spitfire Mk.III was ready to enter production, with the Mk.III being cancelled the Mk.V went on to become the most produced mark of Spitfire with nearly 6500 being constructed, this includes the sub variants.

The Mk.Va retained the same configuration as the earlier variants but the Mk.Vb was fitted with what became known as the B wing, two of the Browning .303s being replaced with a single Hispano 20mm cannon,

it required minor changes to the structure to accommodate the larger gun. The third main iteration was the Mk.Vc which received the C wing, this was supposed to be a universal wing, it could be fitted with a variety of gun configurations, it was easier to construct and the opportunity was taken to slightly modify the undercarriage so that it was a little more stable on the ground. To improve the roll rate of the Spitfire some had the tips of the wings removed, this was to feature on several variants but was known as the clipped wing.

### SUPERMARINE SPITFIRE MK.VC EP193 QJ-U 92 SQUADRON

### SUPERMARINE SPITFIRE MK.VC MH300 KW-S 615 SQUADRON

Flg Off Paul Louis was flying MH300 out of Dohazari, India when he shared a Ki-46 with Flg Off Weggery on January 16, 1944, it was painted in Dark Green and Dark Earth over Ocean Grey.

Consistent with other aircraft operating in North Africa EP193 was painted in Dark Earth and Mid Stone over Azure Blue, it was flown by the leading Australian ace Flt Lt John Waddy who bagged a Bf 109F in it. EP193 later served with 601 and 145 Sqns, it was written off during a landing accident on April 23, 1945.

92 Sqn at RAF Biggin Hill was the first to receive the Mk.V in February 1941, the first were actually re-engined Mk.Ibs although production was limited to only 94 new Mk.Va as the thin wing had insufficient capacity to carry enough ammunition. During early engagements with the Mk.V the Bf 109 pilots had assumed they were the less powerful Mk.I and IIs and were caught unawares.

Due to poor weather 92 Sqn did not fly over France until April but it was the first of many missions over the continent by the Mk.V. As the Castle Bromwich factory increased production more squadrons were converting to the Mk.V, which began escorting bombers and undertaking fighter sweeps over Northern France. These missions continued throughout the war until after D-Day when Mk.V were to be found based at forward airfields on the continent, the last aggressive act by one was on March 12, 1945, when 276 Sqn Spitfires sank a Bieber Class mini

U-boat in the Scheldt Estuary. To cope with hotter climates the enlarged tropical Vokes filter was fitted, performance being slightly impaired due to the reduced airflow into the supercharger. Many of these were destined for squadrons in North Africa where they began replacing the Tomahawks and Kittyhawks from mid 1942. The Spitfires flew a mixture of defence and fighter escort missions during the North Africa campaign. 145 and 601 Squadrons saw particularly heavy action during El Alamein, soon after this 92 Squadron finally joined them, becoming fully operational with the Mk.V.

Tropical Spitfires also found their way to the Far East, where 54 Squadron found themselves up against Japanese fighters having left the UK in mid-1942 to support No 1 Wing of the RAAF, initially based at Darwin. Spitfires were also delivered to India to replacing the aging Hurricane II and Mohawk IV, allowing

## SUPERMARINE SPITFIRE MK.VII MD114 DU-G 602 SQUADRON

Plt Off John 'Ian' Blair was flying MD114 when he shot down a Me 109 at around 38,000ft on February 20, 1944, his log book states it was MD144 but documents state that only MD114 was at RAF Skaebrea at this time. ▼

the squadrons to be on an equal footing with the Ki-43 Oscar and A6M Zero. In Europe the Luftwaffe were using high altitude reconnaissance aircraft, primarily the Ju 86 over Britain, to successfully intercept them a Spitfire capable of flying in the thinner air was required, the Mk.VI was a modified Mk.V with extended wing tips and a pressurised cockpit, eight squadrons ended up being equipped with the type but it was not a particularly successful variant and only produced in small numbers.

Somewhat confusingly the next Spitfire variant to enter service was the Mk.IX in June 1942. It was never the intention to be built in large numbers, even though 5656 were built including sub variants. Instead the

Mk.IX was meant to be an interim solution to the threat posed by the Fw 190 while the Mk.VII was in development. It was fitted with the Merlin 61, a two-stage supercharged engine that gave a top speed of 409mph at 28,000 ft. The Merlin 61 was later replaced with the 63. The first to enter service were modified Mk.Vs but later aircraft included further improvements. In trials against a captured Fw 190 they were found to be almost evenly matched in all areas. The fitting of the Merlin 63 saw the Mk.IX designated the LF IX and a high altitude Merlin 70 powered Spitfire

## SUPERMARINE SPITFIRE LF MK. IXE MJ589 LO-D 602 SQUADRON

MJ589 was flown by the French ace Pierre Clostermann in the summer of 1944 and displays his tally at the time of seven kills, three probable and seven damaged. He was eventually credited with between 29 and 33 victories. ▼

## SUPERMARINE SPITFIRE MK.IXC EN152 QJ-3 92 SQUADRON

On March 14, 1943, 92 Sqn collected their first batch of Mk.IXs. To avoid confusion with the Mk.V, these were allocated numbers instead of individual letters. EN152 was on e of this batch and was probably flown by Sqn Ldr Neville Duke. ▼

| VARIANT | LENGTH | SPAN | HEIGHT | ENGINE |
|---|---|---|---|---|
| **PROTOTYPE** | **29FT 11IN / 9.12M** | **36FT 10IN / 11.23M** | **12FT 8IN / 3.86M** | **MERLIN C** |
| MK I/IA | 29FT 11IN / 9.12M | 36FT 10IN / 11.23M | 11FT 5IN / 3.48M | MERLIN II/III |
| MK IB | 29FT 11IN / 9.12M | 36FT 10IN / 11.23M | 11FT 5½IN / 3.49M | MERLIN III |
| MK IIA | 29FT 11IN / 9.12M | 36FT 10IN / 11.23M | 11FT 5½IN / 3.49M | MERLIN XII |
| MK IIC | 29FT 11IN / 9.12M | 36FT 10IN / 11.23M | 11FT 5½IN / 3.49M | MERLIN XII |
| MK VA,B,C | 29FT 11IN / 9.12M | 36FT 10IN / 11.23M | 11FT 5½IN / 3.49M | MERLIN 45 |
| HF MK VI | 30FT 2IN / 9.19M | 40FT 2IN / 12.24M | 11FT 5½IN / 3.49M | MERLIN 47 |
| MK VII | 31FT 3½ IN / 9.54M | 40FT 2IN / 12.24M | 11FT 8½IN / 3.57M | MERLIN 61, 64, 71 |
| MKVIII | 31FT 3½ IN / 9.54M | 36FT 10IN / 11.23M | 11FT 8½IN / 3.57M | MERLIN 61, 63, 66, 70 |
| MK IX | 30FT 6IN / 9.3M | 36FT 10IN / 11.23M | 11FT 8IN / 3.56M | MERLIN 61,63 |

# SPITFIRE MERLIN

with extended wingtips was the H. F IX.

Four Mk.IX Spitfire squadrons were involved in Operation Jubilee, the raid on Dieppe, with the other Spitfire squadrons using the Mk.V. Despite the small numbers involved it was considered a success for the MK.IX squadrons. They went on to play a significant role in the D-Day invasion.

Following the IX into service was the Mk.VII, the first being completed in August 1942, it featured the pressurised cockpit like the Mk.VI and there

were some improvements but not enough to make a significant difference to existing variants, only 140 were eventually built and it saw limited service. The Mk.VIII was based on the Mk.VII but was fitted with a revised canopy a retractable tail wheel, a Merlin 61 engine and the airframe was strengthened. They were all initially fitted with extended wing tips but the reduced roll rate was not popular with pilots so they reverted to the standard tips. The Mk.VIII proved popular, the pilots generally considered it the best of the Merlin-powered

Spitfires and 1658 were built, going on to serve with 30 squadrons many of which were based in the Mediterranean and Far East.

The Merlin Spitfire is the most well known of all the British fighters and the foresight of Mitchell allowed the basic design to be constantly adapted and revised to cater for improvements in engines, they remained in service for the duration of the war but the Spitfire story did not end with the Mk.IX. ⊙

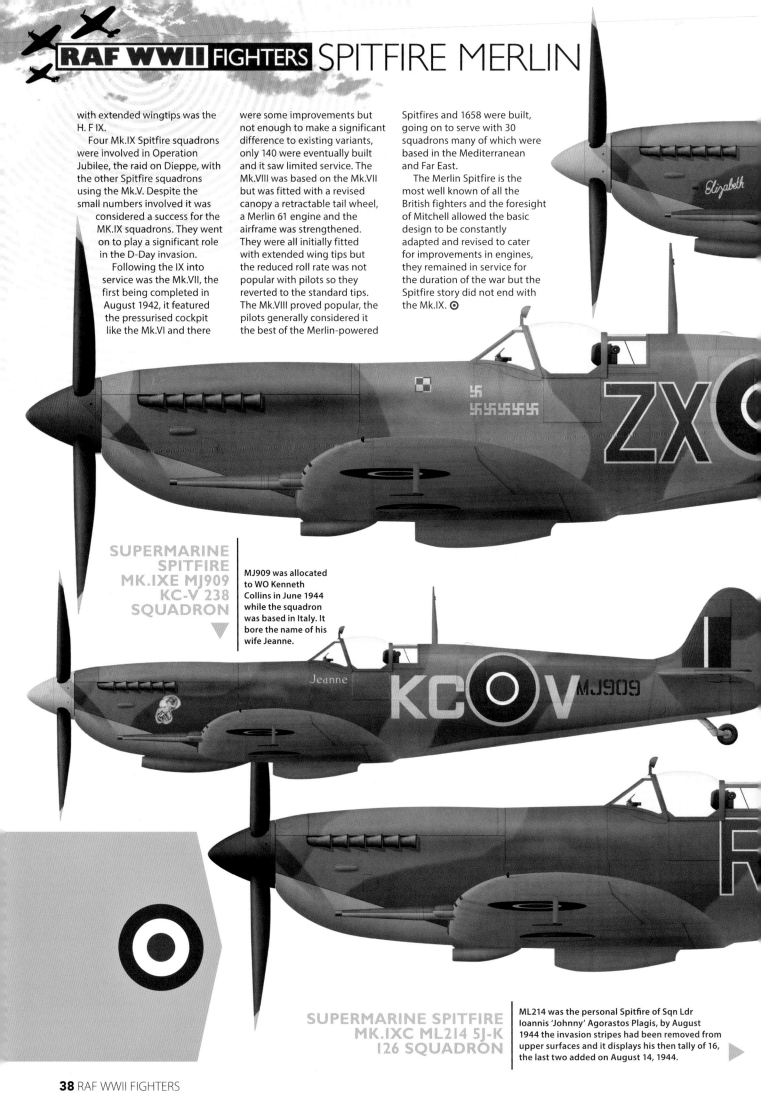

## SUPERMARINE SPITFIRE MK.IXE MJ909 KC-V 238 SQUADRON ▼

MJ909 was allocated to WO Kenneth Collins in June 1944 while the squadron was based in Italy. It bore the name of his wife Jeanne.

## SUPERMARINE SPITFIRE MK.IXC ML214 5J-K 126 SQUADRON

ML214 was the personal Spitfire of Sqn Ldr Ioannis 'Johnny' Agorastos Plagis, by August 1944 the invasion stripes had been removed from upper surfaces and it displays his then tally of 16, the last two added on August 14, 1944.

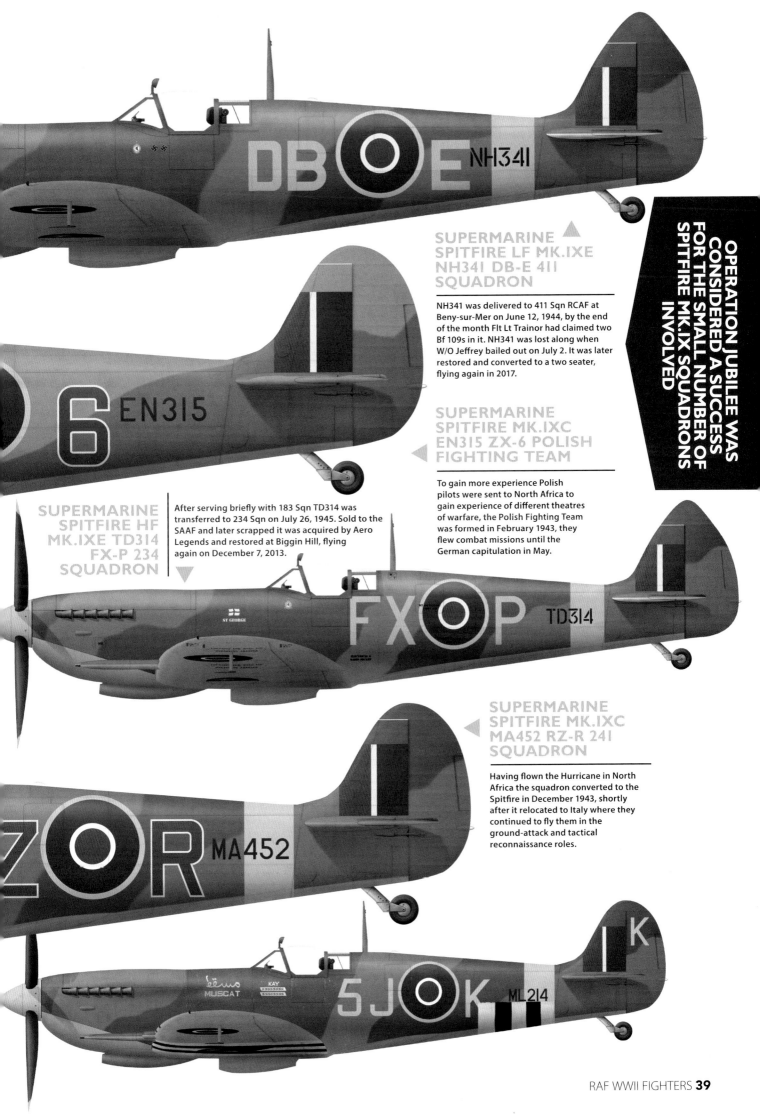

SUPERMARINE SPITFIRE LF MK.IXE NH341 DB-E 411 SQUADRON

NH341 was delivered to 411 Sqn RCAF at Beny-sur-Mer on June 12, 1944, by the end of the month Flt Lt Trainor had claimed two Bf 109s in it. NH341 was lost along when W/O Jeffrey bailed out on July 2. It was later restored and converted to a two seater, flying again in 2017.

SUPERMARINE SPITFIRE MK.IXC EN315 ZX-6 POLISH FIGHTING TEAM

To gain more experience Polish pilots were sent to North Africa to gain experience of different theatres of warfare, the Polish Fighting Team was formed in February 1943, they flew combat missions until the German capitulation in May.

SUPERMARINE SPITFIRE HF MK.IXE TD314 FX-P 234 SQUADRON

After serving briefly with 183 Sqn TD314 was transferred to 234 Sqn on July 26, 1945. Sold to the SAAF and later scrapped it was acquired by Aero Legends and restored at Biggin Hill, flying again on December 7, 2013.

SUPERMARINE SPITFIRE MK.IXC MA452 RZ-R 241 SQUADRON

Having flown the Hurricane in North Africa the squadron converted to the Spitfire in December 1943, shortly after it relocated to Italy where they continued to fly them in the ground-attack and tactical reconnaissance roles.

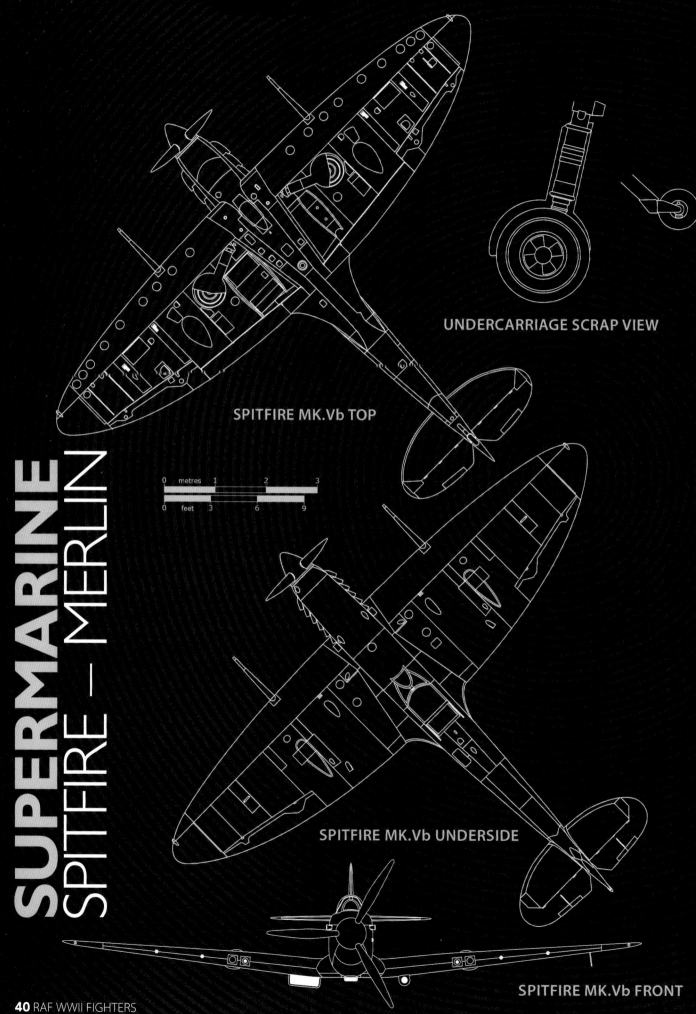

UNDERCARRIAGE SCRAP VIEW

SPITFIRE MK.Vb TOP

**SUPERMARINE**
**SPITFIRE – MERLIN**

metres 0 1 2 3

feet 0 3 6 9

SPITFIRE MK.Vb UNDERSIDE

SPITFIRE MK.Vb FRONT

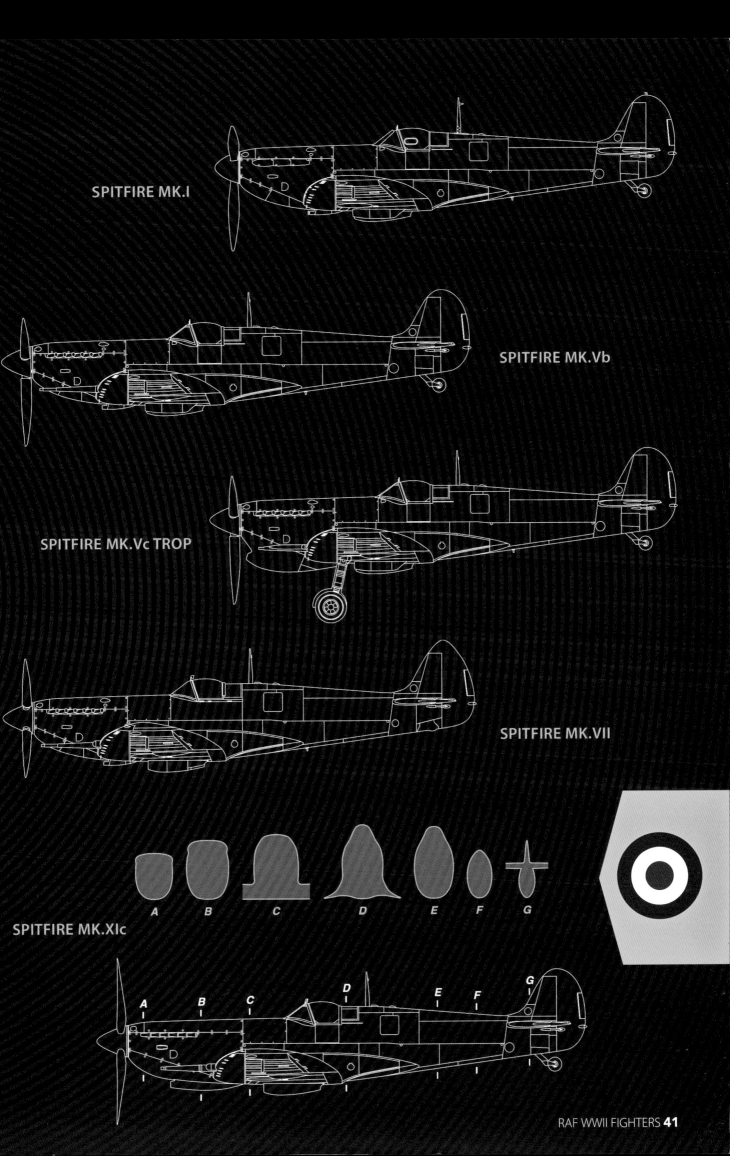

SPITFIRE MK.I

SPITFIRE MK.Vb

SPITFIRE MK.Vc TROP

SPITFIRE MK.VII

SPITFIRE MK.XIc

A  B  C  D  E  F  G

# SUPERMARINE SPITFIRE GRIFFON VARIANTS

## 1942-1955

The Rolls-Royce Merlin was a powerful engine when it was first introduced but the Spitfire airframe still had a lot of potential and the only way this could be realised was with a new power plant that could significantly improve performance – the Rolls-Royce Griffon.

The concept of the Rolls-Royce Griffon began development in 1938. It was initially commissioned by the Fleet Air Arm because it required an engine for new fighters such as the Fairey Firefly and Barracuda. Rolls-Royce introduced a number of improvements and new ideas with the Griffon: it had a hollow crankshaft which improved lubrication efficiency and was a first for aero engines; and it rotated the opposite way to the Merlin so there was some initial confusion by pilots converting from the Merlin powered Spitfires, especially as the swing to the right was so pronounced due to the increase in power.

As early as 1939 the idea of fitting a Spitfire with a Griffon was discussed but it was not until early 1941 that the Air Ministry officially placed an order for two Spitfires to be adapted. For a time they were known as the Mk.IV, then renamed the MK.XX to avoid confusion with the PR version and later the MK.XII, which was retained. The first MK.XII to fly was DP485 which was fitted with a Griffon IIB and flew for the first time on November 27,

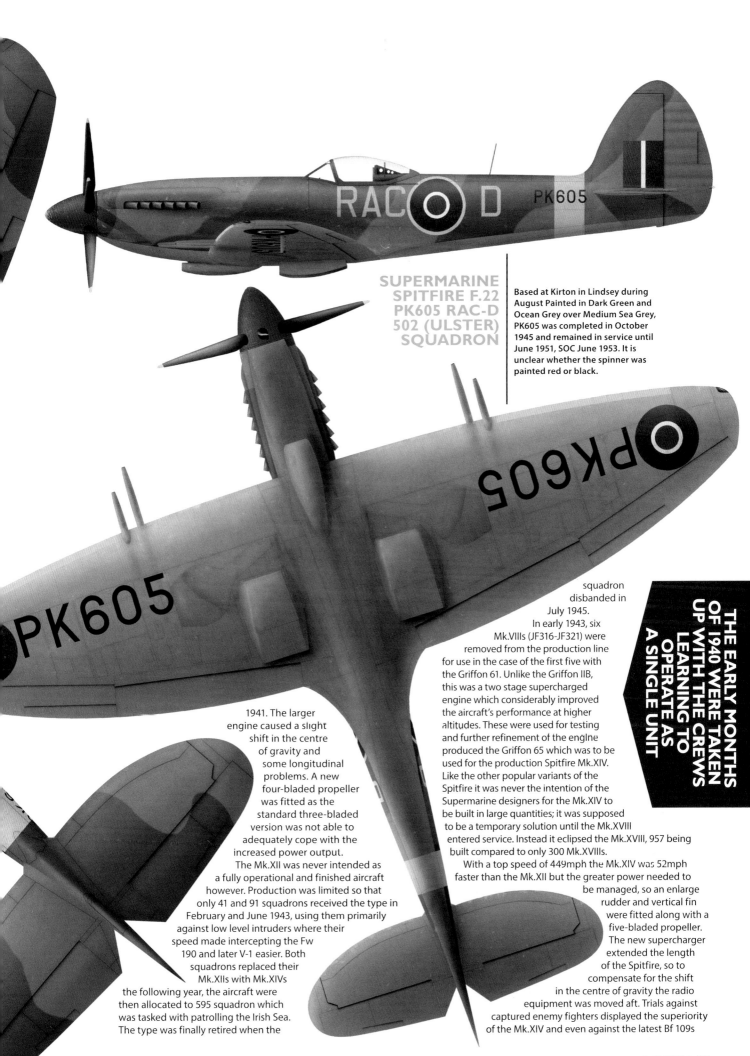

**SUPERMARINE SPITFIRE F.22 PK605 RAC-D 502 (ULSTER) SQUADRON**

Based at Kirton in Lindsey during August Painted in Dark Green and Ocean Grey over Medium Sea Grey, PK605 was completed in October 1945 and remained in service until June 1951, SOC June 1953. It is unclear whether the spinner was painted red or black.

1941. The larger engine caused a slight shift in the centre of gravity and some longitudinal problems. A new four-bladed propeller was fitted as the standard three-bladed version was not able to adequately cope with the increased power output.

The Mk.XII was never intended as a fully operational and finished aircraft however. Production was limited so that only 41 and 91 squadrons received the type in February and June 1943, using them primarily against low level intruders where their speed made intercepting the Fw 190 and later V-1 easier. Both squadrons replaced their Mk.XIIs with Mk.XIVs the following year, the aircraft were then allocated to 595 squadron which was tasked with patrolling the Irish Sea. The type was finally retired when the squadron disbanded in July 1945.

In early 1943, six Mk.VIIIs (JF316-JF321) were removed from the production line for use in the case of the first five with the Griffon 61. Unlike the Griffon IIB, this was a two stage supercharged engine which considerably improved the aircraft's performance at higher altitudes. These were used for testing and further refinement of the engine produced the Griffon 65 which was to be used for the production Spitfire Mk.XIV. Like the other popular variants of the Spitfire it was never the intention of the Supermarine designers for the Mk.XIV to be built in large quantities; it was supposed to be a temporary solution until the Mk.XVIII entered service. Instead it eclipsed the Mk.XVIII, 957 being built compared to only 300 Mk.XVIIIs.

With a top speed of 449mph the Mk.XIV was 52mph faster than the Mk.XII but the greater power needed to be managed, so an enlarge rudder and vertical fin were fitted along with a five-bladed propeller. The new supercharger extended the length of the Spitfire, so to compensate for the shift in the centre of gravity the radio equipment was moved aft. Trials against captured enemy fighters displayed the superiority of the Mk.XIV and even against the latest Bf 109s

## SUPERMARINE SPITFIRE MK.XIVE RN135 YB-A 17 SQUADRON

Most Spitfires were delivered with European Day Fighter markings and would have been repainted in SEAC colours, however this varied from plane to plane within a unit. RN135 was flown by Sqn Ld James H 'Ginger' Lacey, at which time it was repainted in Dark Green and Dark Earth over Medium Sea Grey with the markings reapplied.

## SUPERMARINE SPITFIRE MK.XIV RM619 AP-D 130 SQUADRON

RM619 was delivered to 91 Sqn in July 1944 but was passed to 130 Sqn in October while the unit was based in Holland where it wore the code AP-D and upper invasion stripes had been removed. Transferred to 350 Sqn in January 1945, it was shot down near Aachen on January 16. The pilot, Flt Lt H Smets, became a POW.

## SUPERMARINE SPITFIRE MK.XIV NH654 DL- 91 SQUADRON

Based at RAF Deanland between July and October 1944, 91 Sqn was tasked with intercepting V-1s. Flt Lt Jean-Marie Maridor destroyed a V-1 on July 5 in NH654. Invasion stripes were applied covering all markings except the roundel.

and Fw 190s the Spitfire retained the edge. Fw 190s found the only way to escape was to enter a vertical dive. The first aircraft found their way to 610 (County of Cheshire) Squadron in January 1944 while based at Exeter, 91 and 322 Squadrons received theirs in March.

The Mk.XIV was used in a mixture of home defence against the V-1 and opportunistic tip and run raiders. The first V-1 'Diver' destroyed by a Spitfire

was achieved by Flt Lt H B Moffett on the morning of June 16, 1944. After a 20 mile chase it was finally shot down near Redhill. The Spitfire squadrons failed to achieve the impressive tallies of the Mosquito and Tempest squadrons but the Mk.XIV was still responsible for downing 303 flying bombs. The Mk.XIV also saw extensive action on the offensive with the 2nd Tactical Air Force in Europe, mixing it with the Fw 190, Bf 109 and even the Me 262.

## SUPERMARINE SPITFIRE MK.XIV RB169 MN-F 350 (BELGIAN) SQUADRON

350 Sqn was formed by free Belgians in November 1941. During the summer of 1944 they flew Diver missions against the V-1 from various bases in the South East. Later passed to 612 Sqn RB169 suffered a catastrophic engine fire on August 24, 1947.

## SUPERMARINE SPITFIRE F.21 LA315 EB-O 41 SQUADRON

Postwar Spitfire of 41 Sqn based at RAF Wittering, 1946. The squadron badge within a stylized spear head was carried on the nose, colour of the spearhead varied within the squadron. Red spinner, Sky code letters and band.

Externally the only visual difference between the Mk.XIV and Mk.XVIII was the teardrop canopy, internally there were several improvements, the hollow laminated wing spars had been replaced with solid ones, two 31 gallon tanks were fitted in the rear fuselage. It was intended that the Mk.XVIII should replace the Mk.XIV but in keeping with Spitfire tradition the Mk.XIV surpassed it. 300 were built and only 99 of those were fighters, the rest being the PR.XVIII. Another reason for the smaller numbers was due to the cessation of hostilities in Europe before the first Mk.XVIII had flown. As it entered production, finished machines were initially supplied directly to the Far East, the

first were to 60 Squadron based at Seletar, Singapore soon followed by 11, 28 and 81 Squadrons. Too late to be involved in any serious action, the Mk.XIIIs of 28 and 60 Squadrons were used during the Malayan emergency against guerrilla forces.

The Spitfire Mk.XIII also had the unenviable record of being shot down by Spitfires of another state. 32 and 208

Squadrons were based in Palestine and were being used to provide cover for the British withdrawal. Both the Egyptian and fledgling Israeli air forces were equipped with Spitfires, some flown by ex-RAF pilots and despite the national markings there was inevitably some misidentification. On May 22, 1948, Egyptian Spitfires shot down RAF Spitfires at Ramat David with the loss of four RAF and three Egyptian aircraft.

The final Spitfire variants to be built and serve with the RAF were the F.21 and F.22. The last two 'Super Spitfires' saw a substantial number of changes, so far removed from the original Spitfire that renaming the F.21 the Victor was briefly considered. The wing was extensively modified and introduced laminar flow, while the cannon were offset for better fitting.

It also saw a wider track with the undercarriage being widened and the legs lengthened, providing extra clearance for the Rotol five-bladed propeller and the contra-rotating props fitted to some F.21s. Trials at Boscome Down highlighted a number of problems but many of these could

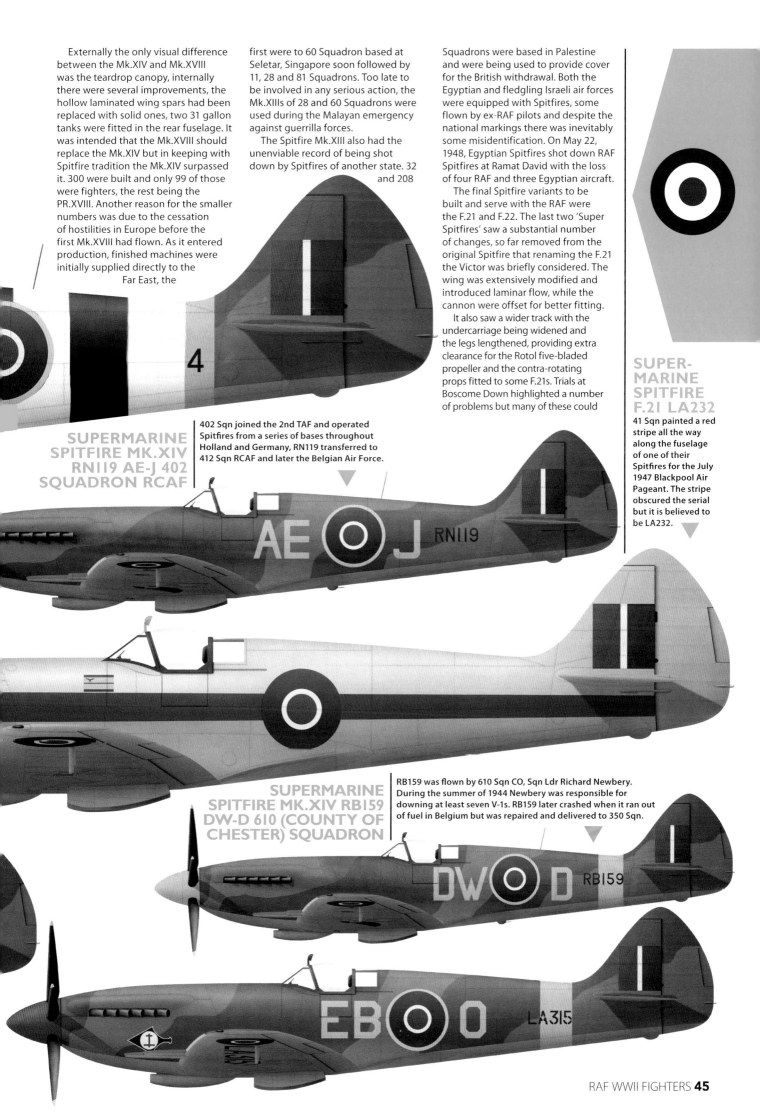

**SUPERMARINE SPITFIRE F.21 LA232**

41 Sqn painted a red stripe all the way along the fuselage of one of their Spitfires for the July 1947 Blackpool Air Pageant. The stripe obscured the serial but it is believed to be LA232.

402 Sqn joined the 2nd TAF and operated Spitfires from a series of bases throughout Holland and Germany, RN119 transferred to 412 Sqn RCAF and later the Belgian Air Force.

**SUPERMARINE SPITFIRE MK.XIV RN119 AE-J 402 SQUADRON RCAF**

AE • J RN119

**SUPERMARINE SPITFIRE MK.XIV RB159 DW-D 610 (COUNTY OF CHESTER) SQUADRON**

RB159 was flown by 610 Sqn CO, Sqn Ldr Richard Newbery. During the summer of 1944 Newbery was responsible for downing at least seven V-1s. RB159 later crashed when it ran out of fuel in Belgium but was repaired and delivered to 350 Sqn.

DW • D RB159

EB • O LA315

be traced back to there being too much power for the control surfaces to cope with. The conclusion drawn by official reports was that there should be no further development of the Spitfire line. Modifications were made and the F.21 was eventually tamed.

Initially an order was placed for 3373 but with the onset of peace only 120 were eventually completed. The first F.21 were delivered to 91 Squadron at RAF Manston in January 1945 and saw limited service, primarily flying reconnaissance missions. The F.21 eventually served with 11 squadrons, remaining with the auxiliary squadrons until May 1955.

The F.22 was almost identical to the F.21 in most regards, but it had the lower back and teardrop canopy; the tail was further enlarged. The F.22 only saw service with one front line squadron, 73 Squadron based in the Middle East for a few months before they were replaced with DH Vampires, the rest of the F.22s served with auxiliary squadrons until they were also replaced with jets. Some F.22s did find a second life as F.24s, along with some newly built, bringing the total to 81. These were the same as the F.22 except for the extra fuel capacity, Griffon 85 and reinforced wings to allow for rockets to be mounted.

Mitchell could never have imagined how far his original design would be developed and evolved, the lineage eventually being traced through the Seafire and Spiteful to the first Supermarine jet, the Attacker, which used some Spitfire elements. A total of 20,351 were built and it served with air forces across the globe. Ultimately, the Spitfire was outclassed by the Meteor and Vampire and so would be consigned to history. It had the looks to capture the imagination and this is reflected in the fascination it still holds for many. In addition, there is a slow but continual increase in the numbers returning to flight, some even being converted to two-seaters allowing anyone to experience the thrill of flying them. ◉

### SUPERMARINE SPITFIRE F.21 LA198 RAI-G 602 (CITY OF GLASGOW) SQUADRON

First flown on August 21, 1944, it was delivered to 1 Sqn and coded JX-C, it then went to 602 Sqn but was damaged in a landing. After some time as a gate guardian it was restored and displayed at Kelvingrove Art Gallery & Museum, Glasgow.

### SUPERMARINE SPITFIRE F.21 LA195 RAV-E 615 (COUNTY OF SURREY) SQUADRON

Having been delivered to the RAF in January 1946 it was not delivered to 615 Sqn until April 25, 1947, painted in Dark Green and Ocean Grey over Medium Sea Grey with the squadron badge on the nose. A year later it was retired and ended up as a target for firing trials.

### SUPERMARINE SPITFIRE F.22 PK602 RAN-O 607 (COUNTY OF DURHAM) SQUADRON

607 Sqn replaced their F.14s with the F.22 in January 1949 with PK602 being delivered on January 27 even though it was completed in October 1945. It was damaged during an air test on August 19, 1950.

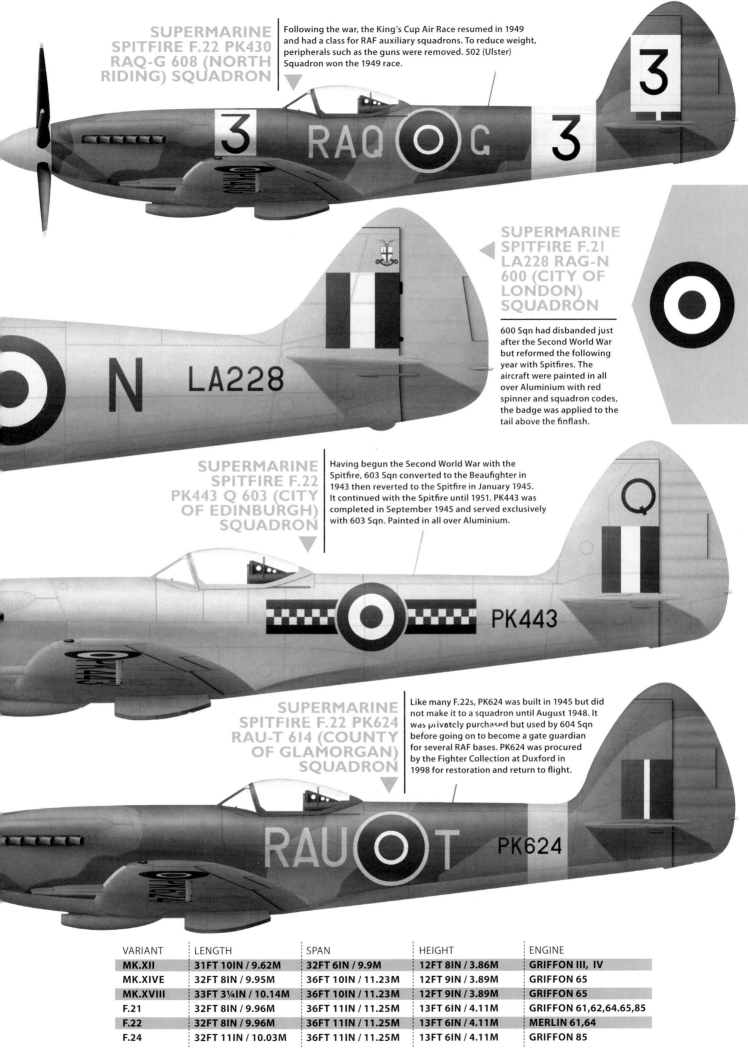

**SUPERMARINE SPITFIRE F.22 PK430 RAQ-G 608 (NORTH RIDING) SQUADRON**

Following the war, the King's Cup Air Race resumed in 1949 and had a class for RAF auxiliary squadrons. To reduce weight, peripherals such as the guns were removed. 502 (Ulster) Squadron won the 1949 race.

**SUPERMARINE SPITFIRE F.21 LA228 RAG-N 600 (CITY OF LONDON) SQUADRON**

600 Sqn had disbanded just after the Second World War but reformed the following year with Spitfires. The aircraft were painted in all over Aluminium with red spinner and squadron codes, the badge was applied to the tail above the finflash.

**SUPERMARINE SPITFIRE F.22 PK443 Q 603 (CITY OF EDINBURGH) SQUADRON**

Having begun the Second World War with the Spitfire, 603 Sqn converted to the Beaufighter in 1943 then reverted to the Spitfire in January 1945. It continued with the Spitfire until 1951. PK443 was completed in September 1945 and served exclusively with 603 Sqn. Painted in all over Aluminium.

**SUPERMARINE SPITFIRE F.22 PK624 RAU-T 614 (COUNTY OF GLAMORGAN) SQUADRON**

Like many F.22s, PK624 was built in 1945 but did not make it to a squadron until August 1948. It was privately purchased but used by 604 Sqn before going on to become a gate guardian for several RAF bases. PK624 was procured by the Fighter Collection at Duxford in 1998 for restoration and return to flight.

| VARIANT | LENGTH | SPAN | HEIGHT | ENGINE |
|---|---|---|---|---|
| MK.XII | 31FT 10IN / 9.62M | 32FT 6IN / 9.9M | 12FT 8IN / 3.86M | GRIFFON III, IV |
| MK.XIVE | 32FT 8IN / 9.95M | 36FT 10IN / 11.23M | 12FT 9IN / 3.89M | GRIFFON 65 |
| MK.XVIII | 33FT 3¼IN / 10.14M | 36FT 10IN / 11.23M | 12FT 9IN / 3.89M | GRIFFON 65 |
| F.21 | 32FT 8IN / 9.96M | 36FT 11IN / 11.25M | 13FT 6IN / 4.11M | GRIFFON 61,62,64.65,85 |
| F.22 | 32FT 8IN / 9.96M | 36FT 11IN / 11.25M | 13FT 6IN / 4.11M | MERLIN 61,64 |
| F.24 | 32FT 11IN / 10.03M | 36FT 11IN / 11.25M | 13FT 6IN / 4.11M | GRIFFON 85 |

# SUPERMARINE SPITFIRE GRIFFON VARIANTS

SPITFIRE F.22 TOP

UNDERCARRIAGE
SCRAP VIEW

SPITFIRE F.22 UNDERSIDE

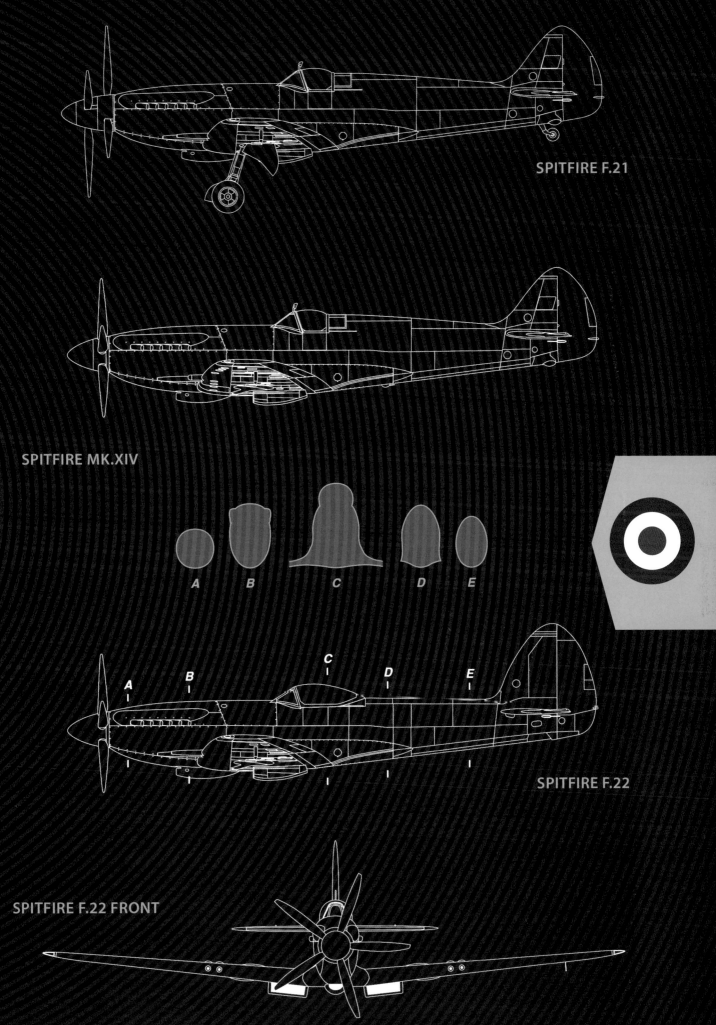

SPITFIRE F.21

SPITFIRE MK.XIV

SPITFIRE F.22

SPITFIRE F.22 FRONT

A    B    C    D    E

The Boulton Paul Defiant was a concept that could not fail in theory but the realities of war proved somewhat different for the fighter. Fitting a turret to a small aeroplane was meant to allow for a wide arc of fire so that the pilot would not be required to get into a precise firing position.

# BOULTON PAUL DEFIANT

**W**hen the Defiant was conceived, single seat fighters normally had their guns harmonised on a point some distance in front of the aircraft and the whole airframe has to be aimed at the target. The turret itself, which was already being seen fitted to bombers such as the Boulton Paul Overstrand, could traverse and target the enemy with much more ease.

The majority of fighters constructed have been single seaters. From early aircraft such as the Sopwith Camel through types such as the Spitfire to jets like the Sea Harrier and Typhoon there has only been a single seat for a lone pilot who does everything. There has however always been an opposing theory that two are better than one and this arrangement has proven successful in aircraft such as the FE.2b, Mosquito, Javelin and Tornado with the second crewmember easing the workload on the pilot.

During the interwar years the speed of aircraft continued to rise and it was apparent that gunners would need some form of protection from the airflow while still being able to accurately fire the guns; the widely used Scarff Ring offering no protection. Boulton Paul was approached by the Air Ministry to investigate using a powered turret in a converted Sidestrand, this resulted in the ungainly Overstrand. Only 28 of these were completed but they did enter service with the RAF. At the same time Fraser Nash had also begun work on turrets, fitting one to

the Hawker Demon fighter.

Several specifications were issued throughout the early to mid-1930s which required a fighter with two crew and a variety of armament configurations. The first of these was F22/33 which was superceded by F5/33 and F7/30, the latter

leading to the Gloster Gladiator. Several companies expressed interest and submitted designs, the most radical being the Westland Pterodactyl V.

Eventually on June 26, 1935, Specification F9/35 was issued for a power operated turret fighter with a top speed of 315mph at 15,000ft that could also carry eight 20lb bombs. Bristol submitted a variation on its existing single engine Type 146 design, while Armstrong Whitworth proposed

the twin engine AW.34. Fairey, Gloster and Supermarine also tendered designs. But it was only the Hawker Hotspur and Defiant which were to proceed, with prototypes of both being ordered by the Air Ministry. A single Hotspur was built but the demands made by the Hurricane meant the company could not commit to development of the Hotspur, leaving only Boulton Paul.

A wooden mock up was constructed at the Boulton Paul factory in Norwich and the SAMM AB.7 was integrated into the design. The turret would be fitted with four Hispano Suiza 20mm cannon. With the design agreed and finalised, work commenced on the first prototype K8130. It was a mix of tubular metal, plywood and a light alloy skin with fabric covered control surfaces.

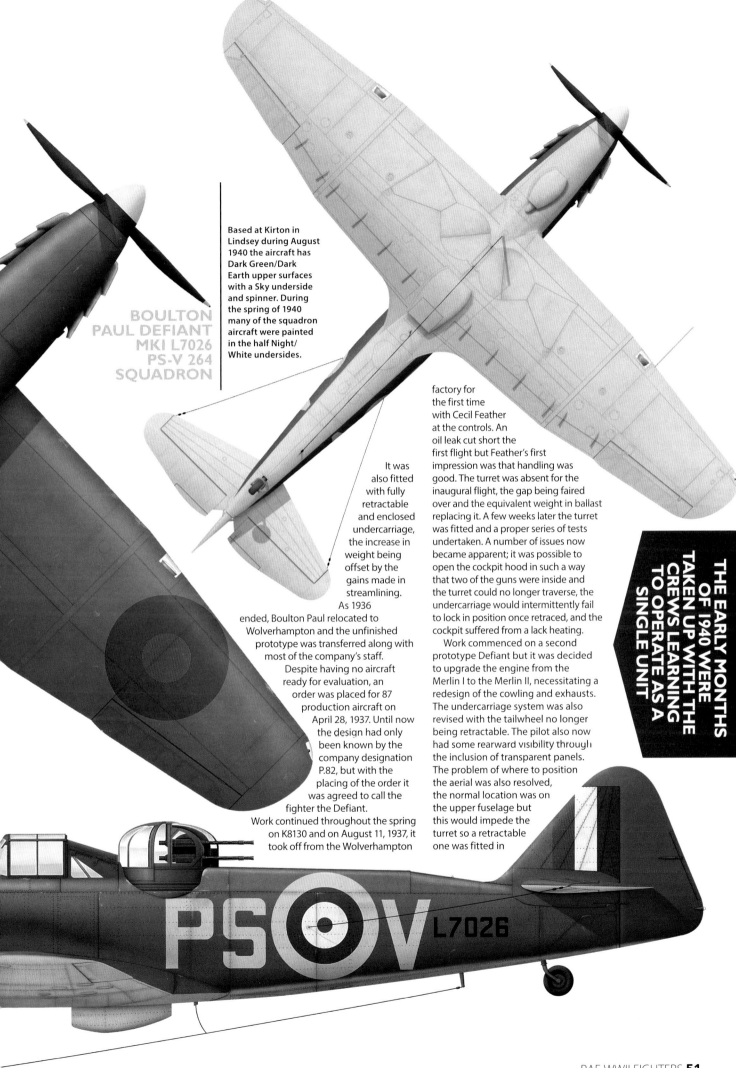

BOULTON
PAUL DEFIANT
MKI L7026
PS-V 264
SQUADRON

Based at Kirton in Lindsey during August 1940 the aircraft has Dark Green/Dark Earth upper surfaces with a Sky underside and spinner. During the spring of 1940 many of the squadron aircraft were painted in the half Night/White undersides.

It was also fitted with fully retractable and enclosed undercarriage, the increase in weight being offset by the gains made in streamlining. As 1936 ended, Boulton Paul relocated to Wolverhampton and the unfinished prototype was transferred along with most of the company's staff. Despite having no aircraft ready for evaluation, an order was placed for 87 production aircraft on April 28, 1937. Until now the design had only been known by the company designation P.82, but with the placing of the order it was agreed to call the fighter the Defiant. Work continued throughout the spring on K8130 and on August 11, 1937, it took off from the Wolverhampton

factory for the first time with Cecil Feather at the controls. An oil leak cut short the first flight but Feather's first impression was that handling was good. The turret was absent for the inaugural flight, the gap being faired over and the equivalent weight in ballast replacing it. A few weeks later the turret was fitted and a proper series of tests undertaken. A number of issues now became apparent; it was possible to open the cockpit hood in such a way that two of the guns were inside and the turret could no longer traverse, the undercarriage would intermittently fail to lock in position once retraced, and the cockpit suffered from a lack heating.

Work commenced on a second prototype Defiant but it was decided to upgrade the engine from the Merlin I to the Merlin II, necessitating a redesign of the cowling and exhausts. The undercarriage system was also revised with the tailwheel no longer being retractable. The pilot also now had some rearward visibility through the inclusion of transparent panels. The problem of where to position the aerial was also resolved, the normal location was on the upper fuselage but this would impede the turret so a retractable one was fitted in

THE EARLY MONTHS OF 1940 WERE TAKEN UP WITH THE CREWS LEARNING TO OPERATE AS A SINGLE UNIT

PS●V L7026

the lower fuselage. The delays caused by the alterations meant that further flight tests did not take place until May 18, 1939, but this was closely followed by the first flight of a production Defiant, L6950, on July 30, 1939.

As aircraft were completed they were delivered for evaluation and testing to A&AEE at Boscombe Down, the Central Flying School at Upavon and the AFDU at RAF Northolt. On October 30, 264 Squadron was re-formed at RAF Sutton Bridge specifically as a Defiant squadron and received the first three aircraft just over a week later.

Like so many pilots converting to the modern monoplanes from fixed undercarriage machines they had to remember to lower the wheels before landing. By the end of the year the squadron had relocated to RAF Martlesham Heath, more aircraft had been delivered, the pilots had qualified on the Defiant and the gunners had arrived.

The early months of 1940 were taken up with the crews learning to operate as a single unit and getting used to flying with a turret, evolving tactics which at the time made sense but which, with hindsight, failed to highlight how weak the Defiant was in a frontal attack. The Merlin III also suffered reliability problems which took time to resolve; the squadron being grounded for a whole week while it was comprehensively dealt with.

During March the squadron once again moved, this time to RAF Wittering where it was declared operational and began flying convoy patrols utilising a detachment which was based at RAF Bircham Newton. At the same time 141 Sqn began replacing their Blenheims with the Defiant at RAF Grangemouth. The timing was fortunate as German forces moved into France and the Low Countries beginning on May 10. Two days later 624 Sqn engaged the Luftwaffe during a fighter sweep when along with Spitfires of 66 Sqn they engaged a Ju 88 and successfully brought it down.

Over the next few weeks the squadron continued to engage the Luftwaffe. Messerschmitt Bf 109 pilots, unfamiliar with the Defiant and often confusing it with the other RAF fighters in France, commonly attacked it from the rear – and flew right into the formidable turret's field of fire. The Defiants continued to patrol over the beaches of Dunkirk throughout the evacuation of the British Expeditionary Force, bringing down Bf 110s, Bf 109s, Ju 88s and He 111s. By this time the squadron was stationed at RAF Manston to reduce the flying time to and from the area of patrol.

The Defiant made its mark in history on May 29. A dozen 264 Sqn aircraft took off in the afternoon, covered by three Hurricane squadrons. As they neared the French coast the Hurricanes encountered a mixed formation

of Bf 110s, Ju 87s and Bf 109s; during the ensuing melee six Bf 109s broke off to engage the Defiants from the rear.

In the confusion it is unclear how many were destroyed but at least half of the attackers were downed. Squadron Leader Philip Hunter then spotted a lone He 111 but as he positioned himself for the attack a formation of Ju 87s came into view with Bf 110s acting as escort, which was a far more appealing target. As the squadron attacked the Ju 87s they were in turn attacked by the Bf 110s. Just like the American settlers forming a wagon circle to defend against Indians the Defiants entered a descending spiral which appeared to work, with three gunners claiming Bf 110s.

Having returned to base to rearm, the squadron took off in the early evening for a second patrol where they again found Ju 87s bombing the British troops on the beaches. This was a very successful engagement with 17 enemy aircraft being claimed (including shared) as destroyed. There was a final opportunity to bag a Ju 88 with a second being damaged before the squadron had to return to base having expended almost all its ammunition. The only loss was a single gunner.

## BOULTON PAUL P.94 K8310

The P.94 prototype wore a variety of schemes during its time in service including this one with a natural metal finish to the nose and painted aluminium all over. It later had the turret removed and faired over as a fighter demonstrator.

The first production Defiant wore the standard camouflage scheme of Dark Green/Dark Earth with Sky undersides but also during this period the port wing was painted black with the aircraft serial in white. It was with A&AEE during September 1939.

## BOULTON PAUL DEFIANT MKI L6950 A&AEE

## BOULTON PAUL DEFIANT MKI N1572 KO-I 2 SQUADRON

While still primarily using the Lysander at Clifton, 2 Sqn was briefly equipped with Defiants between August and September 1940 when the type was used for trials along with the Fairey Battle. The aircraft has Dark Green/Dark Earth upper surfaces with Sky undersides, the spinner being black.

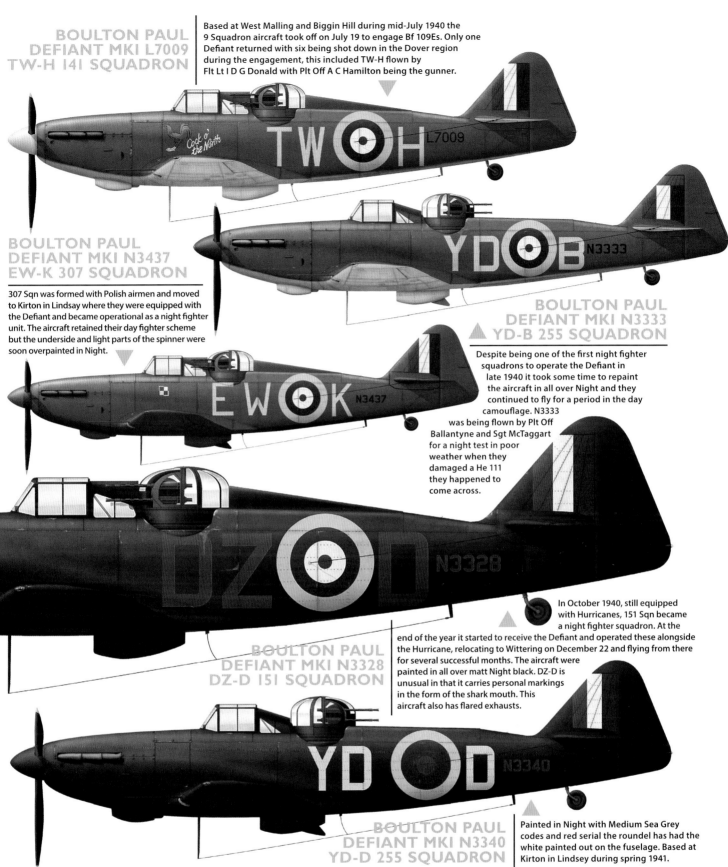

## BOULTON PAUL DEFIANT MKI L7009 TW-H 141 SQUADRON

Based at West Malling and Biggin Hill during mid-July 1940 the 9 Squadron aircraft took off on July 19 to engage Bf 109Es. Only one Defiant returned with six being shot down in the Dover region during the engagement, this included TW-H flown by Flt Lt I D G Donald with Plt Off A C Hamilton being the gunner.

## BOULTON PAUL DEFIANT MKI N3437 EW-K 307 SQUADRON

307 Sqn was formed with Polish airmen and moved to Kirton in Lindsay where they were equipped with the Defiant and became operational as a night fighter unit. The aircraft retained their day fighter scheme but the underside and light parts of the spinner were soon overpainted in Night.

## BOULTON PAUL DEFIANT MKI N3333 YD-B 255 SQUADRON

Despite being one of the first night fighter squadrons to operate the Defiant in late 1940 it took some time to repaint the aircraft in all over Night and they continued to fly for a period in the day camouflage. N3333 was being flown by Plt Off Ballantyne and Sgt McTaggart for a night test in poor weather when they damaged a He 111 they happened to come across.

## BOULTON PAUL DEFIANT MKI N3328 DZ-D 151 SQUADRON

In October 1940, still equipped with Hurricanes, 151 Sqn became a night fighter squadron. At the end of the year it started to receive the Defiant and operated these alongside the Hurricane, relocating to Wittering on December 22 and flying from there for several successful months. The aircraft were painted in all over matt Night black. DZ-D is unusual in that it carries personal markings in the form of the shark mouth. This aircraft also has flared exhausts.

## BOULTON PAUL DEFIANT MKI N3340 YD-D 255 SQUADRON

Painted in Night with Medium Sea Grey codes and red serial the roundel has had the white painted out on the fuselage. Based at Kirton in Lindsey during spring 1941.

A total of 65 kills were claimed during the fall of France, 37 were made on the 29th alone, but the actual number is probably lower due to multiple claims on individual aircraft. Regardless of the actual tally it was the high point of the Defiant's career. As the Luftwaffe pilots became familiar with the aircraft and learned its weaknesses the success rate would drop considerably.

With the intensity beginning to increase in the Battle of Britain, 141 Sqn was moved south to RAF West Malling on July 10 so it could enter the fray.

On the 19th the Defiants took off in response to a raid and were engaged by Bf 110s, but of the nine that took off only two returned safely. Ten crew were lost that day. As the summer progressed, it became increasingly apparent that the Defiant was unsuited to daylight fighter operations despite continuing to get some kills, so it was decided that it should change roles and become exclusively a night fighter.

As the Luftwaffe increased their night time raids during September, a third Defiant squadron was formed

specifically to be a night fighter squadron. 307 Sqn was a Polish unit based at RAF Kirton in Lindsey, this coincided with 264 Sqn beginning to undertake night flying from RAF Northolt. 141 Sqn was posted to RAF Gatwick. All the aircraft were repainted black and had flame dampers fitted so the pilot's night vision would not be impaired.

96, 225 and 226 squadrons were equipped with the Defiant over the following months but poor weather restricted the number of operations

**BOULTON PAUL DEFIANT MKI N1744 JT-S 256 SQUADRON** ▲

Initially based in the south west, 256 Sqn were posted to Squires Gate in March 1941, being tasked with the air defence of Liverpool and Merseyside. The aircraft had been painted Night over the original camouflage but in many cases it began to wear and weather heavily.

**BOULTON PAUL DEFIANT MKI N1801 PS-Y 264 SQUADRON**

Flying from several bases including Debden and Biggin Hill during the winter and spring of 1941 N1801 was frequently flown by Plt Off D Hughes and Sgt F Gash. During this period he shot down three aircraft and became an ace. ▽

**BOULTON PAUL DEFIANT MKI L7011 KJ-A 11 OPERATIONAL TRAINING UNIT**

11 OTU was created to train bomber aircrew and L7011 was utilised for Gunnery Training and Fighter Affiliation duties. All codes in Dull Red. Skatz likely to be in white but possibly in red. ▽

**BOULTON** ▲ **PAUL DEFIANT MKI VIII0 RA-H 410 SQUADRON**

410 Canadian Squadron was based at Drem during the summer of 1941 and unusually for Defiant night fighters had roundels on the lower wings as well.

**DEFENSIVELY THE TURRET CONTINUED TO BE USED ON BOMBERS THROUGHOUT THE WAR AND BEYOND INTO THE COLD WAR**

that could be flow by any of these units, although there were a few successful intercepts such as 255 Sqn claiming three probables during February 1941. The inherent dangers that came with night flying took their toll on the squadrons but as the year progressed so the number of successful intercepts gradually rose. The turning point for 264 Sqn was in the autumn when the first A.I. MkIV (radar) sets were fitted. They were limited to four miles range and suffered badly from ground returns, only being able to pick up trade if the Defiant was below the target aircraft.

The A.I. MkIV was soon superseded by the more powerful and reliable A.I. MkVI which was carried by seven Defiant night fighter squadrons in the upgraded

Defiant MkII. Deliveries began in the autumn and continued until February 1942 when a total of 70 MkIIs had been completed. Despite this the Defiant was being superseded by other aircraft which were more suitable to the night fighting role such as the Beaufighter and Mosquito, which carried a dedicated A.I. operator.

With so many airframes still existing secondary roles were now created for the Defiant. One of these was Air Sea Rescue, where Defiants replaced the Lysander. The aircraft were adapted to carry a dingy under each wing in place of bombs. But even this role was short lived with the aircraft only fulfilling the role from March to December 1942. Eventually the Defiant was relegated to target towing duties, the

turret being removed and replaced with a faired canopy. The target was mounted under the fuselage and a wind operated winch system was fitted. DR863 was selected for the initial conversion and flew in the new configuration for the first time during January 1942. The majority of conversions took place at RAF Desford and over 224 aircraft were eventually altered. Such was the success that this final version of the Defiant ended up seeing service across the globe, from Kenya to India. With the cessation of hostilities the Defiants were surplus to requirements and scrapped, leaving only N1671 which is in the care of the RAF Museum and a second,

L7005 which was restored using a variety of parts from scrapped Defiants.

The turret fighter was an idea that history proved was ultimately impractical with only two types, the Defiant and Blackburn Roc entering service. Despite the flaws 1064 were built and only 37 were shot down by the enemy, while claims were

made for 152. It was an interesting concept but one that could not ultimately survive the advances made in aerial warfare.

Defensively the turret continued to be used on bombers throughout the war and beyond into the Cold War with the Tu-96 Bear and B-52, but as an offensive feature it was no longer practical. ◉

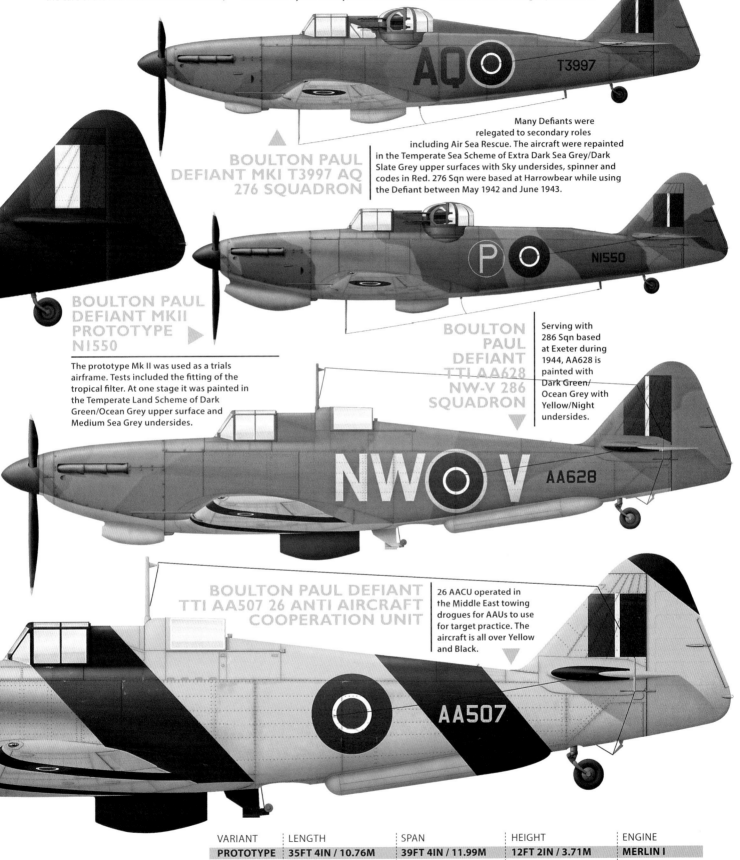

BOULTON PAUL
DEFIANT MKI T3997 AQ
276 SQUADRON

Many Defiants were relegated to secondary roles including Air Sea Rescue. The aircraft were repainted in the Temperate Sea Scheme of Extra Dark Sea Grey/Dark Slate Grey upper surfaces with Sky undersides, spinner and codes in Red. 276 Sqn were based at Harrowbear while using the Defiant between May 1942 and June 1943.

BOULTON PAUL
DEFIANT MKII
PROTOTYPE
N1550

The prototype Mk II was used as a trials airframe. Tests included the fitting of the tropical filter. At one stage it was painted in the Temperate Land Scheme of Dark Green/Ocean Grey upper surface and Medium Sea Grey undersides.

BOULTON
PAUL
DEFIANT
TTI AA628
NW-V 286
SQUADRON

Serving with 286 Sqn based at Exeter during 1944, AA628 is painted with Dark Green/ Ocean Grey with Yellow/Night undersides.

BOULTON PAUL DEFIANT
TTI AA507 26 ANTI AIRCRAFT
COOPERATION UNIT

26 AACU operated in the Middle East towing drogues for AAUs to use for target practice. The aircraft is all over Yellow and Black.

| VARIANT | LENGTH | SPAN | HEIGHT | ENGINE |
|---|---|---|---|---|
| PROTOTYPE | 35FT 4IN / 10.76M | 39FT 4IN / 11.99M | 12FT 2IN / 3.71M | MERLIN I |
| M.I | 35FT 4IN / 10.76M | 39FT 4IN / 11.99M | 12FT 2IN / 3.71M | MERLIN III |
| M.II | 35FT 8IN / 10.87M | 39FT 4IN / 11.99M | 12FT 2IN / 3.71M | MERLIN XX |
| TT.I | 35FT 8IN / 10.87M | 39FT 4IN / 11.99M | 12FT 2IN / 3.71M | MERLIN XX |
| TT.III | 35FT 4IN / 10.76M | 39FT 4IN / 11.99M | 12FT 2IN / 3.71M | MERLIN III |

# RAF WWII FIGHTERS
# BOULTON PAUL
## DEFIANT

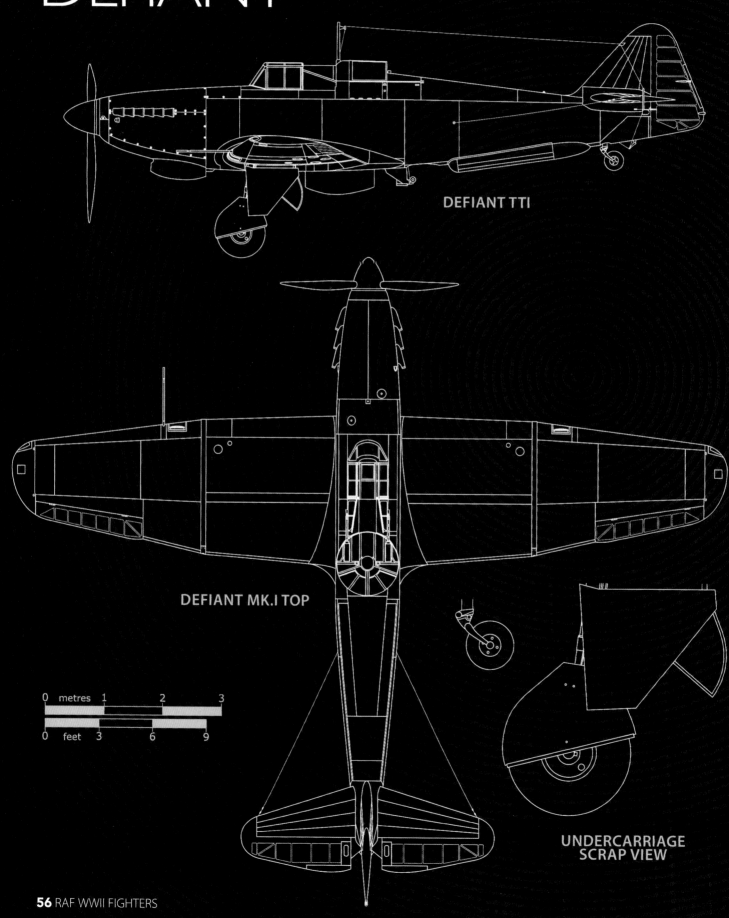

DEFIANT TTI

DEFIANT MK.I TOP

UNDERCARRIAGE
SCRAP VIEW

0   metres   1        2        3

0    feet    3        6        9

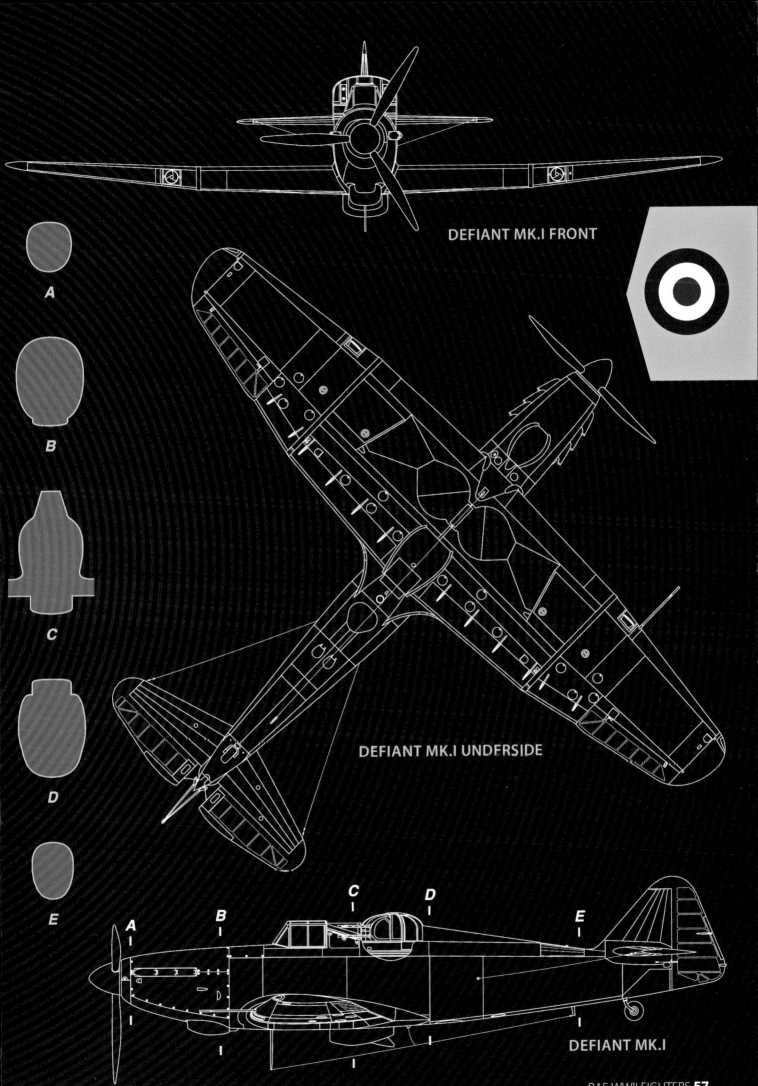

DEFIANT MK.I FRONT

DEFIANT MK.I UNDERSIDE

A

B

C

D

E

C    D

B            E

A

DEFIANT MK.I

The Bell P-39 Airacobra had a poor reputation and a very short service time with the RAF, possibly the shortest of any type despite the revolutionary design features incorporated into it.

## 1938-1951

# BELL P-39 AIRACOBRA

**W**he Airacobra was built around the gun. It was the first fighter to be fitted with tricycle undercarriage and unconventionally had the engine positioned aft of the pilot, radically altering the centre of gravity. The lack of a supercharger meant that compared to the Spitfire or Hurricane the Airacobra, originally intended as an interceptor, was deemed inferior and not suitable to engage Axis forces in the European theatre.

This negative opinion of the aircraft on the part of the RAF meant that Airacobras destined for Britain were redirected to the Russian Air Force. Both Soviet and US pilots embraced the type and it saw extensive action as a low-level combat and ground-attack aircraft. Over 9000 were eventually built.

Work began on the new project in early 1936 when the design team at Bell Aircraft Corporation, headed by Robert J Woods and Harland M Poyer embarked upon the project to design a new fighter for the US Army. The XP-39 was designed around the 37mm cannon which would fire through the propeller hub.

By using the Allison V-1710 12-cylinder liquid-cooled engine combined with a supercharger it was hoped that speeds above 400mph would be attained. Despite the engine being easy to maintain (unlike the rest of the aircraft) by ground crew it faced criticism from pilots who felt the Allison engine was underpowered at altitude due to the eventual omission of the supercharger.

When wind tunnel tests indicated that the XP-39 would suffer from drag and lift issues, a simple solution was to remove the supercharger which solved many of these problems.

With hindsight it seems a strange decision but during the mid-1930s superchargers were unreliable and at the time it made sense.

To accommodate the cannon and ammunition in the nose, the engine was moved aft of the pilot with the driveshaft running between the pilot's feet. The positioning of the engine shifted the centre of gravity much closer to the centre of the aircraft which actually improved handling. While it was radical the P-39 was not the first aircraft built to this configuration, a few years earlier the Westland F.7/30 fighter biplane had a centrally fitted engine and first flew in 1934. Early production models were

SKYLARK XIII

UF

Conveniently incorporating the squadron number in the serial it was inevitable that AH601 would be claimed by Squadron Leader E J Gracie, 601's commanding officer as his personal aircraft for photographic sorties. Instead of wearing an individual letter it had the squadron badge applied prominently on both sides. Painted in Dark Green and Ocean Grey with Medium Sea Grey underside.

BELL P-39
AIRACOBRA
MK.I AH601 601
SQUADRON

A TOP SPEED OF ONLY 359MPH COULD BE REACHED INSTEAD OF THE 392MPH BELL BROCHURES CLAIMED WAS ACHIEVABLE

fitted with the N-2A gun sight but this was phased out in favour of the N-3.

There has been some confusion about when exactly the first flight of the Bell XP-39 took place, with some sources citing April 6, 1938, and some April 6, 1939. By the time the US Army was ready to place an order on August 10, 1939, for 80 aircraft the Airacobra was redesignated the P-45 however it soon reverted to the P-39.

The following April it was announced in Flight that the Anglo-French Purchasing Commission was interested in acquiring a combination of 3000 P-39s and P-40s, although the P-39 had not been released for export at the time of writing. By the end of the month however an order had been placed for the P-39 by the British Government.

To differentiate it from the models destined for the US the British version was originally going to be called the Caribou and was still referred to as the P-400 in America in unofficial documents, by the time it was delivered it was known in the RAF as the Airacobra I.

The main difference was in the armament, the British version saw the six .30 cal machine guns being replaced with the standard RAF weapon, the Browning .303. The main 37mm nose cannon was exchanged for the Hispano-Suiza Mk 404 20mm cannon which carried only 60 rounds. Orders had also been placed by the French but following the fall of France these were combined with the original British order bringing the total the RAF expected to receive to 675.

The first three aircraft were unloaded from Southampton docks and arrived at the Aeroplane &

Armament Experimental Establishment, Boscombe Down and the Air Fighting Unit at RAF Duxford in July 1941 for testing. They had previously been flown by the 31st Pursuit Group, the serials being; DS173 (40-2981), DS174 (40-2983) and DS175 (40-2983).

Early trials proved to be very disappointing in all areas and the problems started on the ground. Entry was found to be difficult as there was no method of keeping the door open during ingress and once in there was minimal clearance, making it very uncomfortable for taller pilots.

The Allison engine was a temperamental thing that needed to be treated with care and respect, the revs needing to be kept between 1000rpm and 1200rpm to minimise vibration. During take off the revs could not be too high as one poor ATA pilot found out when high revs caused the aircraft to crash and explode.

Further to this, the Airacobra required an unusually long take off run compared to the Spitfire and Hurricane. A top speed of only 359mph could be reached instead of the 392mph Bell brochures claimed was achievable, the higher speed was later explained away as the speed of a stripped down

## BELL P-39 AIRACOBRA MK.I AH621 ▲

Originally used for flight trials in the USA, this aircraft was painted using company paints as an interpretation of the required RAF scheme of Dark Green, Dark Earth and Sky, the underside was a light grey and it had a high demarcation line. Fitted with standard exhausts.

## BELL P-39 AIRACOBRA MK.I AH577 601 SQUADRON ▼

Even before the UF squadron code was applied, the Airacobras had the 601 Squadron badge applied on the white of the fin flash. The application may have been for the benefit of a press sortie on August 21, 1941. AH577 was later to wear the code UF-M.

> THE AIRACOBRA COULD NEVER BE CONSIDERED A GREAT AEROPLANE COMPARED TO OTHERS OF THE PERIOD BUT IT DID ACHIEVE SOME POSITIVE RESULTS

airframe specifically modified for high speed flight. The Airacobra may have been able to outperform a captured Bf 109E at below 15,000ft in trials but it was exceptionally poor above 20,000ft, the lack of a supercharger having a detrimental effect on both the performance and climb rate – which was abysmal.

The compass was found to be unreliable and during firing $CO_2$ entered the cockpit. Despite the long list of shortcomings the aircraft did have a few redeeming features. Firstly as a result of the raised seat, visibility was greatly improved in comparison to RAF fighters, it was also quieter than a Spitfire. Basic handling was good with smooth controls and it was considered an enjoyable aeroplane to fly.

With large numbers of Airacobras under construction and destined for Britain, it was inevitable that some would reach a front line squadron. Originally known as the Millionaires'

Squadron due to the wealthy background of the founder members, 601 County of London had started the war with the Bristol Blenheim but spent the Battle of Britain flying the Hurricane. August 6, 1941, was a notable day as it saw the first delivery of a US fighter to a RAF squadron. 601 Sqn was by now at RAF Matlaske, Norfolk, this being a short-lived residency as the squadron relocated to RAF Duxford a little over a week later where the final Hurricanes were exchanged and they began familiarisation with the new aircraft, working up to operational readiness flying a mix of the P-39D and P-400s.

Articles of the time seem to praise the type, with the only criticism being a lack of spare parts and a few landing mishaps but this may well have been for propaganda purposes. In order to ascertain its operational suitability a detachment of four

(AH581, AH583, AH589 and AH595) were sent to RAF Manston to undertake sorties over the channel and French coast, attacking German shipping and flying reconnaissance between October 9 and 11, 1941. Typically the weather did little to aid the situation with visibility being very poor and the serviceability while on detachment was found to be a major hindrance to the operational capabilities of the Airacobra. In the New Year the squadron moved to RAF Acaster

ONE FOR THE ROAD

75

## BELL P-39 AIRACOBRA MK.I AH595 601 SQUADRON ▼

Displaying typical markings for the squadron AH595 was one of the few Airacobras to be used operationally by the RAF, flown by P/O Manak it was used to attack barges close to Dunkirk on October 10, 1940.

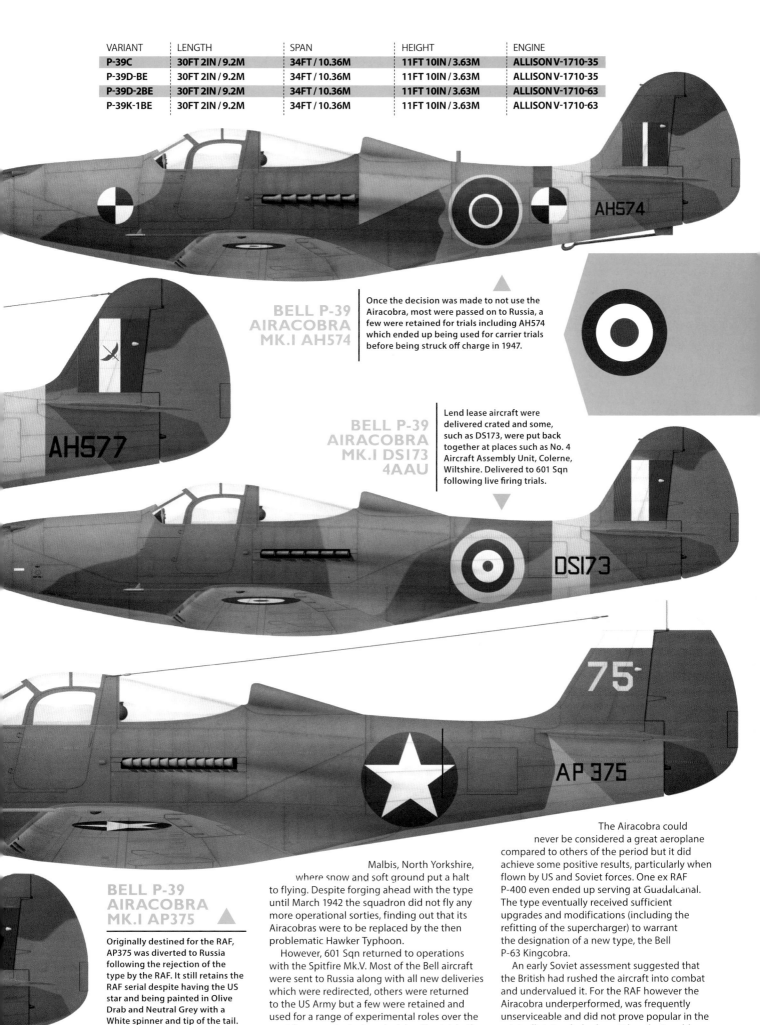

| VARIANT | LENGTH | SPAN | HEIGHT | ENGINE |
|---------|--------|------|--------|--------|
| P-39C | 30FT 2IN / 9.2M | 34FT / 10.36M | 11FT 10IN / 3.63M | ALLISON V-1710-35 |
| P-39D-BE | 30FT 2IN / 9.2M | 34FT / 10.36M | 11FT 10IN / 3.63M | ALLISON V-1710-35 |
| P-39D-2BE | 30FT 2IN / 9.2M | 34FT / 10.36M | 11FT 10IN / 3.63M | ALLISON V-1710-63 |
| P-39K-1BE | 30FT 2IN / 9.2M | 34FT / 10.36M | 11FT 10IN / 3.63M | ALLISON V-1710-63 |

**BELL P-39 AIRACOBRA MK.I AH574**

Once the decision was made to not use the Airacobra, most were passed on to Russia, a few were retained for trials including AH574 which ended up being used for carrier trials before being struck off charge in 1947.

**BELL P-39 AIRACOBRA MK.I DS173 4AAU**

Lend lease aircraft were delivered crated and some, such as DS173, were put back together at places such as No. 4 Aircraft Assembly Unit, Colerne, Wiltshire. Delivered to 601 Sqn following live firing trials.

**BELL P-39 AIRACOBRA MK.I AP375**

Originally destined for the RAF, AP375 was diverted to Russia following the rejection of the type by the RAF. It still retains the RAF serial despite having the US star and being painted in Olive Drab and Neutral Grey with a White spinner and tip of the tail. Unlike other RAF Airacobras it was fitted with the twelve port exhaust system.

Malbis, North Yorkshire, where snow and soft ground put a halt to flying. Despite forging ahead with the type until March 1942 the squadron did not fly any more operational sorties, finding out that its Airacobras were to be replaced by the then problematic Hawker Typhoon.

However, 601 Sqn returned to operations with the Spitfire Mk.V. Most of the Bell aircraft were sent to Russia along with all new deliveries which were redirected, others were returned to the US Army but a few were retained and used for a range of experimental roles over the next few years including deck landing trials, the last Airacobra AH574 was eventually struck off charge in 1947.

The Airacobra could never be considered a great aeroplane compared to others of the period but it did achieve some positive results, particularly when flown by US and Soviet forces. One ex RAF P-400 even ended up serving at Guadalcanal. The type eventually received sufficient upgrades and modifications (including the refitting of the supercharger) to warrant the designation of a new type, the Bell P-63 Kingcobra.

An early Soviet assessment suggested that the British had rushed the aircraft into combat and undervalued it. For the RAF however the Airacobra underperformed, was frequently unserviceable and did not prove popular in the originally intended role so it has the ignoble reputation of having quite probably the shortest frontline career of any RAF fighter. ⊙

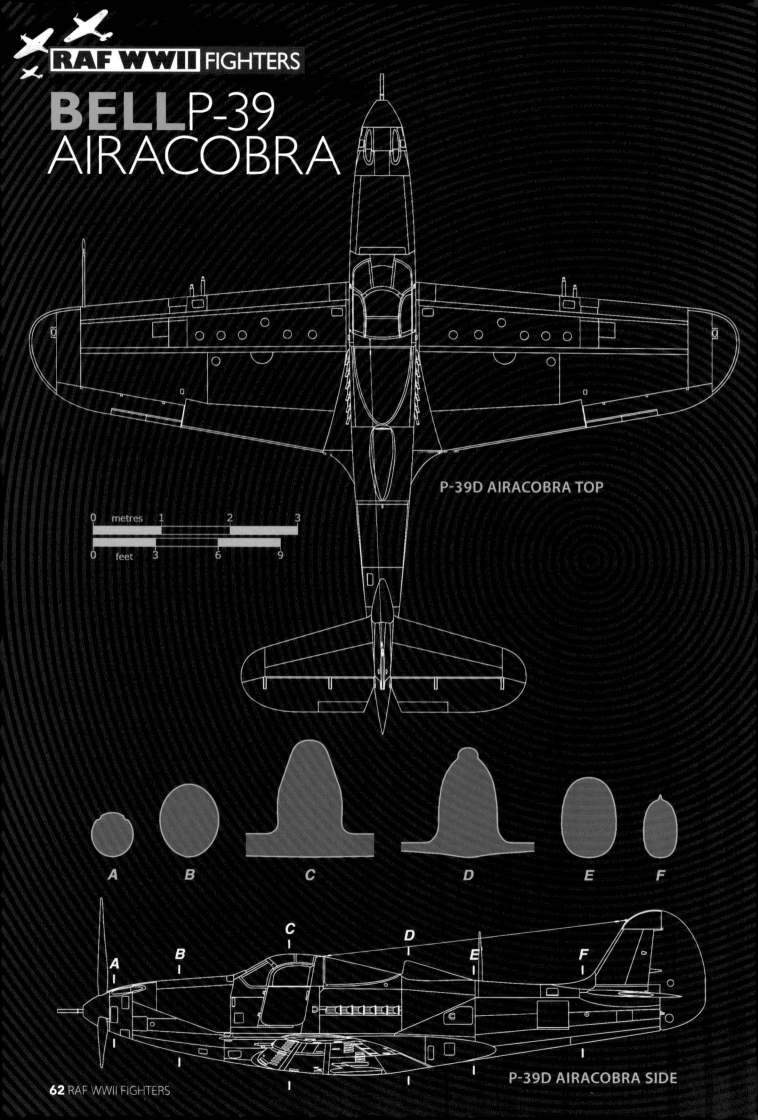

# BELL P-39 AIRACOBRA

P-39D AIRACOBRA TOP

| 0 | metres | 1 | 2 | 3 |
| 0 | feet | 3 | 6 | 9 |

A    B    C    D    E    F

A    B    C    D    E    F

P-39D AIRACOBRA SIDE

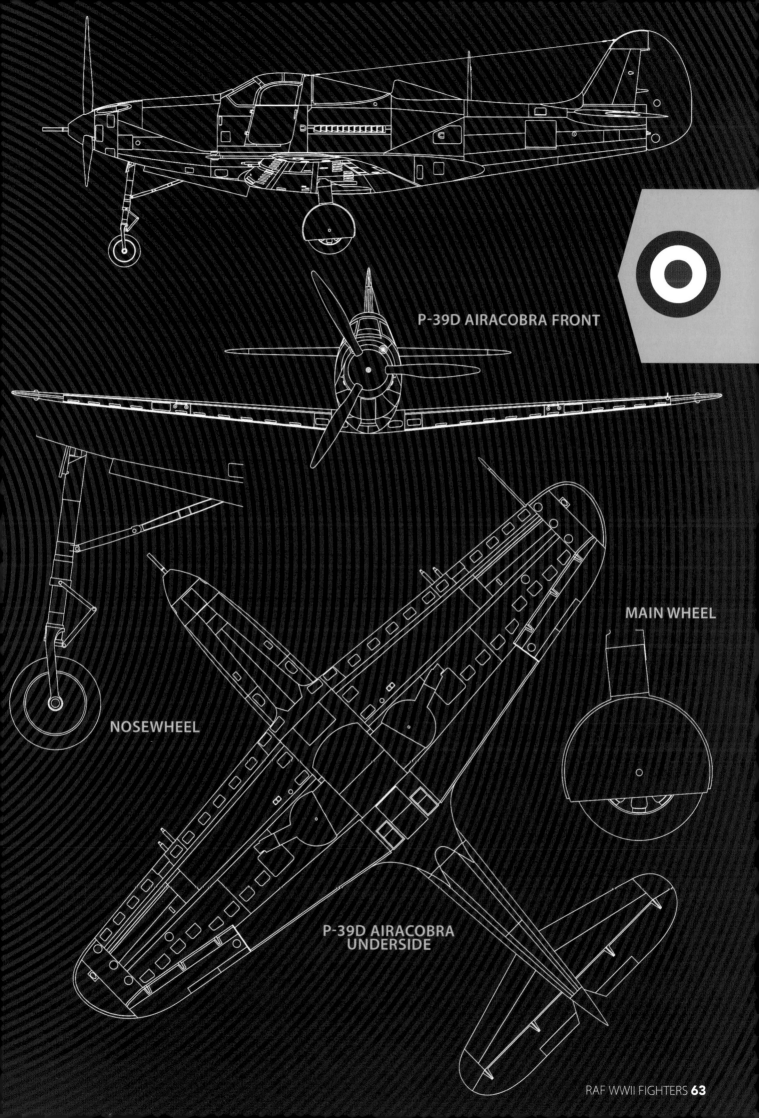

P-39D AIRACOBRA FRONT

MAIN WHEEL

NOSEWHEEL

P-39D AIRACOBRA
UNDERSIDE

There had been high hopes for the Westland Whirlwind yet due to the speed of technological advancement it never became a truly great aeroplane. It was operated by just two squadrons yet had a respectable and distinguished career.

# WESTLAND
## WHIRLWIND

**1940-1943**

**L**ike so many other military aircraft the Whirlwind was built around its weaponry. The Air Ministry recognised the need for an aircraft that could inflict heavy damage, greater than that generated by the machine guns of the early Spitfires and Hurricanes. Therefore on March 30, 1936, specification F37/35 was issued for a high-performance single seater (and initially single engine) fighter that would be capable of carrying four cannon. A top speed of no less than 330mph at 15,000ft, a maximum altitude of at least 33,000ft, enclosed and heated cockpit, variable pitch propellers and

night flying equipment were all necessary. Three companies were contracted to produce prototypes based on their proposals, the others being Boulton Paul and Supermarine. The latter was cancelled at a later date when the Spitfire began to take up the majority of company's resources. The initial cost of the Westland P.9 was estimated at £45,500 and was to be designed by a team headed by the son of one of Westland's founders, W. E. W. 'Teddy' Petter. He was also responsible for the Lysander and

later the Canberra and Lightning. To safely mount the cannons, a rigid frame was constructed in the nose and designed to allow for very easy access to aid reloading.

An early version involved a twin tail layout but this soon altered to a more conventional configuration with a single low tail. Wind tunnel tests showed that in this position the airflow would cause handling issues so it was raised to the upper part of the tail.

To keep drag down, the frontal surface area was kept to a minimum. The two engines were mounted in streamlined nacelles which also housed the main undercarriage, the radiators being accommodated in the wing, inboard of the engines.

An additional benefit of this arrangement was that heating the cockpit was a simple affair due to the close proximity of the radiators. Despite the benefits of these innovative features, one was to cause serious problems and did not make it to the production aircraft. Petter had opted to run the exhaust through the wing past the fuel tanks to ducts in the trailing edge – the theory being that it would contribute a small addition to the top speed.

However concerns were raised by others in the design team and Westland's test pilot Harald Penrose experienced the

## WESTLAND WHIRLWIND P6974 HE-Z 263 SQUADRON

Finished in the later scheme of Dark Green and Ocean Grey over Medium Sea Grey, P6974 served exclusively with 263 Sqn until it was hit during a raid on Cherbourg and made a forced landing at RAF Warmwell, writing it off. During the spoof Operation Starkey all aircraft involved received temporary invasion stripes and a white nose.

problem first-hand when during a flight the ducting became detached, causing an overheating of flying controls. Pressure from the Air Ministry resulted in conventional exhausts being fitted. The powerplant chosen for the new aircraft was the Rolls-Royce Peregrine, which at the time was thought to have great potential. Based on the Kestrel, a highly successful engine used in a wide range of aircraft including the prototype Bf 109, the Peregrine was modified to increase power output and boost levels. It has long been considered the Achilles heel of the Whirlwind and the reason the aircraft was not used more extensively.

Certainly, development was not a high priority for Rolls-Royce when much of the company's time was taken up with the Merlin, which history has proven to be a highly successful engine, but

there were a number of other factors which contributed to the Whirlwind not reaching its full potential.

The Whirlwind moved under its own power for the first time at the Yeovil factory on October 5, 1938. Following three days of trials L6844 was transported to RAF Boscombe Down. On the 11th during one taxi run Penrose was rapidly running out of runway and decided to pull back on the stick, the first flight lasted half an hour and was satisfactory despite highlighting some flaws in the aircraft. At the end of December four A&AEE pilots assessed the aircraft and agreed with Penrose that there were issues with the control surfaces, the brakes were ineffective and the throttles were not synchronised satisfactorily.

## WESTLAND WHIRLWIND L6845

The second prototype Whirlwind was originally finished in all over Aluminium. During testing the airframe evolved considerably. Once testing was complete it was delivered to 25 Sqn in May 1940. It was written off when it collided with a tree during a single engine landing, killing Sgt R. Pacoe of 263 Sqn on June 11, 1941.

Following the short assessment flights, each lasting only 40 minutes, the Air Ministry was encouraged by the reports and placed an order for 200 aircraft in early January 1939. It was over a year later that the first production aircraft were delivered though. This was in part due to the slow development of the engine and the increase in orders for the Lysander which put considerable pressure on the Yeovil factory.

During one test flight Penrose was flying the unarmed fighter up through a layer of cloud and upon exiting the clouds encountered a Bf 109 inadvertently about to intercept him, Penrose claimed that the four guns in the nose must have scared the pilot as they both reacted "I put the nose down, plunging for the safety of cloud. Simultaneously the Bf 109, impressed by guns and twin engines, jerked into a steep turn away from me and dived for the same cloud cover."

Development and refinement of the Whirlwind continued during this period with modifications to the exhaust and the tail acorn being introduced and then enlarged on the tail which

## WESTLAND WHIRLWIND P6966 ▶

The first production aircraft served with both 25 and 263 Sqns until PO McDermott bailed out following a tyre burst during take off on August 7, 1940. It was photographed by Westland before the camouflage scheme was applied in May 1940 when the bare airframe was showing.

## WESTLAND WHIRLWIND L6844

The original prototype was developed extensively by Westland and flew in a variety of schemes during its career. Initially it was painted in all over dark grey but received an all over war scheme of Dark Green and Dark Earth with a White underside, port wing was painted Black.

▲ WESTLAND WHIRLWIND L6844

Continuing as a trials aircraft, L6844, in keeping with prototype aircraft, had the undersides repainted in all over yellow. The aircraft was eventually abandoned at RAF Duxford when it was unserviceable in January 1942. Later reports suggest it may have ended up as an instructional airframe at RAF St Athen.

solved the juddering that was encountered at high speeds. Due to the high speed and inspired by a contemporary Shell Oil advert the aircraft became known around South Somerset as Crikey.

It was not until June 1940 that the first production aircraft, P6966, was completed and delivered to the RAF. 25 Squadron at RAF North Weald was already operating the twin engine Blenheim and received both P6966 and L6845 for use in trials. This early period saw the first appearance of what would become a recurring problem when the tail wheel collapsed, it was to be a major reason

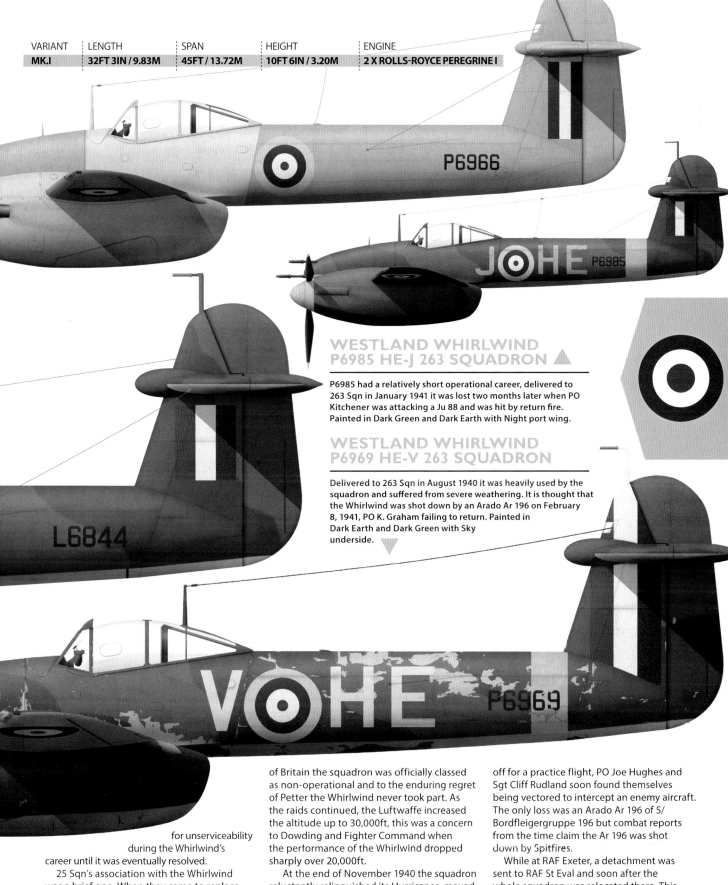

| VARIANT | LENGTH | SPAN | HEIGHT | ENGINE |
|---------|--------|------|--------|--------|
| MK.I | 32FT 3IN / 9.83M | 45FT / 13.72M | 10FT 6IN / 3.20M | 2 X ROLLS-ROYCE PEREGRINE I |

P6966

J⊙HE P6985

### WESTLAND WHIRLWIND
### P6985 HE-J 263 SQUADRON ▲

P6985 had a relatively short operational career, delivered to
263 Sqn in January 1941 it was lost two months later when PO
Kitchener was attacking a Ju 88 and was hit by return fire.
Painted in Dark Green and Dark Earth with Night port wing.

### WESTLAND WHIRLWIND
### P6969 HE-V 263 SQUADRON

Delivered to 263 Sqn in August 1940 it was heavily used by the
squadron and suffered from severe weathering. It is thought that
the Whirlwind was shot down by an Arado Ar 196 on February
8, 1941, PO K. Graham failing to return. Painted in
Dark Earth and Dark Green with Sky
underside. ▽

L6844

V⊙HE P6969

for unserviceability
during the Whirlwind's
career until it was eventually resolved.
25 Sqn's association with the Whirlwind
was a brief one. When they came to replace
the Blenheim it was with the Beaufighter and
the Whirlwinds were instead destined for 263
Sqn. The squadron had recently returned from
Norway where after a successful campaign the
Gladiators and several pilots were lost during
the sinking of HMS *Glorious* on June 8, 1940.
The squadron re-formed at RAF Drem and
took temporary custody of some Hurricanes
for operational duties while re-equipping with
the Whirlwind. For the duration of the Battle

of Britain the squadron was officially classed
as non-operational and to the enduring regret
of Petter the Whirlwind never took part. As
the raids continued, the Luftwaffe increased
the altitude up to 30,000ft, this was a concern
to Dowding and Fighter Command when
the performance of the Whirlwind dropped
sharply over 20,000ft.
At the end of November 1940 the squadron
reluctantly relinquished its Hurricanes, moved
south to Exeter and was finally declared
operational on December 22. Patrols over the
channel commenced at the start of 1941 and
the first enemy intercepted and damaged was
on January 12 when a Ju 88 was encountered
south west of the Scilly Isles by PO David
Stein and Sgt Dennis Mason (a survivor
of the Norway campaign).
It was not until February 8 that the
Whirlwinds claimed a success. Having taken

off for a practice flight, PO Joe Hughes and
Sgt Cliff Rudland soon found themselves
being vectored to intercept an enemy aircraft.
The only loss was an Arado Ar 196 of 5/
Bordfleigergruppe 196 but combat reports
from the time claim the Ar 196 was shot
down by Spitfires.
While at RAF Exeter, a detachment was
sent to RAF St Eval and soon after the
whole squadron was relocated there. This
was followed by time at RAF Filton and
RAF Charmy Down, still all in the West
Country. During the summer the role of the
Whirlwind changed when offensive missions
over occupied France began with attacks
on ground targets, the first of these being
attacks on Luftwaffe airfields on June 13.
The aircraft performed satisfactorily in the
new role, the four nose guns proving more
than adequate when ground strafing at

## WESTLAND WHIRLWIND P7048

Bearing a factory fresh display scheme with Dark Green and Ocean Grey over Medium Sea Grey with Sky spinners and band on fuselage. It went on to serve with 137 Sqn. Following damage it was sold back to Westland and retained by the company as G-AGOI and eventually left to fall into disrepair.

**P7048**

## WESTLAND WHIRLWIND P7055 HE-W 263 SQUADRON BELLOWS ARGENTINA NOI

The first Whirlwind to be purchased with funds raised by the Bellows Fellowship of Argentina, a loose group of wealthy ex-pats and anglophiles based in South America who wanted to aid the Allied war effort. P7055 survived operations and was retired and SOC in September 1944. On the nose was a cartoon version of the squadron crest.

BELLOWS

**WOH**

## WESTLAND WHIRLWIND P7056 PRIDE OF YEOVIL

Bearing the legend of the town where it was built, served with both 137 and 263 Sqns, damaged and returned to Westland where it is thought it was used for spare parts. A replica of P7056 is currently being constructed by the Whirlwind Fighter Project.

THE PRIDE OF YEOVIL

**P7056**

"COMRADES IN ARMS"

attacking enemy shipping. Whirlwinds were also involved in the first low level penetration of Germany during Operation 77 when they acted as fighter escort for Blenheims on the outward leg of the trip. They failed to encounter any enemy aircraft but some Blenheims and Spitfires were lost later in the mission.

During August 1941 a surplus of airframes had built up and it was decided to create a second Whirlwind squadron to join 263 Sqn at RAF Charmy Down. Originally formed during the First World War, 137 Sqn was supposed to have operated the DH9 in France but had been disbanded again before it had a chance, therefore the Whirlwind was the first aircraft it ever flew operationally.

137 Sqn was transferred to 12 Group and posted to East Anglia in November 1941 where the new role was to protect shipping in the area, flying from RAF Coltishall and the satellite airfield RAF Matlaske. It was not until July 25, 1942, that the squadron was able to record its first kill when Sgt John McClure and Robert Smith engaged Ju 88 A-5 8H+KL of 3(F)/122 off the coast of Yarmouth.

At this time it was decided to expand the role of the Whirlwind and after some brief trials at A&AEE

Boscombe Down the Whirlwind was unofficially rechristened the Whirlibomber. Carrying bombs under the outer wing had very little impact on handling, the racks creating more noticeable drag than the actual bombs. Having dropped a few operationally, 263 Sqn was stood down in late August so all the aircraft could be converted.

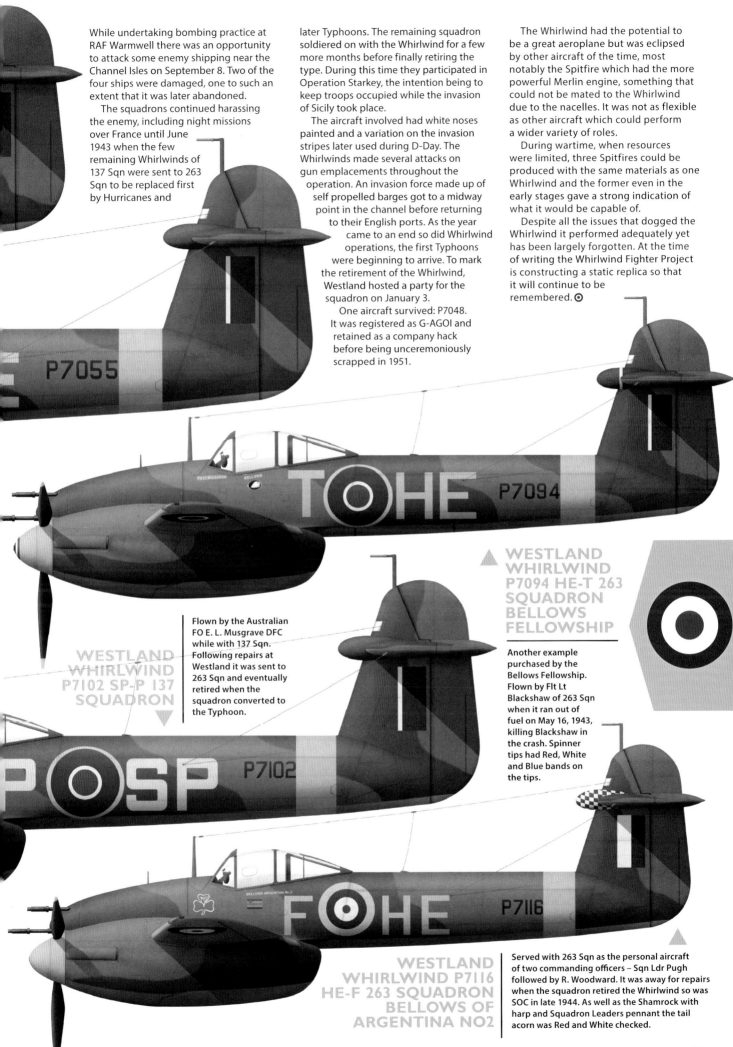

While undertaking bombing practice at RAF Warmwell there was an opportunity to attack some enemy shipping near the Channel Isles on September 8. Two of the four ships were damaged, one to such an extent that it was later abandoned.

The squadrons continued harassing the enemy, including night missions over France until June 1943 when the few remaining Whirlwinds of 137 Sqn were sent to 263 Sqn to be replaced first by Hurricanes and later Typhoons. The remaining squadron soldiered on with the Whirlwind for a few more months before finally retiring the type. During this time they participated in Operation Starkey, the intention being to keep troops occupied while the invasion of Sicily took place.

The aircraft involved had white noses painted and a variation on the invasion stripes later used during D-Day. The Whirlwinds made several attacks on gun emplacements throughout the operation. An invasion force made up of self propelled barges got to a midway point in the channel before returning to their English ports. As the year came to an end so did Whirlwind operations, the first Typhoons were beginning to arrive. To mark the retirement of the Whirlwind, Westland hosted a party for the squadron on January 3.

One aircraft survived: P7048. It was registered as G-AGOI and retained as a company hack before being unceremoniously scrapped in 1951.

The Whirlwind had the potential to be a great aeroplane but was eclipsed by other aircraft of the time, most notably the Spitfire which had the more powerful Merlin engine, something that could not be mated to the Whirlwind due to the nacelles. It was not as flexible as other aircraft which could perform a wider variety of roles.

During wartime, when resources were limited, three Spitfires could be produced with the same materials as one Whirlwind and the former even in the early stages gave a strong indication of what it would be capable of.

Despite all the issues that dogged the Whirlwind it performed adequately yet has been largely forgotten. At the time of writing the Whirlwind Fighter Project is constructing a static replica so that it will continue to be remembered. ◎

**WESTLAND WHIRLWIND P7094 HE-T 263 SQUADRON BELLOWS FELLOWSHIP**

Another example purchased by the Bellows Fellowship. Flown by Flt Lt Blackshaw of 263 Sqn when it ran out of fuel on May 16, 1943, killing Blackshaw in the crash. Spinner tips had Red, White and Blue bands on the tips.

**WESTLAND WHIRLWIND P7102 SP-P 137 SQUADRON**

Flown by the Australian FO E. L. Musgrave DFC while with 137 Sqn. Following repairs at Westland it was sent to 263 Sqn and eventually retired when the squadron converted to the Typhoon.

**WESTLAND WHIRLWIND P7116 HE-F 263 SQUADRON BELLOWS OF ARGENTINA NO2**

Served with 263 Sqn as the personal aircraft of two commanding officers – Sqn Ldr Pugh followed by R. Woodward. It was away for repairs when the squadron retired the Whirlwind so was SOC in late 1944. As well as the Shamrock with harp and Squadron Leaders pennant the tail acorn was Red and White checked.

# WESTLAND WHIRLWIND

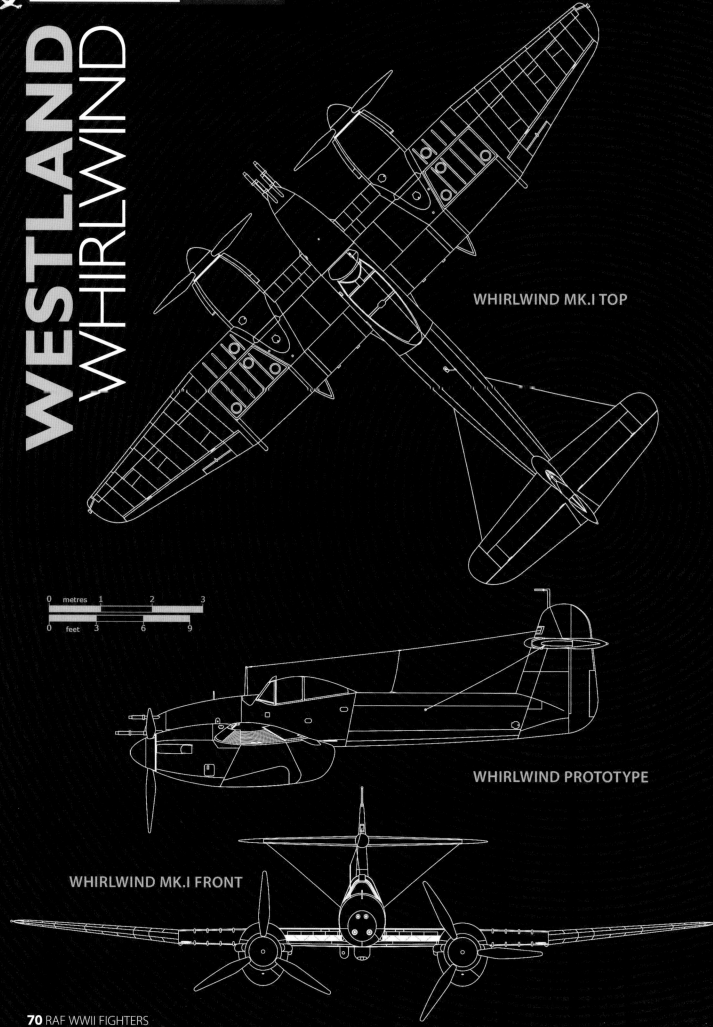

WHIRLWIND MK.I TOP

0  metres  1  2  3

0  feet  3  6  9

WHIRLWIND PROTOTYPE

WHIRLWIND MK.I FRONT

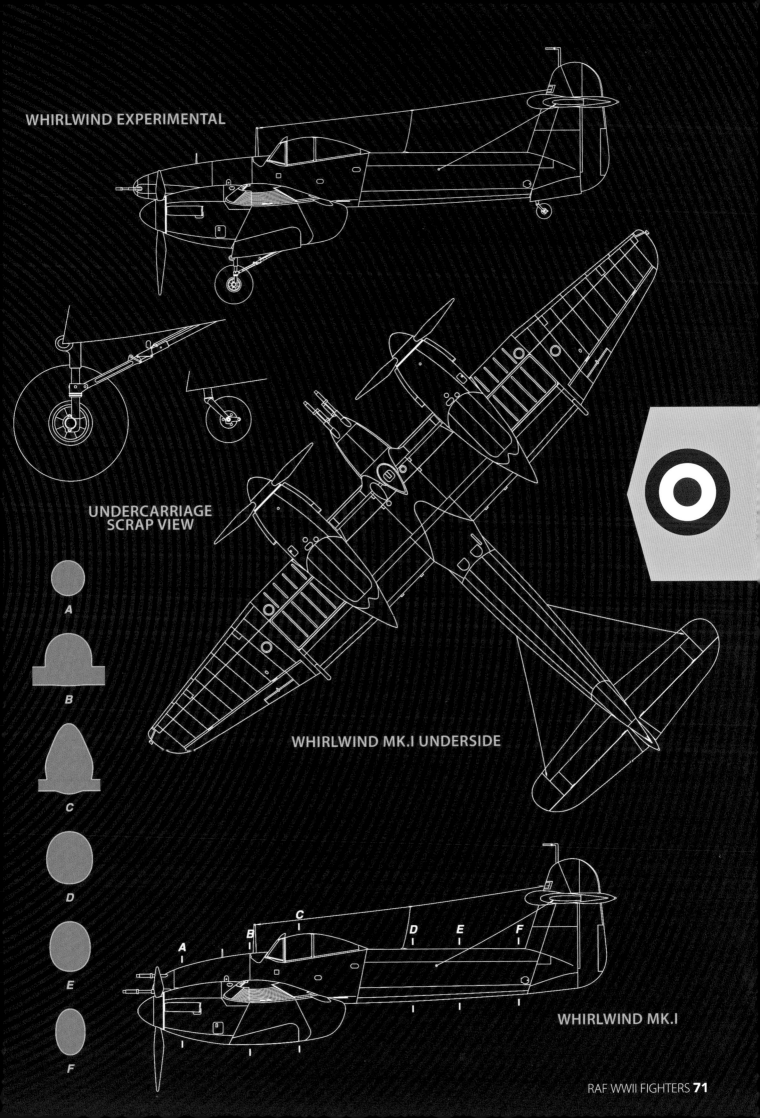

WHIRLWIND EXPERIMENTAL

UNDERCARRIAGE
SCRAP VIEW

A

B

C

D

E

F

WHIRLWIND MK.I UNDERSIDE

C

B

D    E    F

A

WHIRLWIND MK.I

# CURTISS
## P-40A-C TOMAHAWK

**1941–1944**

**Unsuited to conditions in Western Europe the Tomahawk was still a formidable aircraft. It went through many improvements over the years with the biggest being between the P-40C Tomahawk and the P-40D Kittyhawk.**

**T**he P-40 did not begin life on the drawing board as an original concept but was an evolution of earlier Curtiss designs. During the mid-1930s it was becoming clear that there would be a radical change in fighter design before any future conflict with the biplane configuration becoming obsolete. So in anticipation of US Army Air Corps requirements, a private venture was initiated by the Curtiss company and led by Donovan R. Berlin, formerly of Northrop. This project led to the 75 Hawk (also known as the P-36 and the Mohawk by the RAF).

Although the company had already produced monoplanes, the Curtiss 75 was a radical departure from existing designs and employed new construction methods. The most visibly noticeable feature was the method of retracting the undercarriage, instead of either folding aft and having some of the wheel exposed or moving in to the fuselage the wheel actually rotated 90° to sit flush with the wing and reduce drag. This design was created by Boeing which, despite never utilising it in any of its own designs, nevertheless collected fees from Curtiss and later Vought when that

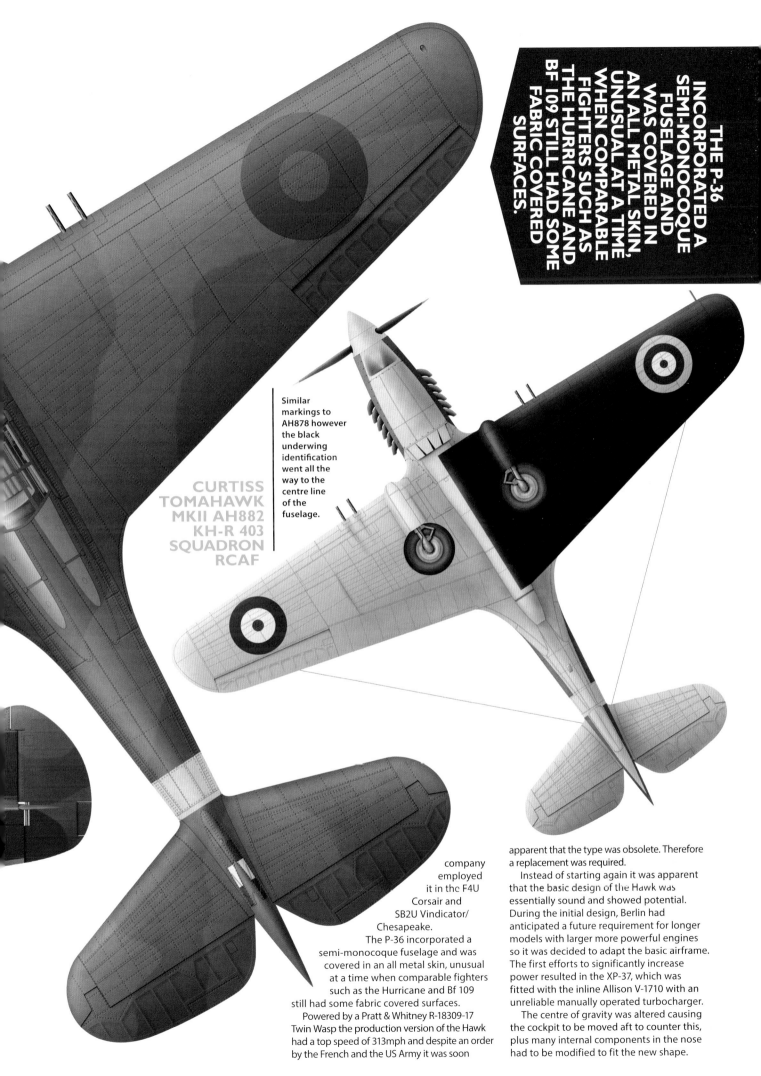

Similar markings to AH878 however the black underwing identification went all the way to the centre line of the fuselage.

CURTISS TOMAHAWK MKII AH882 KH-R 403 SQUADRON RCAF

company employed it in the F4U Corsair and SB2U Vindicator/ Chesapeake.

The P-36 incorporated a semi-monocoque fuselage and was covered in an all metal skin, unusual at a time when comparable fighters such as the Hurricane and Bf 109 still had some fabric covered surfaces.

Powered by a Pratt & Whitney R-18309-17 Twin Wasp the production version of the Hawk had a top speed of 313mph and despite an order by the French and the US Army it was soon

apparent that the type was obsolete. Therefore a replacement was required.

Instead of starting again it was apparent that the basic design of the Hawk was essentially sound and showed potential. During the initial design, Berlin had anticipated a future requirement for longer models with larger more powerful engines so it was decided to adapt the basic airframe. The first efforts to significantly increase power resulted in the XP-37, which was fitted with the inline Allison V-1710 with an unreliable manually operated turbocharger.

The centre of gravity was altered causing the cockpit to be moved aft to counter this, plus many internal components in the nose had to be modified to fit the new shape.

While it was an improvement on the previous model there were still a number of issues with the XP-37 which were never fully resolved.

P-36 serial 38-10 was removed from the production line and heavily modified forward of the firewall to. It received the Allison V-1710-19 but was fitted with a supercharger which made a big difference to performance and reliability when compared to the P-36 and XP-37. The main structure and profile remained unchanged but the inline engine required a revision of the coolant system, having it very close to the engine and truncated interconnecting lines.

One unexpected benefit of this was increased combat survivability. It was harder to sever the lines and even with heavy damage to the fuselage the engine could to continue functioning sufficiently to allow the aircraft to return to base. The alterations also resulted in a new gun configuration being fitted in the upper nose. Finally on October 14, 1938, the polished metal XP-40 was rolled out at Buffalo and assistant chief test pilot Edward Elliot took it on the first test flight.

The climb rate may have been lower than that of the P-36 and the initial top speed was only 299mph during the test flight but during a subsequent test it flew 300 miles in 57 minutes. It eventually managed to reach 340mph which was still considered not fast enough for a pursuit plane. Curtiss managed to eke out a few more mph with modifications to the nose and coolant intakes but considerable work was required to bring it up to the 360mph required by the Army Air Corps.

Even though the required speed had not yet been reached the US government was sufficiently impressed with the XP-40 to place an order for 524 P-40s, worth a total of $13 million, on April 26, 1939.

Further alterations, which included an expanded radiator scoop and the Allison V-1710-33 engine, allowed the XP-40 to reach a 366mph top speed in level flight at 15,000ft. By the time it was ready to enter production the

Operated by 26 Sqn from February 1941 as part of RAF Army Cooperation Command, the aircraft operated over France in the reconnaissance role. The aircraft were received from 403 Sqn RCAF. The aircraft is standard Dark Earth, Dark Green with Sky Blue underside and a black wing (not extended as far as the undercarriage) for identification purposes. The squadron badge is on the white bar of the fin flash. With some aircraft the original 403 Sqn codes are still visible.

## CURTISS TOMAHAWK MKII AH791 RM-E 26 SQUADRON

## CURTISS TOMAHAWK MKII AH973

Curtiss painted the aircraft destined for the RAF before being transported in a variation of the Dark Earth, Dark Green scheme using similar colours which were available at the Curtiss factory. Arrived in the UK with only the serial number and no squadron codes.

## CURTISS TOMAHAWK MKII AH878 KH-G 403 SQUADRON RCAF

The only squadron to employ the Tomahawk in a fighter role in the European Theatre, 403 Sqn received them on March 1, 1941, when formed at RAF Baginton. After 29 operational sorties the aircraft were deemed unsuitable for the fighter role and were replaced by Spitfires. During this time the aircraft received identification markings of a black wing, though this was hastily painted over on many of the aircraft later on, including AH878.

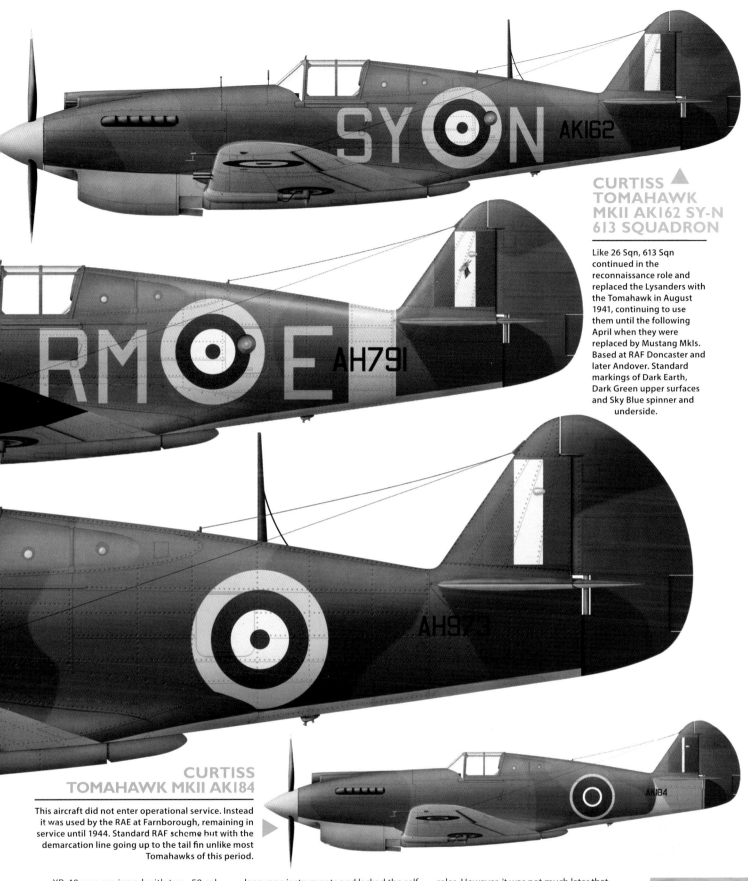

## CURTISS ▲ TOMAHAWK MKII AK162 SY-N 613 SQUADRON

Like 26 Sqn, 613 Sqn continued in the reconnaissance role and replaced the Lysanders with the Tomahawk in August 1941, continuing to use them until the following April when they were replaced by Mustang MkIs. Based at RAF Doncaster and later Andover. Standard markings of Dark Earth, Dark Green upper surfaces and Sky Blue spinner and underside.

## CURTISS TOMAHAWK MKII AK184

This aircraft did not enter operational service. Instead it was used by the RAE at Farnborough, remaining in service until 1944. Standard RAF scheme but with the demarcation line going up to the tail fin unlike most Tomahawks of this period.

XP-40 was equipped with two .50 cal machine guns in the upper nose and a single .30 cal gun in each wing.

With tensions rising rapidly in Europe, France had placed an order for 140 of the aircraft, designated the H-81A. The first of 200 destined for the USAAC was completed in March 1940 and once this order had been met production switched to the French order. With the fall of France and the commencement of the Battle of Britain, the RAF took receipt of the order instead. Early aircraft arrived with French language instruments and lacked the self-sealing tanks that were fitted as standard in all subsequent versions. Of the original 200 intended for France, a total of 140 were delivered.

As the aircraft, dubbed the Tomahawk I, began arriving they were sent to various aircraft manufacturers such as Westland to un-crate and prepare for flight, the first of these was AH741 and they ran concurrently through to AH880. These early P-40s were deemed lacking in firepower so were relegated to training roles. However, it was not much later that the RAF started receiving the Tomahawk II which had seen improvements from the lessons learnt during the fall of France and Battle of Britain.

Space for an additional gun was added to each wing so that upon arrival in the UK .303 Brownings could be fitted, armour plating and a bulletproof windscreen were added and self-sealing tanks were fitted. This resulted in an increase in weight and slight drop in performance but the benefits were

# P-40 TOMAHAWK

| VARIANT | LENGTH | SPAN | HEIGHT | ENGINE |
|---|---|---|---|---|
| P-40 TOMAHAWK MK I | 31FT 9IN / 9.68M | 37FT 3½ IN / 11.37M | 12FT 4IN / 9.66M | ALLISON V-1710-33 |
| P-40B TOMAHAWK MK IIA | 31FT 9IN / 9.68M | 37FT 3½ IN / 11.37M | 12FT 4IN / 9.66M | ALLISON V-1710-33 |
| P-40C TOMAHAWK MK IIB | 31FT 9IN / 9.68M | 37FT 3½ IN / 11.37M | 12FT 4IN / 9.66M | ALLISON V-1710-33 |

**CURTISS TOMAHAWK MKII AH940 XV-U 2 SQUADRON**

As with other squadrons the Tomahawk replaced the Lysander in 1940, the squadron aircraft wore standard markings with the codes in Medium Sea Grey. 'A' flight had red tipped spinners. AH940 made a wheels-up landing at Sawbridgeworth in late 1941.

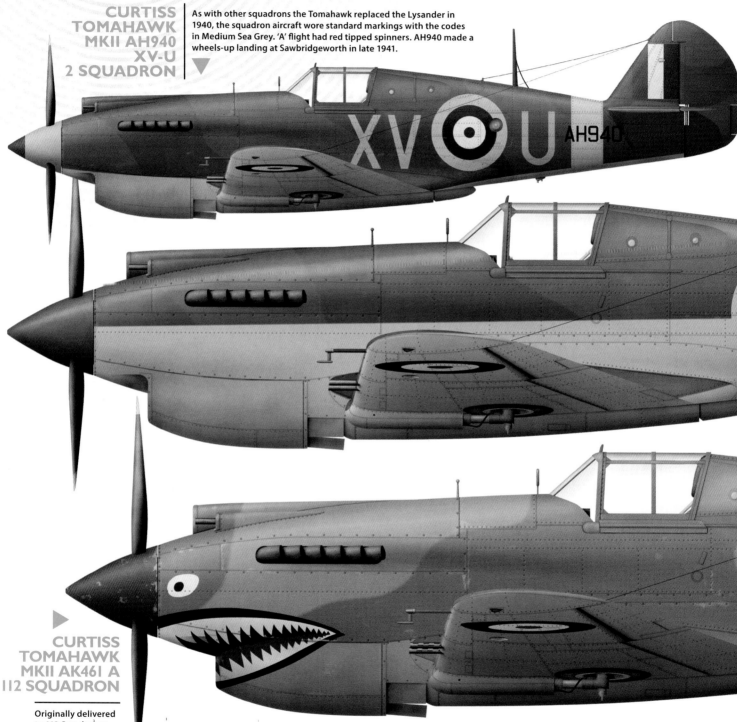

**CURTISS TOMAHAWK MKII AK461 A 112 SQUADRON**

Originally delivered to 112 Sqn during July 1941 wearing standard European camouflage it was repainted in Mid Stone, Dark Earth upper surfaces with Azure Blue underside. 112 Sqn soon applied the shark's mouth to all their aircraft and led to others including the AVG adopting the design.

thought to outweigh the losses. II AC squadron became the first RAF unit based in the UK to receive the Tomahawk during June 1941 following conversion courses for the pilots who had until then been used to flying the Westland Lysander. Just like the P-39, the RAF pilots were not impressed with early versions of the Tomahawk and returned to using the Lysander for operations while only using the Tomahawk for exercises until they began receiving the P-51 in spring 1942.

Clearly unsuitable for the European Theatre, the Tomahawk IIs were allocated to squadrons based in the Middle East once they had worked up to operational readiness in the UK. During this time the only action they were involved in was when one 410 RCAF aircraft flew an unauthorised strafing mission over occupied Europe.

During the summer of 1941 a shipment of 300 was sent to the Desert Air Force via Takoradi, West Africa. The aircraft were delivered to 112 & 250

Squadrons RAF, 2,4 & 5 Squadrons SAAF and 3 Squadron RAAF, where they were gratefully received by the pilots who unlike those in 2 Sqn were highly impressed with the rugged durability, reliable handling and clean lines of the Tomahawk.

250 Sqn had the honour of being the first squadron to use the Tomahawk in combat on May 14, 1941, when two aircraft flown by Flg Off Aldridge and Flg Off Wolsey took off from Aqir, Egypt to escort

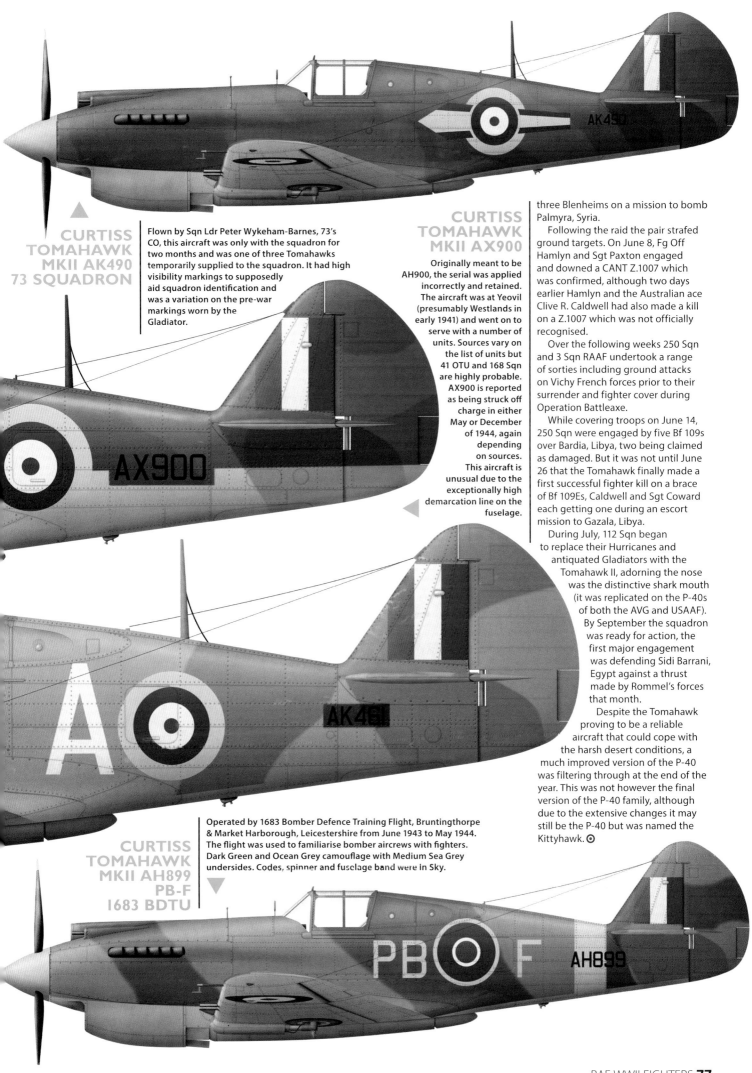

**CURTISS TOMAHAWK MKII AK490 73 SQUADRON**

Flown by Sqn Ldr Peter Wykeham-Barnes, 73's CO, this aircraft was only with the squadron for two months and was one of three Tomahawks temporarily supplied to the squadron. It had high visibility markings to supposedly aid squadron identification and was a variation on the pre-war markings worn by the Gladiator.

**CURTISS TOMAHAWK MKII AX900**

Originally meant to be AH900, the serial was applied incorrectly and retained. The aircraft was at Yeovil (presumably Westlands in early 1941) and went on to serve with a number of units. Sources vary on the list of units but 41 OTU and 168 Sqn are highly probable. AX900 is reported as being struck off charge in either May or December of 1944, again depending on sources. This aircraft is unusual due to the exceptionally high demarcation line on the fuselage.

three Blenheims on a mission to bomb Palmyra, Syria.

Following the raid the pair strafed ground targets. On June 8, Fg Off Hamlyn and Sgt Paxton engaged and downed a CANT Z.1007 which was confirmed, although two days earlier Hamlyn and the Australian ace Clive R. Caldwell had also made a kill on a Z.1007 which was not officially recognised.

Over the following weeks 250 Sqn and 3 Sqn RAAF undertook a range of sorties including ground attacks on Vichy French forces prior to their surrender and fighter cover during Operation Battleaxe.

While covering troops on June 14, 250 Sqn were engaged by five Bf 109s over Bardia, Libya, two being claimed as damaged. But it was not until June 26 that the Tomahawk finally made a first successful fighter kill on a brace of Bf 109Es, Caldwell and Sgt Coward each getting one during an escort mission to Gazala, Libya.

During July, 112 Sqn began to replace their Hurricanes and antiquated Gladiators with the Tomahawk II, adorning the nose was the distinctive shark mouth (it was replicated on the P-40s of both the AVG and USAAF). By September the squadron was ready for action, the first major engagement was defending Sidi Barrani, Egypt against a thrust made by Rommel's forces that month.

Despite the Tomahawk proving to be a reliable aircraft that could cope with the harsh desert conditions, a much improved version of the P-40 was filtering through at the end of the year. This was not however the final version of the P-40 family, although due to the extensive changes it may still be the P-40 but was named the Kittyhawk. ◉

**CURTISS TOMAHAWK MKII AH899 PB-F 1683 BDTU**

Operated by 1683 Bomber Defence Training Flight, Bruntingthorpe & Market Harborough, Leicestershire from June 1943 to May 1944. The flight was used to familiarise bomber aircrews with fighters. Dark Green and Ocean Grey camouflage with Medium Sea Grey undersides. Codes, spinner and fuselage band were in Sky.

# CURTISS P-40A-C
# TOMAHAWK

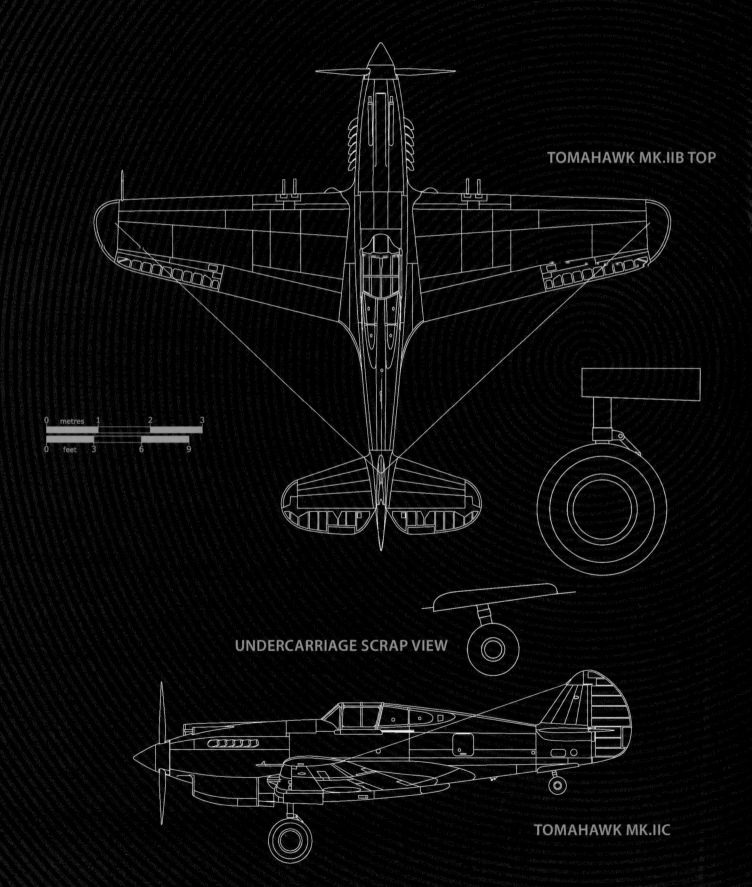

TOMAHAWK MK.IIB TOP

metres
0    1    2    3
feet
0    3    6    9

UNDERCARRIAGE SCRAP VIEW

TOMAHAWK MK.IIC

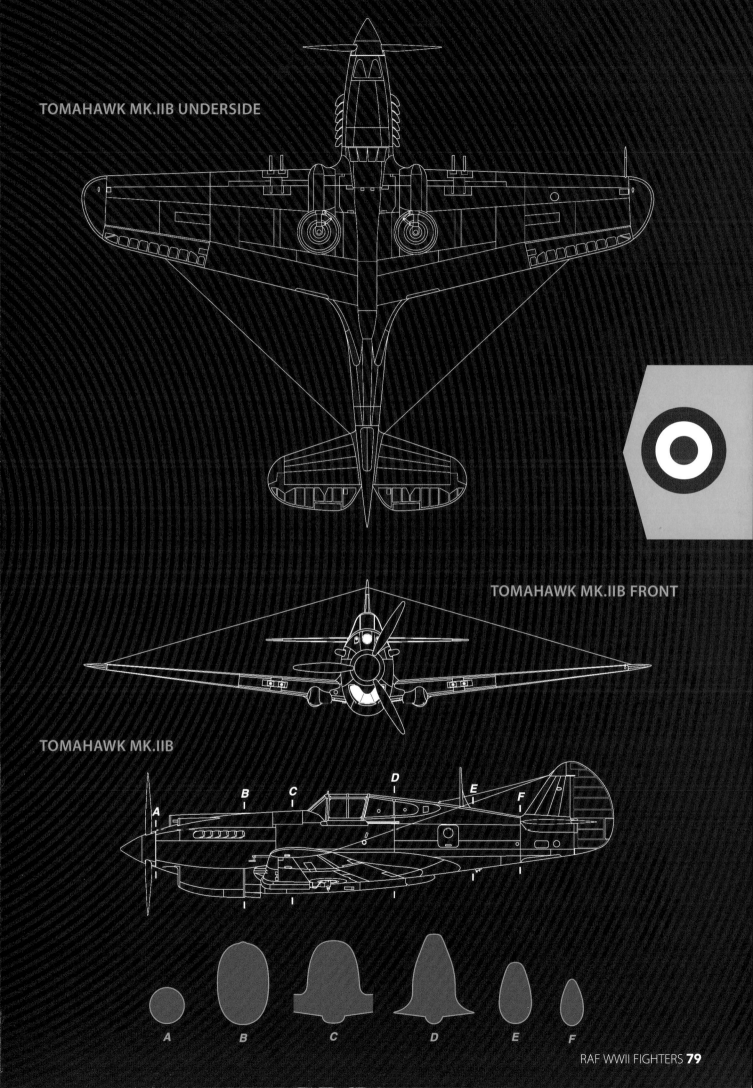

TOMAHAWK MK.IIB UNDERSIDE

TOMAHAWK MK.IIB FRONT

TOMAHAWK MK.IIB

## 1942-1944

The development of the Allison V-1710-33 engined Tomahawk continued as the war progressed and before long sufficient changes had been made to warrant a new name – the Kittyhawk retained the same P-40 code though.

# CURTISS
## P-40D-N KITTYHAWK

**J**ust like its predecessor the Kittyhawk was built in vast numbers and although it was not suited to conditions in Western Europe it was highly successful in all other theatres of conflict during the Second World War. With the RAF and Commonwealth forces, it is North Africa with which the Kittyhawk is primarily associated.

The P-40D (Mark I) was produced by Curtiss in an effort to improve performance. It was visibly different to the Tomahawk due to the fuselage cross section being reduced in an effort to cut drag. It also had the strength to carry a centreline 500lb bomb or external tank as well as a 100lb bomb under each wing. The nose guns were removed and after the first 20 were completed two more Browning .50 cal guns were mounted in the wings to compensate. The number of rounds was increased to 615 per gun, providing greater firepower and for longer. British aircraft had their rear cockpit windows changed in size and shape to improve rear visibility for the pilot. He also benefitted from

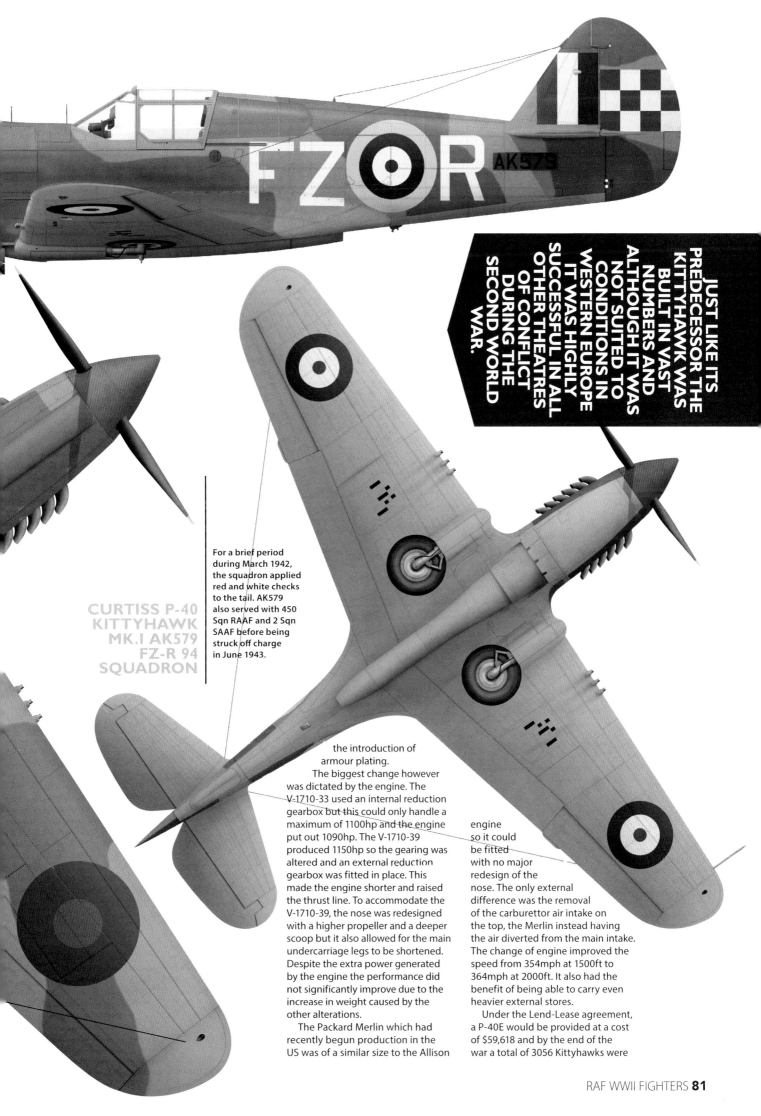

For a brief period during March 1942, the squadron applied red and white checks to the tail. AK579 also served with 450 Sqn RAAF and 2 Sqn SAAF before being struck off charge in June 1943.

CURTISS P-40
KITTYHAWK
MK.I AK579
FZ-R 94
SQUADRON

the introduction of armour plating.

The biggest change however was dictated by the engine. The V-1710-33 used an internal reduction gearbox but this could only handle a maximum of 1100hp and the engine put out 1090hp. The V-1710-39 produced 1150hp so the gearing was altered and an external reduction gearbox was fitted in place. This made the engine shorter and raised the thrust line. To accommodate the V-1710-39, the nose was redesigned with a higher propeller and a deeper scoop but it also allowed for the main undercarriage legs to be shortened. Despite the extra power generated by the engine the performance did not significantly improve due to the increase in weight caused by the other alterations.

The Packard Merlin which had recently begun production in the US was of a similar size to the Allison engine so it could be fitted with no major redesign of the nose. The only external difference was the removal of the carburettor air intake on the top, the Merlin instead having the air diverted from the main intake. The change of engine improved the speed from 354mph at 1500ft to 364mph at 2000ft. It also had the benefit of being able to carry even heavier external stores.

Under the Lend-Lease agreement, a P-40E would be provided at a cost of $59,618 and by the end of the war a total of 3056 Kittyhawks were

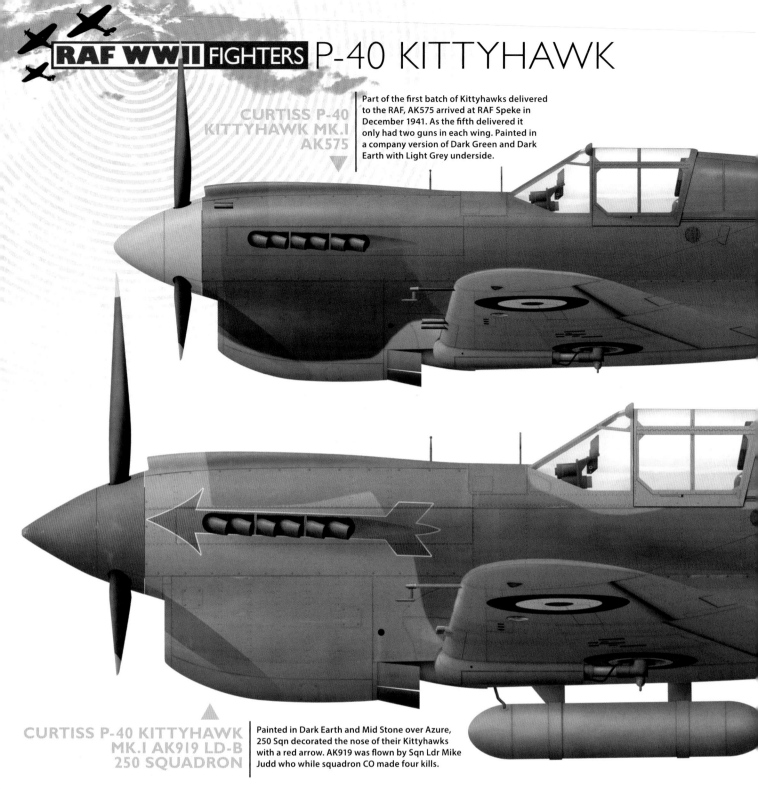

**CURTISS P-40 KITTYHAWK MK.I AK575**

Part of the first batch of Kittyhawks delivered to the RAF, AK575 arrived at RAF Speke in December 1941. As the fifth delivered it only had two guns in each wing. Painted in a company version of Dark Green and Dark Earth with Light Grey underside.

**CURTISS P-40 KITTYHAWK MK.I AK919 LD-B 250 SQUADRON**

Painted in Dark Earth and Mid Stone over Azure, 250 Sqn decorated the nose of their Kittyhawks with a red arrow. AK919 was flown by Sqn Ldr Mike Judd who while squadron CO made four kills.

**AS THE TOMAHAWK HAD ALREADY PROVED MORE SUITED TO DESERT CONDITIONS THE ONLY KITTYHAWKS TO BE SEEN IN BRITAIN WERE THOSE DELIVERED TO RAF SPEKE**

provided although 300 were diverted to the USSR and some were lost at sea. As the Tomahawk had already proved more suited to desert conditions the only Kittyhawks to be seen in Britain were those delivered to RAF Speke. Apart from a few retained for trials, all were forwarded on to replace the Tomahawks in the fighter and ground-attack roles.

Aircraft began arriving in late 1941 in the Middle East and 3 Squadron RAAF became the first Commonwealth unit to operate to the Kittyhawk on December 17, due to similarities in types and the necessities of war there was no conversion process, the squadron soon found itself flying missions and on New Year's Day the squadron's nine P-40Ds destroyed a Bf 109 and a Ju 87, several more were damaged in the fight near Agedabia, Libya.

During January, 112 Squadron became the second Kittyhawk squadron when they also replaced their Tomahawks. Just like 3 Squadron

RAAF, 112 Squadron had made a trip to Agedabia when they first used the Kittyhawk in combat. Having escorted a flight of Blenheims tasked with bombing Agedabia, the nine P-40s were returning when they encountered five Bf 109s west of Msus. During the mêlée Sgt Plt 'Bleu' Leu made a head-on attack and the Bf 109 was later seen to crash. This was confirmed in a combat report made by Neville Duke. It was Leu's fifth claim and made him an ace.

The two squadrons continued to chalk up victories over the Luftwaffe and Regia Aeronautica during the following weeks. They were joined by 250 Squadron and 450 Squadron RAAF on March 1, 1942, when 239 Wing was formed and commanded by Wg Cdr H C Mayers. A second wing comprising of a mix of Kittyhawk and Tomahawk squadrons was also formed (all the Tomahawks were eventually replaced), 233 Wing contained 2, 5 and 5 Squadrons SAAF along with 94 and 260 Squadrons.

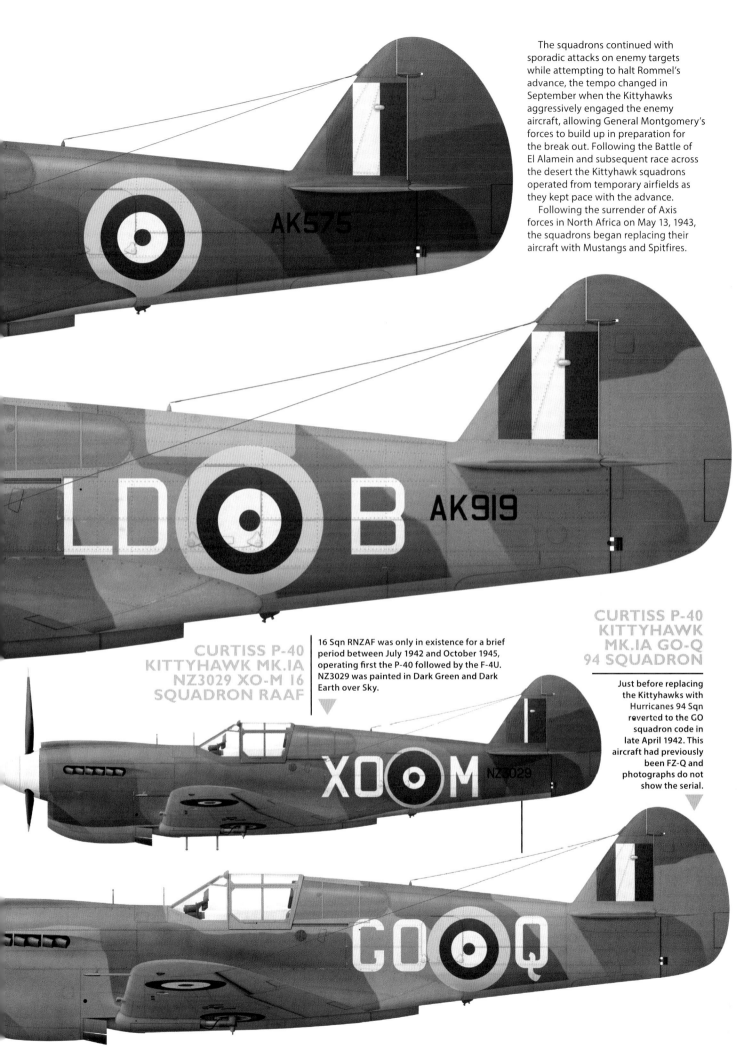

The squadrons continued with sporadic attacks on enemy targets while attempting to halt Rommel's advance, the tempo changed in September when the Kittyhawks aggressively engaged the enemy aircraft, allowing General Montgomery's forces to build up in preparation for the break out. Following the Battle of El Alamein and subsequent race across the desert the Kittyhawk squadrons operated from temporary airfields as they kept pace with the advance.

Following the surrender of Axis forces in North Africa on May 13, 1943, the squadrons began replacing their aircraft with Mustangs and Spitfires.

AK575

LD ⊙ B AK919

CURTISS P-40
KITTYHAWK MK.IA
NZ3029 XO-M 16
SQUADRON RAAF

16 Sqn RNZAF was only in existence for a brief period between July 1942 and October 1945, operating first the P-40 followed by the F-4U. NZ3029 was painted in Dark Green and Dark Earth over Sky.

XO ⊙ M NZ3029

CURTISS P-40
KITTYHAWK
MK.IA GO-Q
94 SQUADRON

Just before replacing the Kittyhawks with Hurricanes 94 Sqn reverted to the GO squadron code in late April 1942. This aircraft had previously been FZ-Q and photographs do not show the serial.

GO ⊙ Q

P-40 KITTYHAWK

112 Squadron retained their P-40s until June 1944, by which time they had flown through Sicily and Italy. The last aerial action for the Kittyhawk was when a dozen 112 Squadron aircraft attacked some Fw 190s taking off from Rieti, Italy, on April 7. The rest of the missions until the end of June were against ground targets and several pilots were lost, the last being Sgt Davis on June 30.

Commonwealth Kittyhawks were not limited to North Africa and Italy, a substantial number being sent to eight RAAF squadrons and seven RNZAF squadrons where they operated throughout the South Pacific. The first posting for 15 Squadron RAAF was to Tonga, relieving the USAAF squadron and allowing it to undertake combat operations. As the campaign

continued the squadron island hopped and began encountering Zeros while providing fighter cover over the Russell Islands. Due to the manoeuvrability of the Zeros, the Kittyhawk pilots developed tactics to avoid prolonged dogfights, instead they employed high-speed diving attacks which found some success.

Squadrons from both the RAAF and RNZAF were involved in heavy combat during June 1943 when the Japanese launched a series of bombing raids on Guadalcanal. During this phase of the war a mix of E, K, M and Ns were used by the squadrons supporting the US Marine forces. As aircraft became available the number of squadrons also increased. The method of defending an island and aiding in the invasion of the next continued until the Japanese

surrender on August 15, 1945, by which time the Kittyhawk had proven itself a versatile and capable combat aircraft.

Although the P-40 was outclassed in many areas by the end of the war, it had the benefit of comparatively simple construction and low cost production allowing large numbers to be pressed into service quickly. The improvements made to the Tomahawk meant that the Kittyhawk was suited to the ground-attack bomber role. Pilots learned how to exploit the strengths of their aircraft in order to gain results although there was understandable relief when they exchanged their P-40s for later superior fighters. ⊙

**CURTISS P-40 KITTYHAWK MK.II FL308 CV-V 3 SQUADRON RAAF**

FL308 was the second Kittyhawk to be flown by the Australian ace 'Bobby' Gibbes. Both ET953 and FL308 wore variations of the same nose art and his code letter V. Having returned to Australia he undertook a second tour in the Pacific.

| VARIANT | LENGTH | SPAN | HEIGHT | ENGINE |
|---|---|---|---|---|
| P-40D KITTYHAWK MK I | 31FT 2IN / 9.50M | 37FT 3½ IN / 11.37M | 12FT 4IN / 9.66M | ALLISON V-1710-39 |
| P-40E KITTYHAWK MK IA | 31FT 2IN / 9.50M | 37FT 3½ IN / 11.37M | 12FT 4IN / 9.66M | ALLISON V-1710-39 |
| P-40F KITTYHAWK MK II | 31FT 8¾IN / 9.67M | 37FT 3½ IN / 11.37M | 12FT 4IN / 9.66M | PACKARD V-1650-1 MERLIN |
| P-40K KITTYHAWK MK III | 31FT 8½IN / 9.66M | 37FT 3½ IN / 11.37M | 12FT 4IN / 9.66M | ALLISON V-1710-39 |
| P-40L KITTYHAWK MK II/III | 33FT 4IN / 10.16M | 37FT 3½ IN / 11.37M | 12FT 4IN / 9.66M | PACKARD V-1650-1 MERLIN |
| P-40M KITTYHAWK MK III | 33FT 4IN / 10.16M | 37FT 3½ IN / 11.37M | 12FT 4IN / 9.66M | PACKARD V-1650-1 MERLIN |
| P-40N KITTYHAWK MK IV | 33FT 4IN / 10.16M | 37FT 3½ IN / 11.37M | 12FT 4IN / 9.66M | ALLISON V-1710-81 |

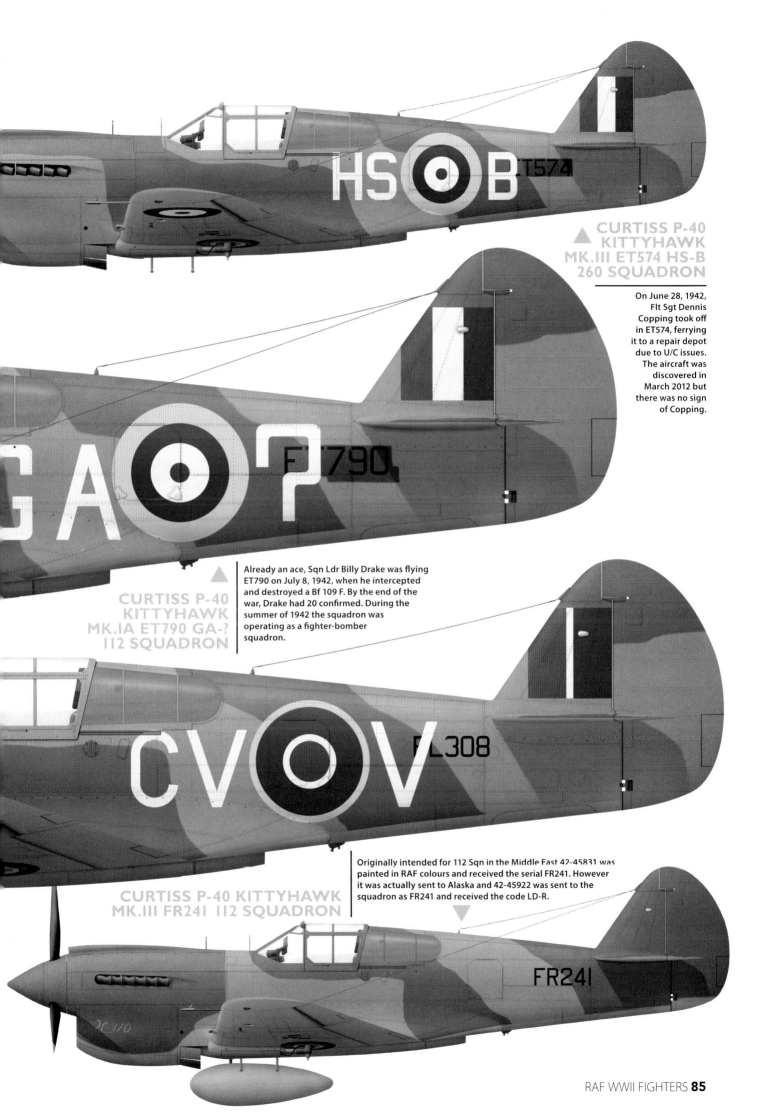

CURTISS P-40
KITTYHAWK
MK.III ET574 HS-B
260 SQUADRON

On June 28, 1942, Flt Sgt Dennis Copping took off in ET574, ferrying it to a repair depot due to U/C issues. The aircraft was discovered in March 2012 but there was no sign of Copping.

CURTISS P-40
KITTYHAWK
MK.IA ET790 GA-?
112 SQUADRON

Already an ace, Sqn Ldr Billy Drake was flying ET790 on July 8, 1942, when he intercepted and destroyed a Bf 109 F. By the end of the war, Drake had 20 confirmed. During the summer of 1942 the squadron was operating as a fighter-bomber squadron.

CURTISS P-40 KITTYHAWK
MK.III FR241 112 SQUADRON

Originally intended for 112 Sqn in the Middle East 42-45831 was painted in RAF colours and received the serial FR241. However it was actually sent to Alaska and 42-45922 was sent to the squadron as FR241 and received the code LD-R.

# CURTISS P-40D-N
# KITTYHAWK

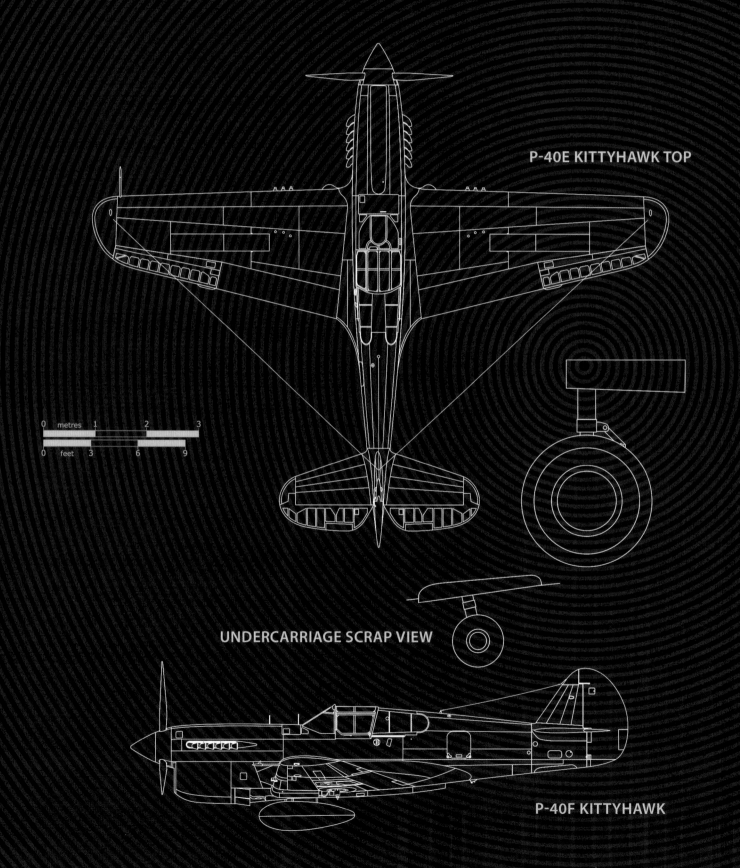

P-40E KITTYHAWK TOP

UNDERCARRIAGE SCRAP VIEW

P-40F KITTYHAWK

P-40E KITTYHAWK UNDERSIDE

P-40E KITTYHAWK FRONT

P-40E KITTYHAWK

A  B  C  D  E  F

# BRISTOL
## BEAUFIGHTER

**Bristol followed up its successful Blenheim with a more powerful aircraft which it hoped would be both a successful bomber and fighter. The Beaufighter may have had drawbacks but went on to become a formidable night fighter and served with the RAF in various roles for 20 years.**

## 1940-1960

**T**he Beaufighter was to an extent based on the existing Bristol Beaufort (Type 152), a torpedo bomber that itself was based on the Bristol Blenheim (Type 150). The Beaufort came about through Air Ministry Specification M15/35 which was for a land based torpedo bomber; a second Specification G24/35 was for a reconnaissance aircraft.

By altering the nose, replacing the Mercury engines and relocating the turret to retain the centre of gravity, extending the wingspan and modifying the bomb bay to accommodate a partially enclosed torpedo, the Blenheim was adapted into the Beaufort. Due to delays with the Westland Whirlwind, the Air Ministry was concerned about the lack of a suitable cannon fighter. Both the Spitfire and Hurricane were considered for the role but tests proved troublesome and it was quite a long time before either aircraft successfully had cannon fitted. Having already successfully converted the Blenheim into a twin engine fighter the Bristol design team led by Leslie Frise looked into the feasibility of repeating it with the Beaufort. Unlike the Blenheim, which was converted with the simple addition of a gun pack under the bomb bay, the new aircraft required much more than just adapting a Beaufort fuselage which was the original plan.

Of all the proposals submitted, Bristol's was the strongest on paper and the company was given permission to proceed with the Type 156 prototype. Utilising many of the existing Beaufort elements reduced development time and speeded up delivery of production

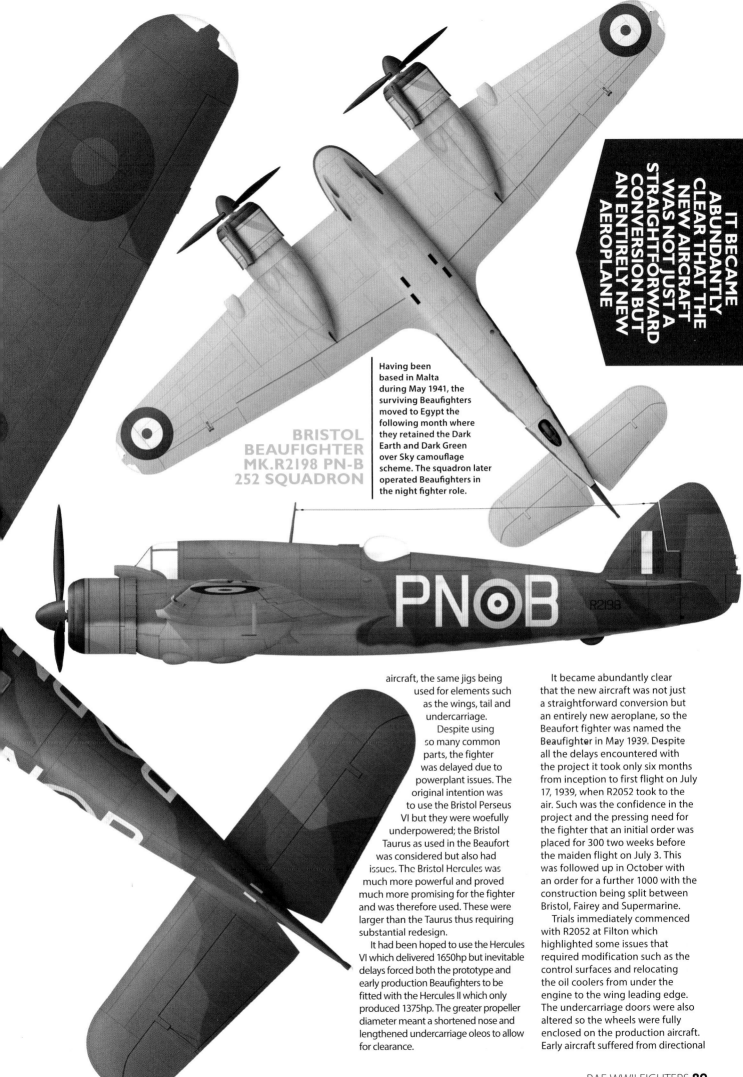

Having been based in Malta during May 1941, the surviving Beaufighters moved to Egypt the following month where they retained the Dark Earth and Dark Green over Sky camouflage scheme. The squadron later operated Beaufighters in the night fighter role.

**BRISTOL BEAUFIGHTER MK.R2198 PN-B 252 SQUADRON**

aircraft, the same jigs being used for elements such as the wings, tail and undercarriage.

Despite using so many common parts, the fighter was delayed due to powerplant issues. The original intention was to use the Bristol Perseus VI but they were woefully underpowered; the Bristol Taurus as used in the Beaufort was considered but also had issues. The Bristol Hercules was much more powerful and proved much more promising for the fighter and was therefore used. These were larger than the Taurus thus requiring substantial redesign.

It had been hoped to use the Hercules VI which delivered 1650hp but inevitable delays forced both the prototype and early production Beaufighters to be fitted with the Hercules II which only produced 1375hp. The greater propeller diameter meant a shortened nose and lengthened undercarriage oleos to allow for clearance.

It became abundantly clear that the new aircraft was not just a straightforward conversion but an entirely new aeroplane, so the Beaufort fighter was named the Beaufighter in May 1939. Despite all the delays encountered with the project it took only six months from inception to first flight on July 17, 1939, when R2052 took to the air. Such was the confidence in the project and the pressing need for the fighter that an initial order was placed for 300 two weeks before the maiden flight on July 3. This was followed up in October with an order for a further 1000 with the construction being split between Bristol, Fairey and Supermarine.

Trials immediately commenced with R2052 at Filton which highlighted some issues that required modification such as the control surfaces and relocating the oil coolers from under the engine to the wing leading edge. The undercarriage doors were also altered so the wheels were fully enclosed on the production aircraft. Early aircraft suffered from directional

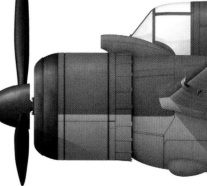

## BRISTOL BEAUFIGHTER MK.IC T4800 ND-C 236 SQUADRON

On June 12, 1942, Wg Cdr Gatward in T4800 took off for a unique mission to spoil a Gestapo parade in Paris. Flying at low level the aircraft arrived to find no parade so it circled the Eiffel Tower, dropped a Tricolour over the Arc de Triomphe and strafed the Naval Ministry before returning to RAF Northolt.

stability issues but this was resolved by adding 12° of dihedral to the tail.

It was introduced to some of the early marks and was standard on later marks, though confusingly photographs show that some later Beaufighters were fitted with the early flat tail.

After six months the first two prototypes were handed over to A&AEE in February 1940 where testing was continued and live firing trials undertaken using the four Hispano 20mm cannon.

Initially the cannons were drum fed and it fell to the navigator/AI operator to change drums. The task was challenging at the best of times but at night in a dark fuselage, being thrown around by the pilot, it was very difficult so later cannons were belt fed. The first 50 production aircraft were just fitted with the cannons but later aircraft were also fitted with six .303in Brownings in the wings.

The Beaufighter was ready to enter series production but there were not enough Hercules engines to meet demand, plus the majority were allocated to the Short Stirling which meant that the delivery rate would be much lower than originally intended for the Beaufighter.

## BRISTOL BEAUFIGHTER MK.IF R2101 NG-R 604 COUNTY OF MIDDLESEX SQUADRON

The squadron replaced its Blenheim night fighters with Beaufighters in September 1940. R2101 was flown by John Cunningham with Jimmy Rawnsley as his AI operator; Cunningham gaining 10 of his 20 victories in R2101.

## BRISTOL BEAUFIGHTER MK.IF X7540 V 46 SQUADRON ▶

This aircraft was the first to be completed by the Bristol factory at Oldmixon, Weston-super-Mare and first flew on February 20, 1941. It was first used for trials by A&AEE before serving with 68 and 46 Squadrons. Painted in Night, by the end it was heavily weathered.

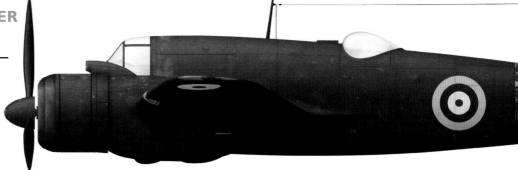

**BRISTOL BEAUFIGHTER MK.IF R2069 ZK-H 25 SQUADRON**

One of the first squadrons to receive the Beaufighter. R2069 was an early production model which retained the spinners. Despite being a night fighter squadron, aircraft retained the day scheme. R2069 was flown by the New Zealand ace Plt Off Mike Herrick.

**BRISTOL BEAUFIGHTER MK.II R2270**

R2270 was the first p roduction Mk.II to be built and features the angled tail that was not present on most Mk.Is. It first flew on March 22, 1941, and Mk.II deliveries to the squadrons commenced the following month.

**BRISTOL BEAUFIGHTER MK.II R2402 YD-G 255 SQUADRON**

255 Sqn was re-formed on November 23, 1940, as a night fighter squadron, having flown the Defiant and Blenheim, the squadron converted to the Beaufighter Mk.II in March 1941 but replaced them the following March. Painted in all over Night the aircraft weathered heavily while in service.

With the need for the fighter becoming increasingly urgent, an alternative was required. Both the Wright Cyclone and Rolls-Royce Griffon were candidates but Bristol instead selected the Merlin which was already developed and had more potential in the short term. Three aircraft were selected to take the engine with the modification being undertaken during the spring of 1940, this variant became known as the Mk.II but was short-lived as the Merlin was in demand for a wide variety of aircraft and Hercules production gradually improved. One

advantage the Mk.II had over other types was the slightly improved visibility the pilot had, the larger Hercules cowlings reducing the view considerably.

As the Beaufighter entered production, AI sets were beginning to prove themselves as more than just a theory having been introduced in the Blenheim. There was some early success but the lack of power had a detrimental effect on results of the night fighter. The Beaufighter was naturally selected to replace the Blenheim in this duty. The AI operator could also fulfil the role of armourer, replacing the drums containing the ammunition of the four cannons.

The first Beaufighters began filtering through to the Blenheim squadrons in September 1940, the logic being that the aircraft were similar

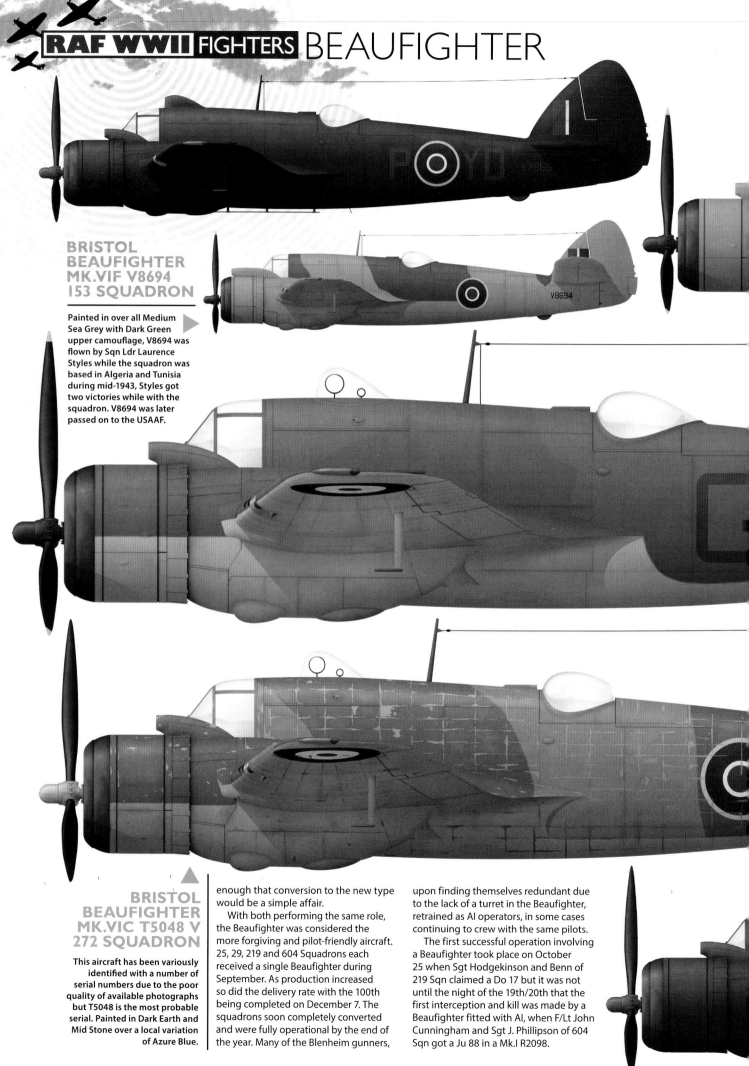

## BRISTOL BEAUFIGHTER MK.VIF V8694 153 SQUADRON

Painted in over all Medium Sea Grey with Dark Green upper camouflage, V8694 was flown by Sqn Ldr Laurence Styles while the squadron was based in Algeria and Tunisia during mid-1943, Styles got two victories while with the squadron. V8694 was later passed on to the USAAF.

## BRISTOL BEAUFIGHTER MK.VIC T5048 V 272 SQUADRON

This aircraft has been variously identified with a number of serial numbers due to the poor quality of available photographs but T5048 is the most probable serial. Painted in Dark Earth and Mid Stone over a local variation of Azure Blue.

enough that conversion to the new type would be a simple affair.

With both performing the same role, the Beaufighter was considered the more forgiving and pilot-friendly aircraft. 25, 29, 219 and 604 Squadrons each received a single Beaufighter during September. As production increased so did the delivery rate with the 100th being completed on December 7. The squadrons soon completely converted and were fully operational by the end of the year. Many of the Blenheim gunners,

upon finding themselves redundant due to the lack of a turret in the Beaufighter, retrained as AI operators, in some cases continuing to crew with the same pilots.

The first successful operation involving a Beaufighter took place on October 25 when Sgt Hodgekinson and Benn of 219 Sqn claimed a Do 17 but it was not until the night of the 19th/20th that the first interception and kill was made by a Beaufighter fitted with AI, when F/Lt John Cunningham and Sgt J. Phillipson of 604 Sqn got a Ju 88 in a Mk.I R2098.

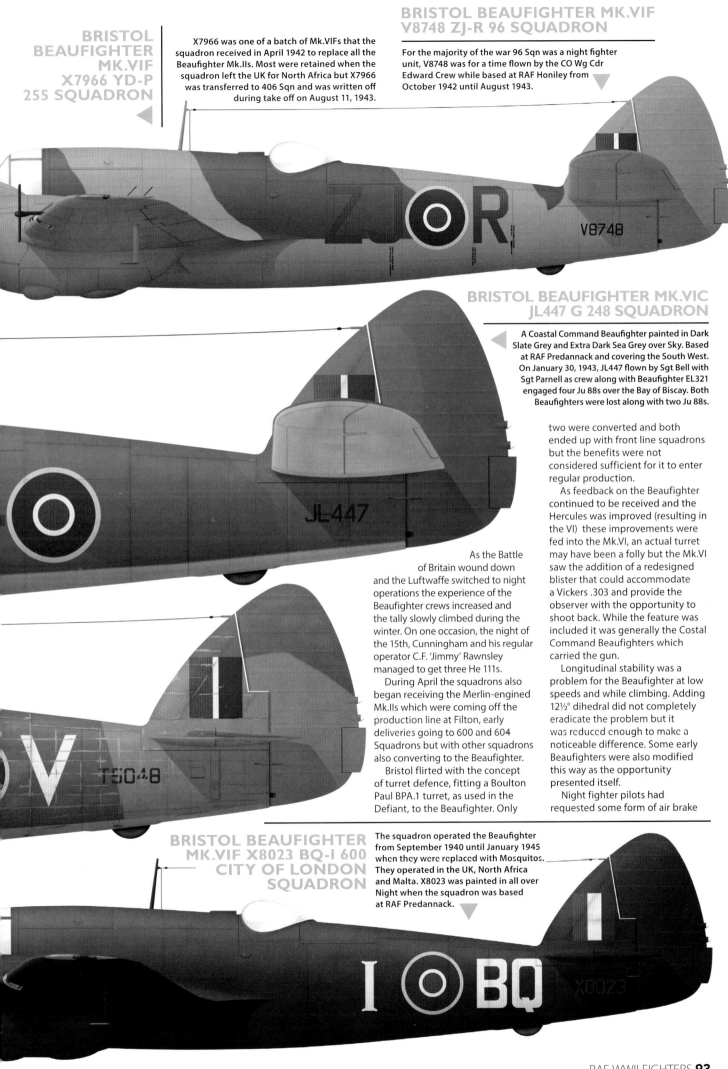

## BRISTOL BEAUFIGHTER MK.VIF X7966 YD-P 255 SQUADRON

X7966 was one of a batch of Mk.VIFs that the squadron received in April 1942 to replace all the Beaufighter Mk.IIs. Most were retained when the squadron left the UK for North Africa but X7966 was transferred to 406 Sqn and was written off during take off on August 11, 1943.

## BRISTOL BEAUFIGHTER MK.VIF V8748 ZJ-R 96 SQUADRON

For the majority of the war 96 Sqn was a night fighter unit, V8748 was for a time flown by the CO Wg Cdr Edward Crew while based at RAF Honiley from October 1942 until August 1943.

## BRISTOL BEAUFIGHTER MK.VIC JL447 G 248 SQUADRON

A Coastal Command Beaufighter painted in Dark Slate Grey and Extra Dark Sea Grey over Sky. Based at RAF Predannack and covering the South West. On January 30, 1943, JL447 flown by Sgt Bell with Sgt Parnell as crew along with Beaufighter EL321 engaged four Ju 88s over the Bay of Biscay. Both Beaufighters were lost along with two Ju 88s.

As the Battle of Britain wound down and the Luftwaffe switched to night operations the experience of the Beaufighter crews increased and the tally slowly climbed during the winter. On one occasion, the night of the 15th, Cunningham and his regular operator C.F. 'Jimmy' Rawnsley managed to get three He 111s.

During April the squadrons also began receiving the Merlin-engined Mk.IIs which were coming off the production line at Filton, early deliveries going to 600 and 604 Squadrons but with other squadrons also converting to the Beaufighter.

Bristol flirted with the concept of turret defence, fitting a Boulton Paul BPA.1 turret, as used in the Defiant, to the Beaufighter. Only

two were converted and both ended up with front line squadrons but the benefits were not considered sufficient for it to enter regular production.

As feedback on the Beaufighter continued to be received and the Hercules was improved (resulting in the VI) these improvements were fed into the Mk.VI, an actual turret may have been a folly but the Mk.VI saw the addition of a redesigned blister that could accommodate a Vickers .303 and provide the observer with the opportunity to shoot back. While the feature was included it was generally the Costal Command Beaufighters which carried the gun.

Longitudinal stability was a problem for the Beaufighter at low speeds and while climbing. Adding 12½° dihedral did not completely eradicate the problem but it was reduced enough to make a noticeable difference. Some early Beaufighters were also modified this way as the opportunity presented itself.

Night fighter pilots had requested some form of air brake

## BRISTOL BEAUFIGHTER MK.VIF X8023 BQ-I 600 CITY OF LONDON SQUADRON

The squadron operated the Beaufighter from September 1940 until January 1945 when they were replaced with Mosquitos. They operated in the UK, North Africa and Malta. X8023 was painted in all over Night when the squadron was based at RAF Predannack.

## BRISTOL BEAUFIGHTER MK.X NT950 MB-T 236 SQUADRON

- 236 Sqn was part of Coastal Command, based at RAF North Coates where it was used for anti shipping patrols. The wing sunk over 150,000 tons of shipping by the end of the war. Painted in Medium Sea Grey and Dark Green with Sky underside. ▼

to avoid overshooting during an interception so Bristol investigated split flaps but this also caused a reduction in speed which was not appropriate for any fighter. However, lowering the undercarriage had a similar effect.

Costal Command had slightly different requirements for their aircraft where the Beaufighter was more likely to be found at low level attacking shipping. Range was extended by fitting a 50 gallon tank in the starboard wing and a 24 gallon tank in the port wing, both in place of the guns.

The Hercules XVII was a modified VI which produced greater power at low altitude; the Coastal Command version received the C suffix. A few Mk.VIs were also adapted to carry torpedoes, the normal tactic being for a Torbeau to

fly with two Mk.VICs providing fighter support during anti-shipping missions.

More than 1800 were built and the type served in all theatres of the war with many being sent to the Middle East, North Africa and the Mediterranean where they flew patrols from Malta. Many more were sent Far East where they were operated by the RAAF primarily in the ground-attack role and due to the

## BRISTOL BEAUFIGHTER MK.VIF V8965 ZQ-F FIGHTER INTERCEPTION UNIT ▲

The FIU was used to evaluate methods of interception including AI. Although based at RAF Tangmere the unit operated across the UK including RAF Wittering where V8965 was used for trails of the Mk.VIIIA centimetric radar fitted in the extended nose.

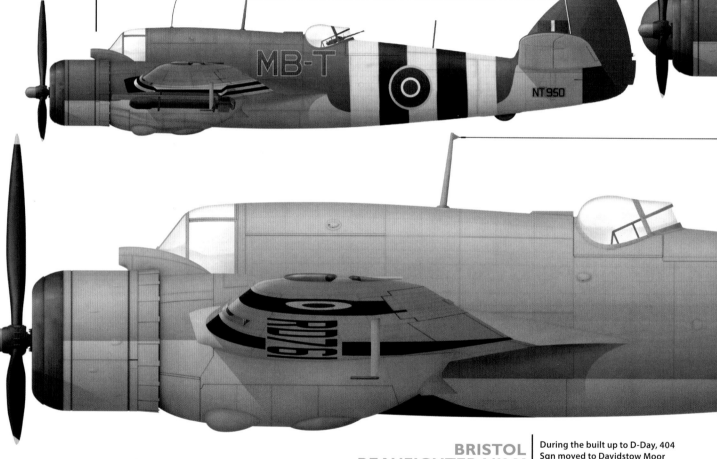

## BRISTOL BEAUFIGHTER MK.X NE355 EE-H 404 SQUADRON

During the built up to D-Day, 404 Sqn moved to Davidstow Moor to provide cover to the Western Approaches with 144 Sqn. Following the invasion the squadron code of 2 was replaced with EE. ▼

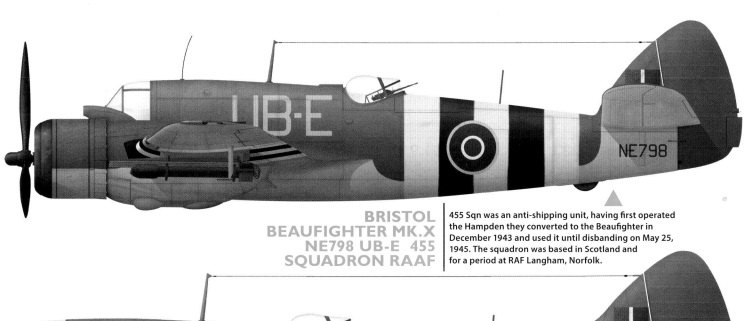

**BRISTOL BEAUFIGHTER MK.X NE798 UB-E 455 SQUADRON RAAF**

455 Sqn was an anti-shipping unit, having first operated the Hampden they converted to the Beaufighter in December 1943 and used it until disbanding on May 25, 1945. The squadron was based in Scotland and for a period at RAF Langham, Norfolk.

**BRISTOL BEAUFIGHTER TF MK.X RD351 F-QM 254 SQUADRON**

Painted in all over Dark Grey and Sky, RD351 operated by 254 Sqn Coastal Command, North Coates strike wing which used the Beaufighter from March 1940 until October 1946.

**BRISTOL BEAUFIGHTER TT.10 RD761 1574 FLIGHT**

Converted from a TF.X and used for target tug duties at RAF Seletar, Singapore following the war. On May 12, 1960, RD761 undertook the last flight by a RAF Beaufighter and was broken up shortly after by 390 MU. Painted in Aluminium with Yellow and Black underside.

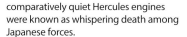

comparatively quiet Hercules engines were known as whispering death among Japanese forces.

The Mk.VI was followed by the Mk.X. The early production aircraft were visually very similar to the Mk.VI with the exception of the nose, which was extended to accommodate the AI Mk.VII and Mk.VIII on most airframes. The aircraft were also all fitted with the Hercules XVII, like the Beaufighter Mk.VIC. Later Mk.Xs were fitted with the distinctive extended dorsal fin, part of the continual effort by Bristol to resolve the handling issues that had plagued the Beaufighter. To expand the capabilities of the Beaufighter, the wings were strengthened to allow up to a 1000lb bomb to be carried on the outer wings, two 500lb bombs, a torpedo or 200 gallon drop tank under the fuselage. The Mk.X was the last iteration of the Beaufighter to be used in combat and can be considered a success with 2368 being built in total.

Inevitably with the introduction of more advanced aircraft such as the Mosquito the Beaufighter was phased out of service. Like so many other obsolete combat aircraft there many left that still had plenty flying hours remaining in them so Beaufighters were relegated to target tug duties and continued flying across the world until May 12, 1960, when RD761, a converted Mk.X took off from RAF Selatar, Singapore for a final operational flight.

Although it was built as a fighter the Beaufighter could not shake off the bomber lineage it had inherited from the Beafort. Just like the Blenheim it replaced, the Beaufighter was heavy and slow in combat and unable to compete equally with the Spitfires and Hurricanes that fought during the day.

It was, however, an ideal night fighter. The pilot and navigator / AI operator worked well in tandem, with the Beaufighter providing a stable gun platform that could bring formidable firepower to bear on enemy intruders.

It served well in a range of secondary roles from anti-shipping raids to ground-attack, especially in the Far East. It is a testament to the type that nearly 6000 were built and (including Commonwealth forces) served with 11 nations in a career lasting 20 years. ◉

| VARIANT | LENGTH | SPAN | HEIGHT | ENGINE |
|---|---|---|---|---|
| PROTOTYPE | 41FT 4IN / 12.6M | 57FT 10IN / 17.63M | 15FT 10IN / 4.83M | 2 X HERCULES II |
| MK.IF | 41FT 4IN / 12.6M | 57FT 10IN / 17.63M | 15FT 10IN / 4.83M | 2 X HERCULES II |
| MK.II | 42FT 6IN / 12.95M | 57FT 10IN / 17.63M | 15FT 10IN / 4.83M | 2 X R-R MERLIN XX |
| MK.VI | 41FT 8IN / 12.7M | 56FT 4IN / 17.17M | 15FT 10IN / 4.83M | 2 X HERCULES VI OR XVI |
| MK.X | 41FT 4IN / 12.6M | 57FT 10IN / 17.63M | 15FT 10IN / 4.83M | 2 X HERCULES XVII |

# BRISTOL BEAUFIGHTER

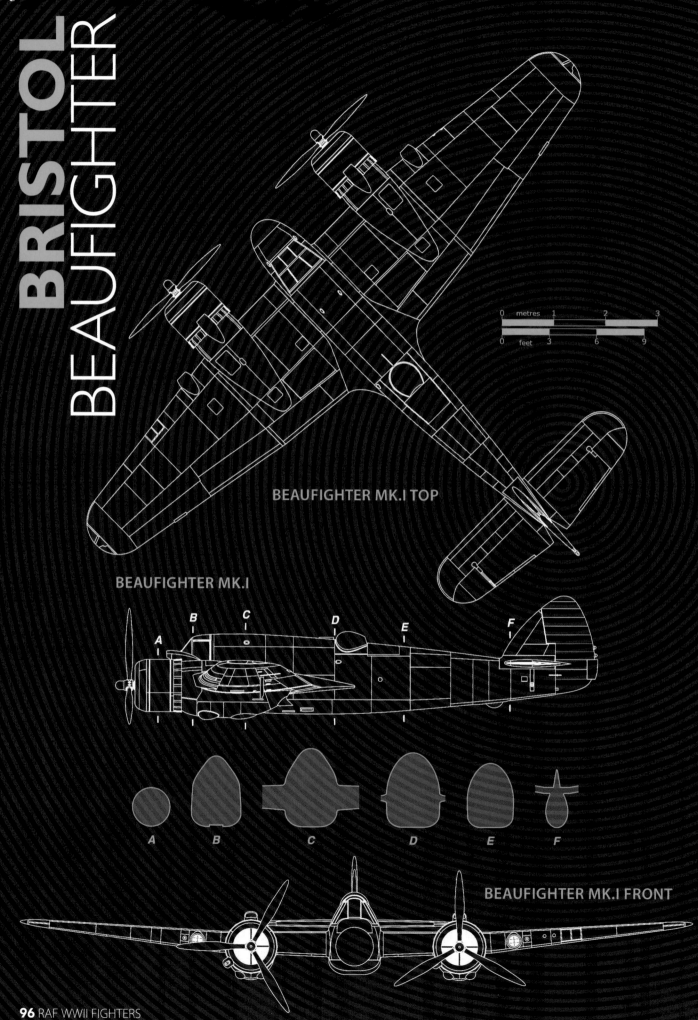

BEAUFIGHTER MK.I TOP

BEAUFIGHTER MK.I

A   B   C   D   E   F

A   B   C   D   E   F

BEAUFIGHTER MK.I FRONT

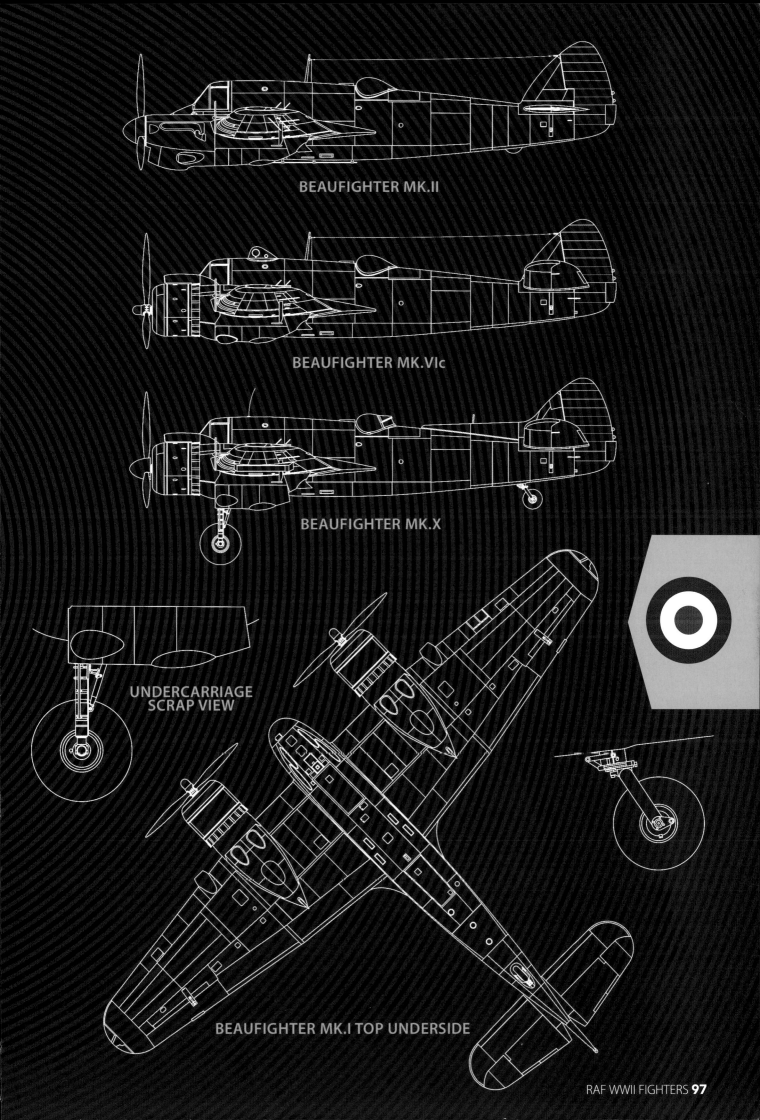

BEAUFIGHTER MK.II

BEAUFIGHTER MK.VIc

BEAUFIGHTER MK.X

UNDERCARRIAGE
SCRAP VIEW

BEAUFIGHTER MK.I TOP UNDERSIDE

**1941-1945**

The Hawker Typhoon was rushed into production before it had been truly perfected. Combining advanced construction techniques and a new engine design, the Typhoon was flawed aircraft but is best remembered for its role during the months following D-Day as a tank buster.

# HAWKER
## TYPHOON

**A**s has been discussed elsewhere Hawker had already had a lot of experience with successful fighters and during war there was a pressing need to stay one step ahead of the technological progression made by the Axis aircraft manufacturers. The Hurricane was the first successful British mono plane but in many regards it was very closely tied to its biplane predecessors both in design and construction. A replacement was required.

Sydney Camm began considering a successor to the Hurricane as early as 1937, putting forward an initial proposal to the Air Ministry in July 1937 only 21 months after the maiden flight of the Hurricane. The Hawker Tornado was supposed to be a vastly superior fighter to the Hurricane and two power plants were considered for it. The first Rolls-Royce Vulture, which was in essence two Kestrel engines joined together by inverting one of them. The second engine incorporated a new design which was a big step away from existing aero engines; the Napier Sabre used a sleeve valve instead of the more common poppet valve design.

Unlike the Vulture, which was beset with problems due to a lack of resources (the Merlin being the priority for Rolls-Royce), the Sabre eventually went into the Typhoon and Tempest production models. Although the Sabre produced impressive results once it was fully developed the precision required during the manufacture of the sleeves caused problems when it went into mass production with many engines failing.

Aside from the engine, the main difference between the Hurricane and the Tornado was in their construction. The Hurricane's tube structure was carried over in the forward fuselage but aft of the cockpit a semi-monocoque design was used and all metal wings were used from the outset. Unlike the Hurricane, which was entered through the sliding hood, a car door style entry was fitted to the prototypes and early production models.

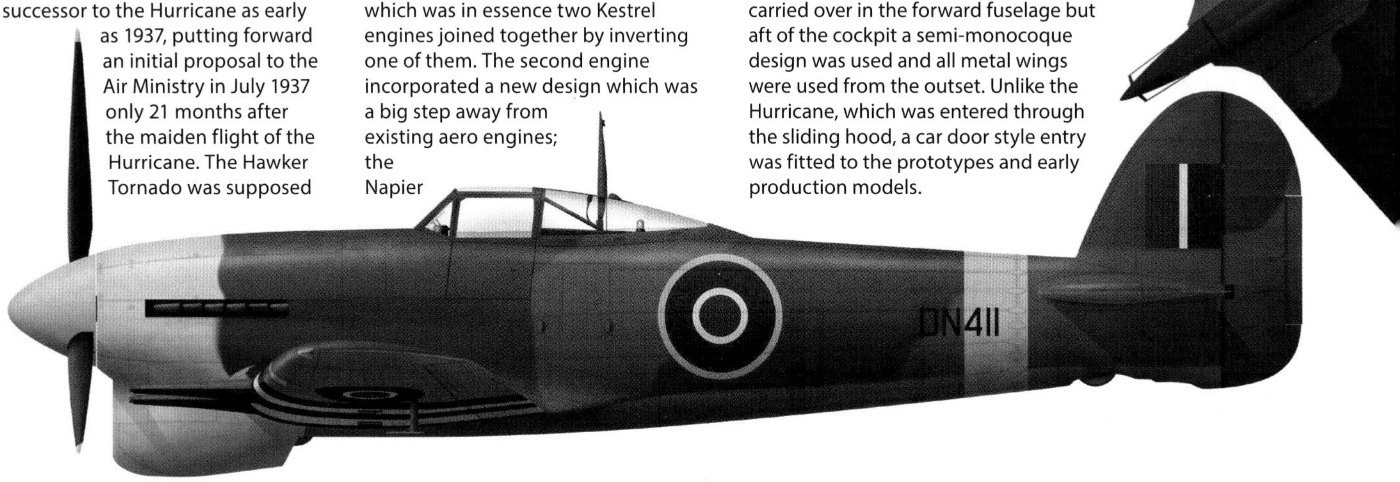

DN411

In an effort to avoid confusion with the Fw 190 a number of recognition schemes were trialled including painting the entire nose section white, a few aircraft including DN411 wore this during November 1942

SYDNEY CAMM BEGAN CONSIDERING A SUCCESSOR TO THE HURRICANE AS EARLY AS 1937, PUTTING FORWARD AN INITIAL PROPOSAL TO THE AIR MINISTRY IN JULY 1937

Eventually the Air Ministry issued Specification F.18/37 for a fighter capable of exceeding 400mph and fitted with a dozen .303 machine guns. Several companies tendered for it, Supermarine putting forward a twin-engined design with the wings closely mirroring those of the Spitfire. The only serious contender and the one around which F.18/37 was written was Hawker's so it was inevitable that the company would win the contract to build prototypes.

In March 1938, the Air Ministry gave Hawker the green light to proceed with four prototypes, two with the Sabre, known initially as the Hawker N-Type and two with the Vulture, the Hawker R-Type. Eventually in keeping with the tradition of naming fighters after winds the Sabre engine prototypes became Typhoons and the Vulture-engined aircraft the Tornado. Construction was undertaken at the Kingston factory

and was comparatively straightforward, the two aircraft being of identical design apart from essential differences that the two engines dictated, saving considerable time and resources.

The Tornado, P5219, first flew on October 6, 1939, and the first Typhoon, P5212, the following year on February 24, 1940. From the outset the test pilots were critical of the Vulture engine; it was underpowered, overweight and prone to mechanical failure. Work on the Vulture meant that another Rolls-Royce project had been put on hold but as the shortcomings of the Vulture became apparent the decision was taken to resurrect the Griffon project while cancelling the Vulture. The result of this was the termination of the Tornado project all together, Hawker choosing instead to develop the Typhoon which appeared to have much greater potential.

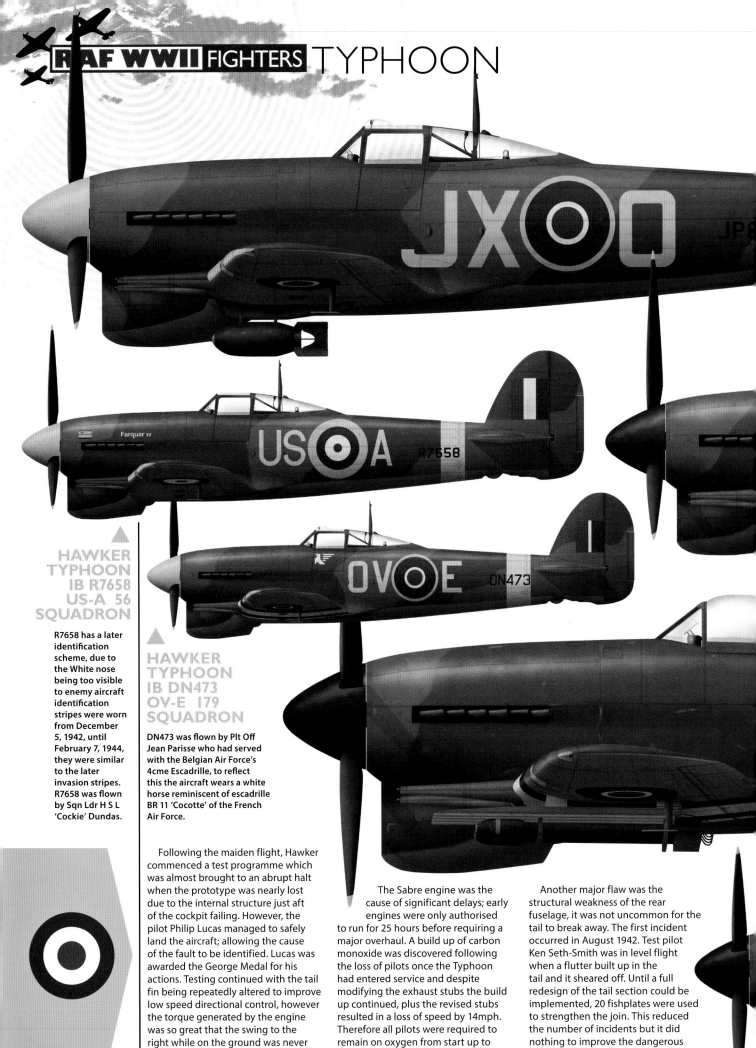

## HAWKER TYPHOON IB R7658 US-A 56 SQUADRON

R7658 has a later identification scheme, due to the White nose being too visible to enemy aircraft identification stripes were worn from December 5, 1942, until February 7, 1944, they were similar to the later invasion stripes. R7658 was flown by Sqn Ldr H S L 'Cockie' Dundas.

## HAWKER TYPHOON IB DN473 OV-E 179 SQUADRON

DN473 was flown by Plt Off Jean Parisse who had served with the Belgian Air Force's 4cme Escadrille, to reflect this the aircraft wears a white horse reminiscent of escadrille BR 11 'Cocotte' of the French Air Force.

Following the maiden flight, Hawker commenced a test programme which was almost brought to an abrupt halt when the prototype was nearly lost due to the internal structure just aft of the cockpit failing. However, the pilot Philip Lucas managed to safely land the aircraft; allowing the cause of the fault to be identified. Lucas was awarded the George Medal for his actions. Testing continued with the tail fin being repeatedly altered to improve low speed directional control, however the torque generated by the engine was so great that the swing to the right while on the ground was never adequately resolved.

The Sabre engine was the cause of significant delays; early engines were only authorised to run for 25 hours before requiring a major overhaul. A build up of carbon monoxide was discovered following the loss of pilots once the Typhoon had entered service and despite modifying the exhaust stubs the build up continued, plus the revised stubs resulted in a loss of speed by 14mph. Therefore all pilots were required to remain on oxygen from start up to shut down.

Another major flaw was the structural weakness of the rear fuselage, it was not uncommon for the tail to break away. The first incident occurred in August 1942. Test pilot Ken Seth-Smith was in level flight when a flutter built up in the tail and it sheared off. Until a full redesign of the tail section could be implemented, 20 fishplates were used to strengthen the join. This reduced the number of incidents but it did nothing to improve the dangerous reputation the Typhoon had gained.

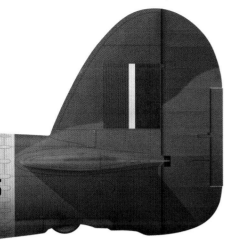

## HAWKER TYPHOON IB JP865 JX-O 1 SQUADRON

JX-O was flown by John F D 'Tim' Elkington when the squadron was based at RAF Acklington, having previously been shot down in Hurricane P3137 (also JX-O). Following a posting to Russia he returned to 1 Sqn to fly the Typhoon during August 1942. The aircraft is painted in Dark Green and Ocean Grey with Medium Sea Grey underside. Spinner, letters and fuselage band are Sky Blue.

An urgent increase in Hurricane production during the summer of 1940 meant that the second Typhoon, P5216 was not completed and flown until May 3, 1941 (over a year after P5212). Due to the necessities of wartime secrecy it was only the next day that the public became aware the Typhoon – when Philip Lucas inadvertently mentioned it during an interview with the Sunday Chronicle. The second prototype was soon followed by the first production Typhoon on May 27.

Eventually aircraft were delivered to RAE and A&AEE in August. The following month a pair of Typhoons were used for tactical trials by the Air Fighting Development Unit at RAF Duxford. It soon became apparent that despite the advantages gained by the speed and power of the Typhoon, visibility was still a major issue. The closed cockpit offered a very poor rear view, a potentially fatal design flaw for a fighter. Blown single piece canopies were beginning to appear on other aircraft so it was logical that Hawker follow suit, but it was not until 1943 that the revised design was finalised and began being fitted to the IB and IIB.

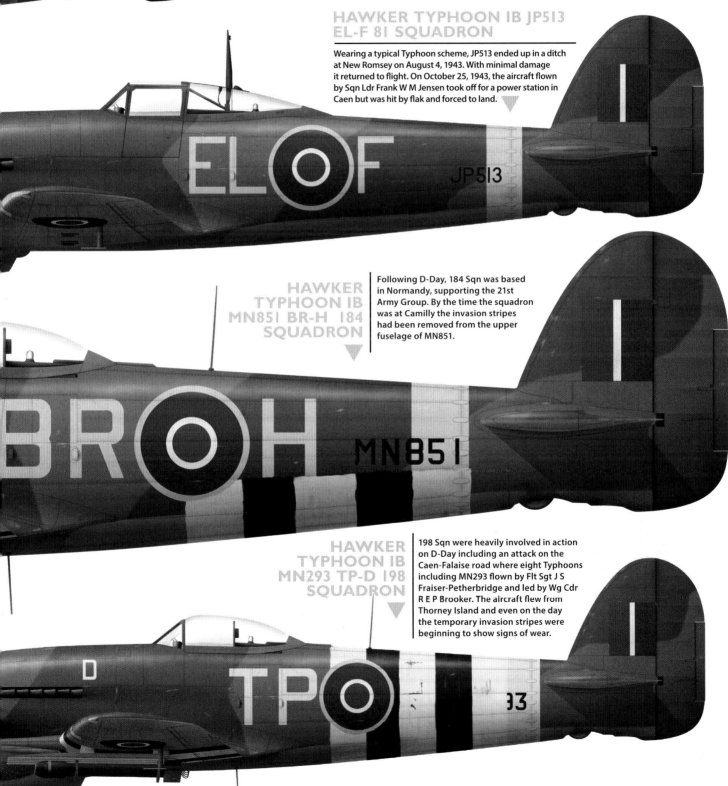

## HAWKER TYPHOON IB JP513 EL-F 81 SQUADRON

Wearing a typical Typhoon scheme, JP513 ended up in a ditch at New Romsey on August 4, 1943. With minimal damage it returned to flight. On October 25, 1943, the aircraft flown by Sqn Ldr Frank W M Jensen took off for a power station in Caen but was hit by flak and forced to land.

## HAWKER TYPHOON IB MN851 BR-H 184 SQUADRON

Following D-Day, 184 Sqn was based in Normandy, supporting the 21st Army Group. By the time the squadron was at Camilly the invasion stripes had been removed from the upper fuselage of MN851.

## HAWKER TYPHOON IB MN293 TP-D 198 SQUADRON

198 Sqn were heavily involved in action on D-Day including an attack on the Caen-Falaise road where eight Typhoons including MN293 flown by Flt Sgt J S Fraiser-Petherbridge and led by Wg Cdr R E P Brooker. The aircraft flew from Thorney Island and even on the day the temporary invasion stripes were beginning to show signs of wear.

## HAWKER TYPHOON IB EK273 JE-DT 195 SQUADRON

EK273 is unusual in that as well as bearing the squadron code (JT) it also has the initials of the pilot, Sqn Ldr Don 'Butch' Taylor. On July 6, 1943, the ace Wg Cdr A C Rabagliati borrowed EK273 but was hit by flak over the Netherlands, forced to ditch he bailed out but was killed.

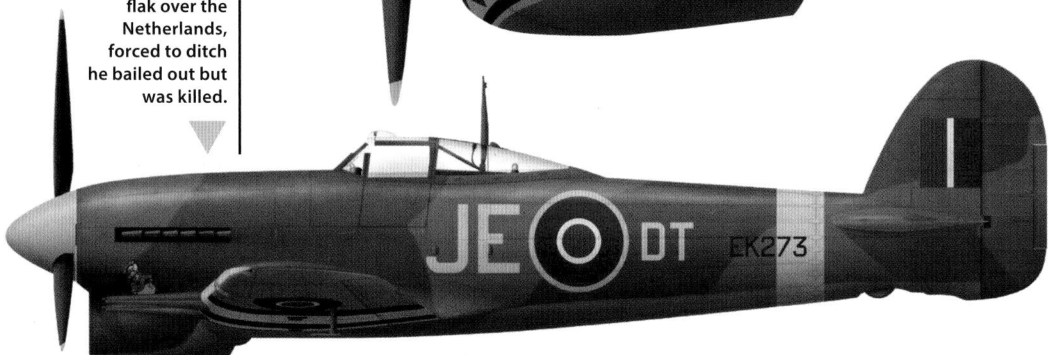

JE DT EK273

## HAWKER TYPHOON IB RB389 I8-P 440 SQUADRON RCAF

Several Typhoons coded I8-P were known as 'Pulverizer' including Pulverizer II MP149, Pulverizer III RB342 and Pulverizer IV RB389 which wore the legend in the closing months of the war. RB389 completed 96 missions by the end of the war but was later scrapped.

PULVERIZER IV I8 P RB33

## HAWKER TYPHOON IB R7695 ZH-Z 226 SQUADRON

When it first converted to the Typhoon the squadron letters were UO but this was soon changed to ZH. Being the second squadron to convert to the Typhoon it initially had the Type A roundel which was replaced with a smaller Type 'C'.

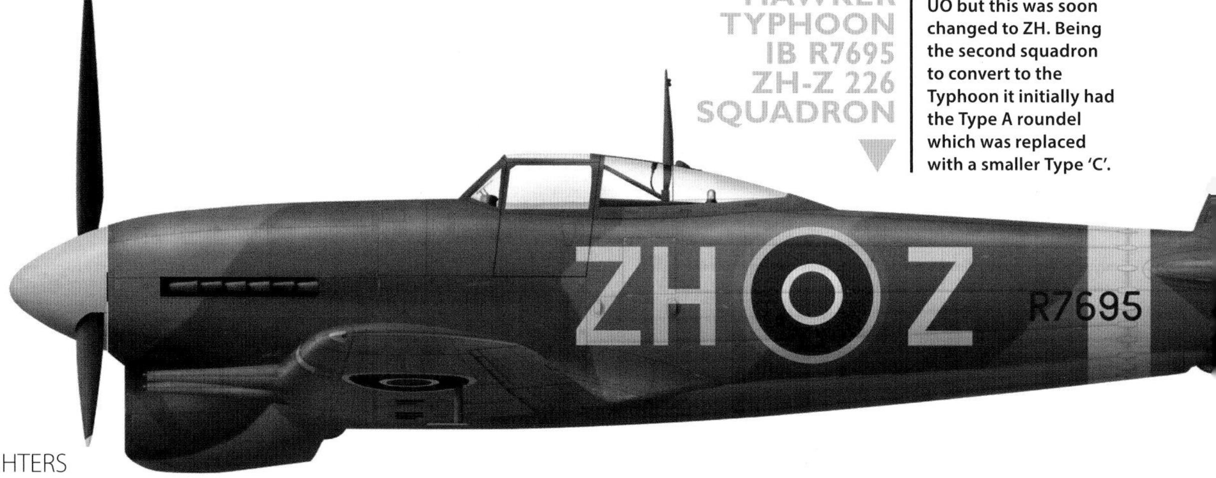

ZH Z R7695

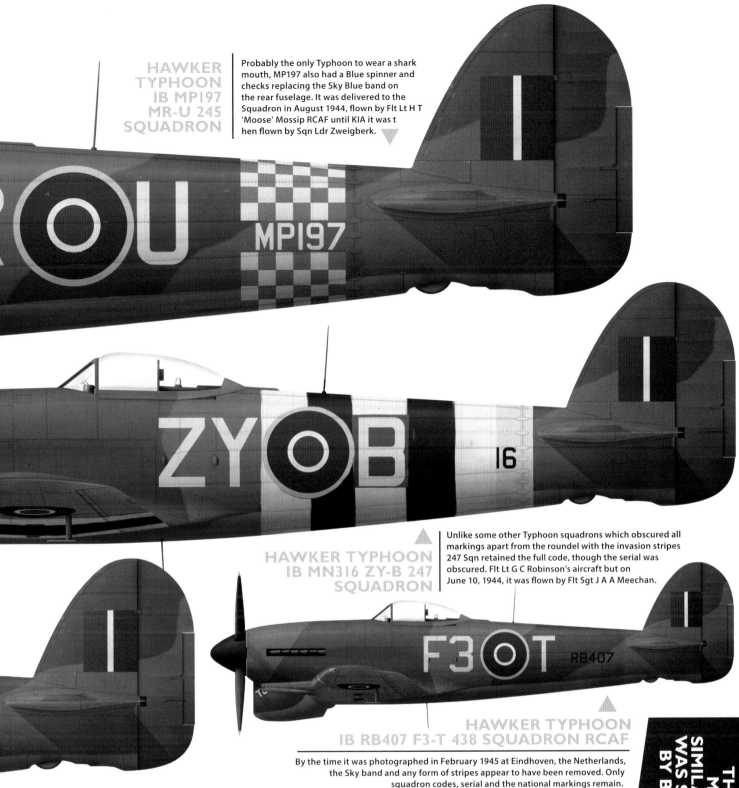

HAWKER TYPHOON IB MP197 MR-U 245 SQUADRON

Probably the only Typhoon to wear a shark mouth, MP197 also had a Blue spinner and checks replacing the Sky Blue band on the rear fuselage. It was delivered to the Squadron in August 1944, flown by Flt Lt H T 'Moose' Mossip RCAF until KIA it was t hen flown by Sqn Ldr Zweigberk.

Unlike some other Typhoon squadrons which obscured all markings apart from the roundel with the invasion stripes 247 Sqn retained the full code, though the serial was obscured. Flt Lt G C Robinson's aircraft but on June 10, 1944, it was flown by Flt Sgt J A A Meechan.

HAWKER TYPHOON IB MN316 ZY-B 247 SQUADRON

HAWKER TYPHOON IB RB407 F3-T 438 SQUADRON RCAF

By the time it was photographed in February 1945 at Eindhoven, the Netherlands, the Sky band and any form of stripes appear to have been removed. Only squadron codes, serial and the national markings remain.

The Typhoon eventually reached a front line squadron on September 11, 1941, when 56 Squadron based at Duxford began receiving them with some trepidation as the already dangerous reputation preceded the aircraft. The first aircraft to arrive were Mk.IAs fitted with the Browning .303s but before the squadron had even become operational again they were replaced by the Mk.IB with 20mm Hispano cannon.

Once they were in use with an active squadron, a plethora of further problems arose with both the aircraft and the troubled engine. Not only was there the carbon monoxide poisoning but the Napier Sabre had a tendency to cut out especially during final approach and on occasions in the air. The oil cooler was prone to failure, further compounding the engine issues, and serviceability was an issue.

The Typhoon also bore more than a passing similarity to the Fw 190 and was sometimes misidentified by both Allied pilots and ground forces. The first Typhoons lost were R7678 and R8199 of 56 Squadron, which were shot down by Spitfires on June 1, 1942, during an early combat patrol. A number of solutions were explored, including painting the nose all white, black and white stripes on the wings long before Operation Overlord, and blue spinners and a yellow band on the leading edge.

Early deliveries were slow so it was not until February 1941 that 266 Rhodesia Squadron received their first Typhoon, 609 Squadron was the third squadron to convert in April, thus completing the Duxford Typhoon Wing led by W/C Denys Gillam DFC. On August 9, 1942, two aircraft of 266 Squadron downed a Ju 88 off the Norfolk coast, the first aerial victory by a Typhoon. Ten days later the wing was providing cover during the failed Dieppe raid but for the squadrons involved it was a success with several claims being made.

With daylight raids in decline, 56 Squadron was able to undertake sweeps over Holland, targeting flak batteries and shipping. Meanwhile, 609 Squadron moved to the south

THE TYPHOON ALSO BORE MORE THAN A PASSING SIMILARITY TO THE FW 190 AND WAS SOMETIMES MISIDENTIFIED BY BOTH ALLIED PILOTS AND GROUND FORCES

## HAWKER TYPHOON IB JP853 SA-K 486 SQUADRON RNZAF

**Based at RAF Tangmere between October 1942 and January 1944, 486 Sqn was involved in extensive action over France. On October 27, 1943, JP853 undertook an aerial photographic sortie and is well documented.**

coast, and tasked with intercepting Fw 190 fighter-bombers that were making hit and run raids on the coastal towns. To make it harder, the raiders were flying at almost sea level to avoid radar, cutting the response time to a minimum for the RAF.

As the production rate gradually increasing two fighter-bomber squadrons were formed, 181 and 182 Squadrons. Further squadrons converted during the following months, eventually bring the total to 27 RAF Typhoon squadrons. The strength of the wing allowed the Typhoon to carry a 250lb or 500lb bomb under each wing. These were used for precision raids on a range of targets including factories, shipping and airfields. The Typhoon was also cleared to carry the 3in rocket with the

squadrons rotating away from the front line to allow for the rails to be fitted. It took practice to master the fine art of firing rockets due to their high drop off rate. But by 1944 experienced pilots were using them with devastating effect on such targets as trains, bridges and tanks.

On D-Day the Typhoons concentrated on the ground-attack role and in the following weeks flew in close support of ground troops, in particular General Patton's forces as they attempted to close the Falaise Pocket. As the allies progressed through France and into Germany the Typhoon squadrons followed, operating from airfields on the continent and using a cab rank technique where aircraft would orbit around the front line until called upon

by an RAF liaison officer on the ground.

While most squadrons were destined for the continent, 137 and 263 Squadrons were retained for the defence of Britain. 137 Squadron may have intercepted 30 V-1 flying bombs, but the Mosquito and Tempest squadrons had a far higher success rate. Apart from a few aircraft that were used for unsuccessful tropical trials such as DN323 of RAAF, the Typhoon was used exclusively in the European Theatre of Operations. With the cessation of hostilities and superior aircraft such as the Tempest and Meteor in service there was no place for the Typhoon in the postwar RAF.

As with any aircraft it was only through active

## HAWKER TYPHOON IB DN323 Y 451 SQUADRON RAAF

**One of three Typhoons (R8891 & EJ906 being the others) that were sent to 451 Sqn in the Middle East for operational trials. Before the evaluation was completed the squadron converted to Spitfires. Painted in Mid Stone and Dark Earth with Azure Blue undersides.**

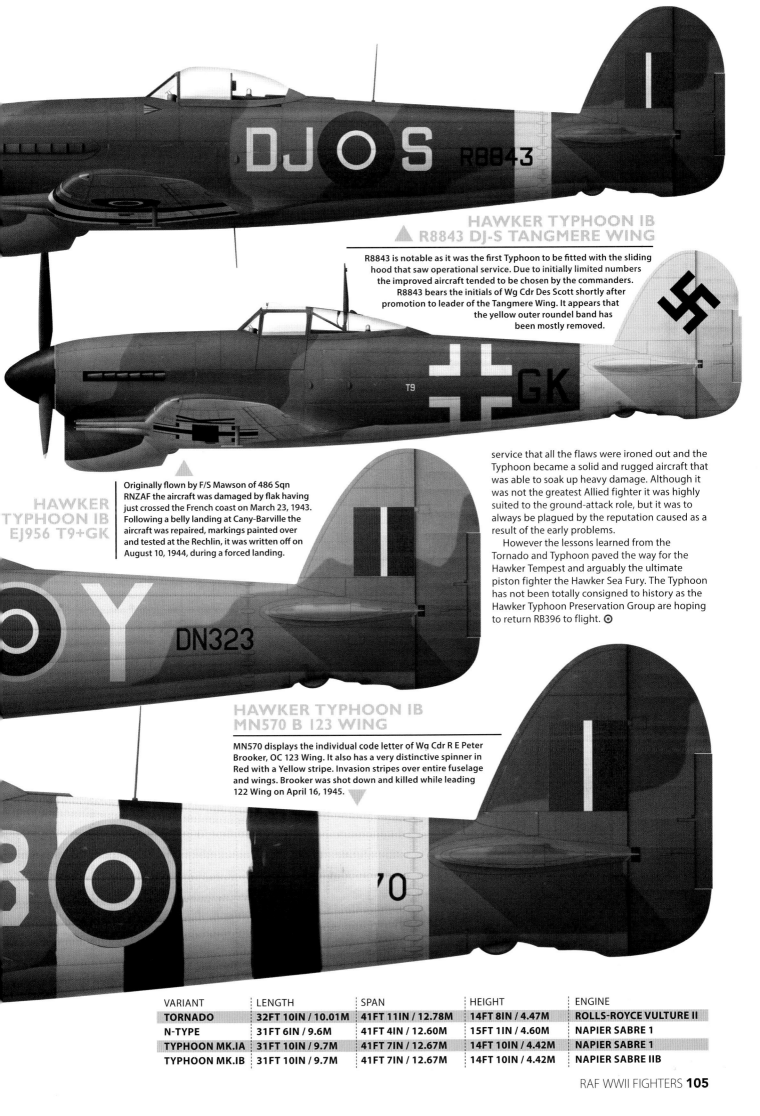

## HAWKER TYPHOON IB
### R8843 DJ-S TANGMERE WING

R8843 is notable as it was the first Typhoon to be fitted with the sliding hood that saw operational service. Due to initially limited numbers the improved aircraft tended to be chosen by the commanders. R8843 bears the initials of Wg Cdr Des Scott shortly after promotion to leader of the Tangmere Wing. It appears that the yellow outer roundel band has been mostly removed.

## HAWKER TYPHOON IB
### EJ956 T9+GK

Originally flown by F/S Mawson of 486 Sqn RNZAF the aircraft was damaged by flak having just crossed the French coast on March 23, 1943. Following a belly landing at Cany-Barville the aircraft was repaired, markings painted over and tested at the Rechlin, it was written off on August 10, 1944, during a forced landing.

## HAWKER TYPHOON IB
### MN570 B 123 WING

MN570 displays the individual code letter of Wg Cdr R E Peter Brooker, OC 123 Wing. It also has a very distinctive spinner in Red with a Yellow stripe. Invasion stripes over entire fuselage and wings. Brooker was shot down and killed while leading 122 Wing on April 16, 1945.

service that all the flaws were ironed out and the Typhoon became a solid and rugged aircraft that was able to soak up heavy damage. Although it was not the greatest Allied fighter it was highly suited to the ground-attack role, but it was to always be plagued by the reputation caused as a result of the early problems.

However the lessons learned from the Tornado and Typhoon paved the way for the Hawker Tempest and arguably the ultimate piston fighter the Hawker Sea Fury. The Typhoon has not been totally consigned to history as the Hawker Typhoon Preservation Group are hoping to return RB396 to flight.

| VARIANT | LENGTH | SPAN | HEIGHT | ENGINE |
|---|---|---|---|---|
| TORNADO | 32FT 10IN / 10.01M | 41FT 11IN / 12.78M | 14FT 8IN / 4.47M | ROLLS-ROYCE VULTURE II |
| N-TYPE | 31FT 6IN / 9.6M | 41FT 4IN / 12.60M | 15FT 1IN / 4.60M | NAPIER SABRE 1 |
| TYPHOON MK.IA | 31FT 10IN / 9.7M | 41FT 7IN / 12.67M | 14FT 10IN / 4.42M | NAPIER SABRE 1 |
| TYPHOON MK.IB | 31FT 10IN / 9.7M | 41FT 7IN / 12.67M | 14FT 10IN / 4.42M | NAPIER SABRE IIB |

# HAWKER
# TYPHOON

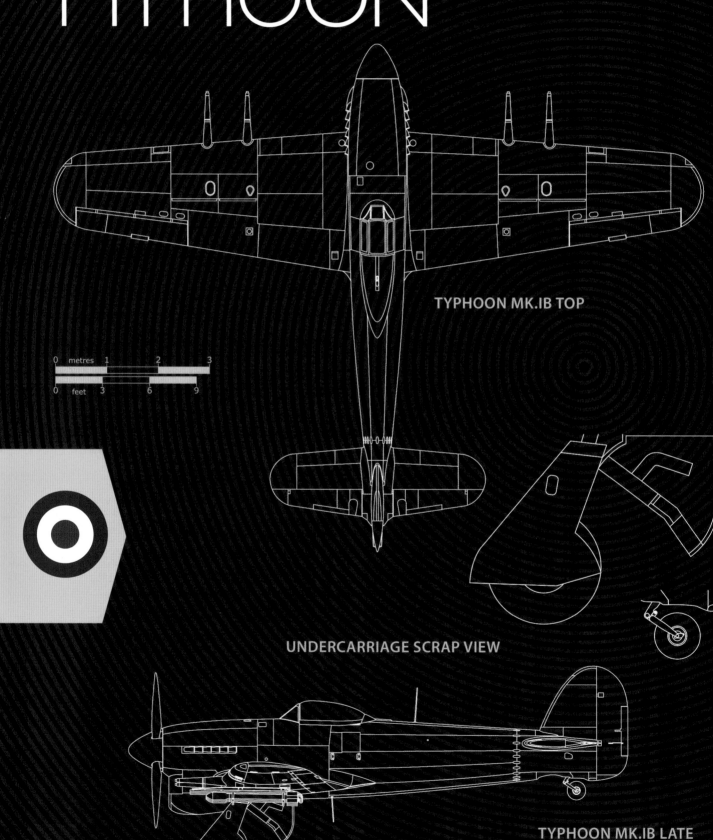

TYPHOON MK.IB TOP

UNDERCARRIAGE SCRAP VIEW

TYPHOON MK.IB LATE

0 metres 1 2 3
0 feet 3 6 9

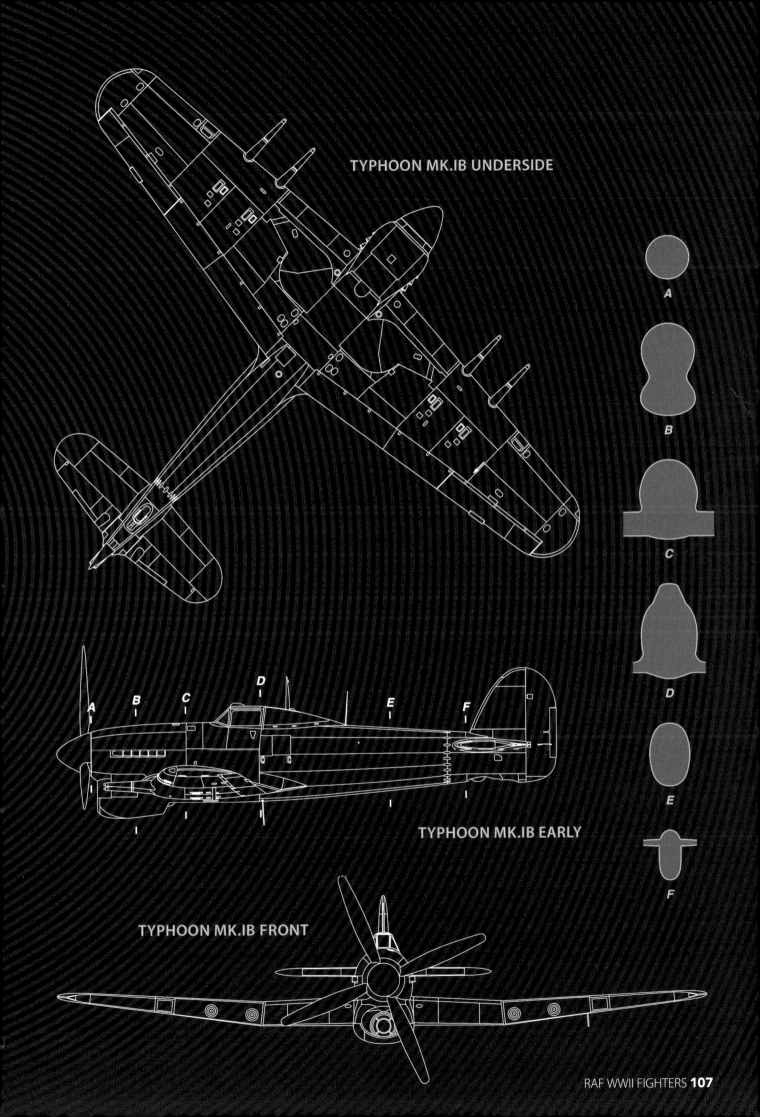

TYPHOON MK.IB UNDERSIDE

TYPHOON MK.IB EARLY

TYPHOON MK.IB FRONT

A

B

C

D

E

F

# NORTH AMERICAN P-51 MUSTANG

1942-1947

The Mustang is perhaps the most iconic, recognisable and arguably successful fighter used by the United States during the war, but without the British it may never have existed. Then without further intervention by the British it would not have realised its potential.

**AS** a response to German rearmament, France had placed with Curtiss a substantial order for the P-40 and Britain was poised to do the same but there were concerns that Curtiss would not be in a position to fulfil all the orders. North American was approached by US officials to consider constructing the P-40 under licence, the reasoning being that North American was a comparatively young company with no experience of fighter design and it already had a relationship with the British Government having provided the highly successful trainer that the RAF called the Harvard.

However, North American was not enamoured with the idea of building someone else's fighter, especially when its designers thought they could create a better aircraft using the same Allison V-1710 engine.

They made the British representatives aware of their intentions. Britain urgently needed fighters and the initial proposal was convincing enough for a prototype to be commissioned and an order for 400 aircraft was placed in April 1940. The following month, North American's chief engineer John Leland Atwood wrote to the head of the British Purchasing Commission, Sir Henry Self, to confirm that by no later than September 30, 1941, the first 320 production aircraft would be delivered. The company also secured an export licence that month but with the caveat that two production aircraft would be supplied to the Army Air Corps for testing, kindly being paid for by the British.

As work commenced on the design, North American acquired wind tunnel date from Curtiss based on their work on the XP-46. This not only provided the design

team with valuable data but it is possible that it influenced the positioning of the radiator intake scoop, one of the defining features of the Mustang.

One unexpected benefit of the scoop was that as the air passed through it was warmed and expanded, adding a little extra thrust. Another new feature was the laminar flow wing, aviation companies were aware of the technology but an absolutely smooth finish to the surfaces was required and considered to be too much work. North American intended to achieve a smooth finish during the painting process.

Once the official confirmation had been received from the British to proceed, the company wasted no time and on August 30,

1940, at the California plant NA-73X, the first prototype was rolled out. Due to demands for the British war effort, most engines were destined for the P-40 which meant a slight delay to the programme, eventually an Allison V-1710-39 was fitted and the NA-73X undertook taxiing trials during the first weeks of October, the inaugural flight was on the 26th with Vance Breese at the controls for the five minute flight.

For the fifth flight on November 20, Paul Balfour was the pilot and it is reported that beforehand Breese made a bet that Balfour would crash during his first flight. During the flight B

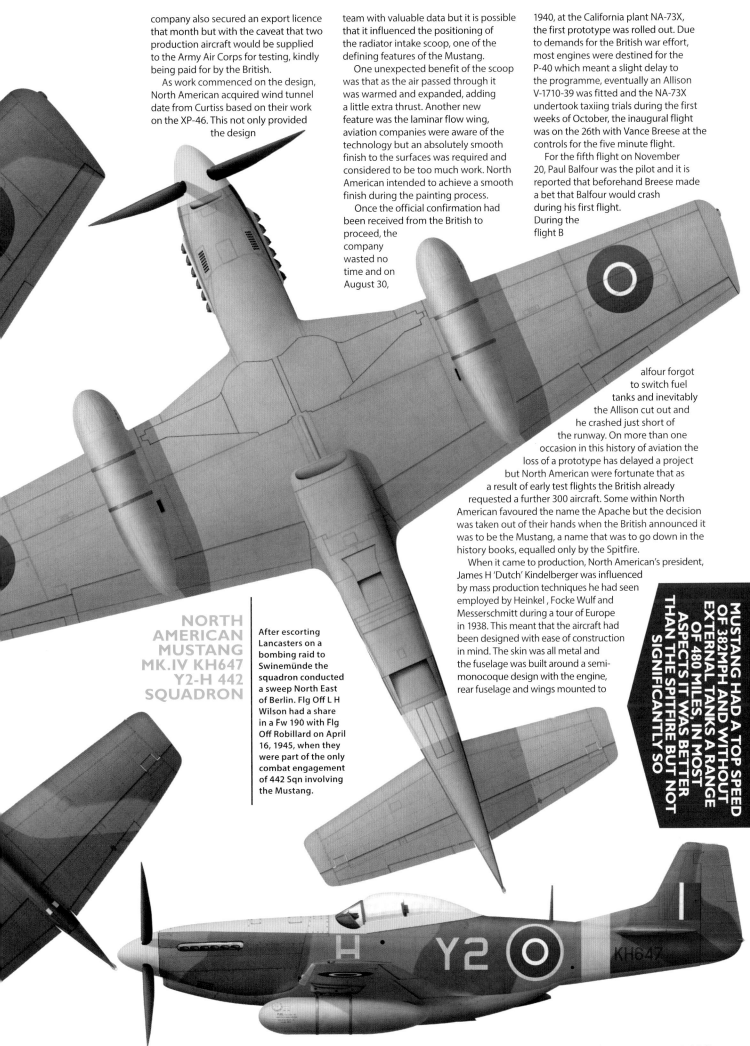

**NORTH AMERICAN MUSTANG MK.IV KH647 Y2-H 442 SQUADRON**

After escorting Lancasters on a bombing raid to Swinemünde the squadron conducted a sweep North East of Berlin. Flg Off L H Wilson had a share in a Fw 190 with Flg Off Robillard on April 16, 1945, when they were part of the only combat engagement of 442 Sqn involving the Mustang.

alfour forgot to switch fuel tanks and inevitably the Allison cut out and he crashed just short of the runway. On more than one occasion in this history of aviation the loss of a prototype has delayed a project but North American were fortunate that as a result of early test flights the British already requested a further 300 aircraft. Some within North American favoured the name the Apache but the decision was taken out of their hands when the British announced it was to be the Mustang, a name that was to go down in the history books, equalled only by the Spitfire.

When it came to production, North American's president, James H 'Dutch' Kindelberger was influenced by mass production techniques he had seen employed by Heinkel , Focke Wulf and Messerschmitt during a tour of Europe in 1938. This meant that the aircraft had been designed with ease of construction in mind. The skin was all metal and the fuselage was built around a semi-monocoque design with the engine, rear fuselage and wings mounted to

MUSTANG HAD A TOP SPEED OF 382MPH AND WITHOUT EXTERNAL TANKS A RANGE OF 480 MILES, IN MOST ASPECTS IT WAS BETTER THAN THE SPITFIRE BUT NOT SIGNIFICANTLY SO

## NORTH AMERICAN MUSTANG MK.I AG345

The first production Mustang completed by North American was made to subsequent production in the American equivalent of Dark Green and Dark Earth over a variation of Sky. AG345 was retained by the company for testing and struck off charge on December 3, 1946.

it. The undercarriage opened outwards providing much better stability on the ground than the Spitfire. At 13,700ft the Mustang had a top speed of 382mph and without external tanks a range of 480 miles, in most aspects it was better than the Spitfire but not significantly so.

Trials continued with NA-73X and the only major modification that was made to subsequent production aircraft was a redesign of the scoop to improve the cooling and airflow. It was only one year after the Mustang was commissioned that AG345 flew for the first time on April 23, 1941. This was the first production Mk.I and despite being finished in RAF colours it was retained by the company for ongoing testing. AG345 was configured to carry two Browning 0.5s in the nose and another Browning in each wing, which also had a pair of 0.3 machine guns bringing the total to eight guns.

Although the original schedule called for deliveries to commence in January 1941 it is still a considerable feat that AG346 arrived at Liverpool docks on October 24, 1941, closely followed by more deliveries. AG346's fate is unclear but AG351 was certainly delivered to Aeroplane and Armament Experimental Establishment at Boscombe Down for trials. Compared to the Spitfire Vb the Mustang was found to have a considerably longer take off and landing run.

The rate of climb for the Allison engine aircraft was slightly slower than the Spitfire and it had a greater rate of turn at low altitude, however it was faster in the dive and better at retaining speed. The engine also restricted combat operations at high

altitude where much of the combat over the continent took place. In time a solution was found, however.

Having started the war operating the slow Lysander, 26 Squadron replaced them with Tomahawks in February 1941, continuing in its role as part of Army Co-operation Command. While it may have been an improvement to the Lysander, the Tomahawk failed to successfully fulfil the role so 26 Squadron became the first unit to operate the Mustang when the first aircraft were delivered in January 1942. The transition was fully completed on May 10 when a Mustang (fitted with two F.24 cameras) piloted by Flg Off G N Dawson undertook a reconnaissance sortie

AG345

## NORTH AMERICAN MUSTANG MK.I AG457 UG-F 16 SQUADRON

Most Mustangs were repainted with Dark Green and Ocean Grey over Medium Sea Grey with revised national markings. 16 Sqn had operated Lysanders in the reconnaissance role and continued in these duties when they were replaced by the Mk.I Mustang in April 1942.

XV-S AL995

## NORTH AMERICAN MUSTANG MK.I AL995 XV-S 2 SQUADRON

Having already operated the P-40, the squadron replaced them with another American fighter in July 1942 when the Mustangs were delivered. Standard markings with a Sky spinner and band on the fuselage, Dark Green and Ocean Grey over Medium Sea Grey.

UG-F AG457

RM-T AG365

## NORTH AMERICAN MUSTANG MK.I AG365 RM-T 26 SQUADRON

Early Mustangs delivered by North American were painted in Dark Earth and Dark Green over Sky with a variation of the A1 roundel on the fuselage as depicted by AG365 of 26 Sqn at RAF Duxford during spring 1942.

## NORTH AMERICAN MUSTANG MK.I AG511 RZ-C 241 SQUADRON

On July 1, all RAF fighters were to be repainted with Ocean Grey replacing Dark Earth, however a shortage of Ocean Grey meant that squadrons had to improvise, it was advised to use 7/8 Medium Sea Grey to 1/8 Black as a temporary solution.

RZ-C AG511

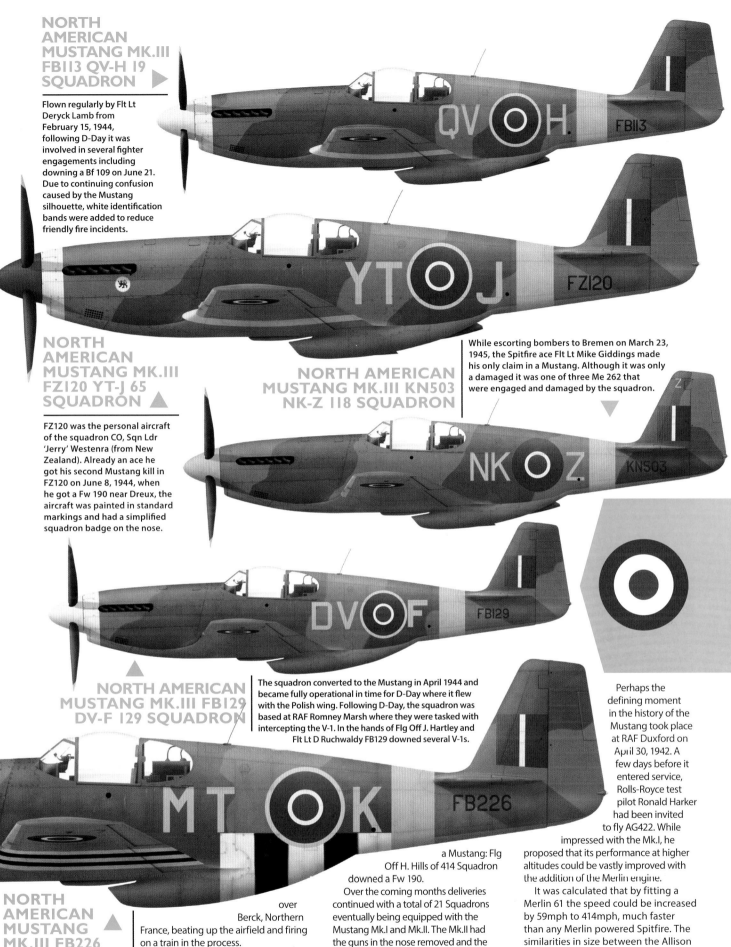

## NORTH AMERICAN MUSTANG MK.III FB113 QV-H 19 SQUADRON ▶

Flown regularly by Flt Lt Deryck Lamb from February 15, 1944, following D-Day it was involved in several fighter engagements including downing a Bf 109 on June 21. Due to continuing confusion caused by the Mustang silhouette, white identification bands were added to reduce friendly fire incidents.

## NORTH AMERICAN MUSTANG MK.III FZ120 YT-J 65 SQUADRON ▲

FZ120 was the personal aircraft of the squadron CO, Sqn Ldr 'Jerry' Westenra (from New Zealand). Already an ace he got his second Mustang kill in FZ120 on June 8, 1944, when he got a Fw 190 near Dreux, the aircraft was painted in standard markings and had a simplified squadron badge on the nose.

## NORTH AMERICAN MUSTANG MK.III KN503 NK-Z 118 SQUADRON

While escorting bombers to Bremen on March 23, 1945, the Spitfire ace Flt Lt Mike Giddings made his only claim in a Mustang. Although it was only a damaged it was one of three Me 262 that were engaged and damaged by the squadron. ▼

## NORTH AMERICAN MUSTANG MK.III FB129 DV-F 129 SQUADRON ▲

The squadron converted to the Mustang in April 1944 and became fully operational in time for D-Day where it flew with the Polish wing. Following D-Day, the squadron was based at RAF Romney Marsh where they were tasked with intercepting the V-1. In the hands of Flg Off J. Hartley and Flt Lt D Ruchwaldy FB129 downed several V-1s.

## NORTH AMERICAN MUSTANG MK.III FB226 MT-K 122 SQUADRON ▲

122 Sqn used the Mustang Mk.III from February 1944 until the end of hostilities in Europe, FB226 was flown occasionally by the Malayan national and ace Cyril L F 'Jimmy' Talalla during the summer of 1944.

over Berck, Northern France, beating up the airfield and firing on a train in the process.

By the time of Operation Jubilee in August sufficient Mustangs had been delivered to equip four squadrons; 26, 239, 400 and 414, although these were not all at full strength there were sufficient aircraft to be involved. Several were lost during the raid on Dieppe but perhaps fittingly it was an American flying with the RAF that got the first aerial victory in a Mustang: Flg Off H. Hills of 414 Squadron downed a Fw 190.

Over the coming months deliveries continued with a total of 21 Squadrons eventually being equipped with the Mustang Mk.I and Mk.II. The Mk.II had the guns in the nose removed and the improved Allison V-1710-81 engine fitted but this was still not providing the performance that pilots required to compete with the latest variants of the Fw 190. Regardless of this the Allison engined Mustangs continued to serve with 26 and 268 Squadrons right up until the end of the war in Europe, providing vital intelligence in the tactical reconnaissance role.

Perhaps the defining moment in the history of the Mustang took place at RAF Duxford on April 30, 1942. A few days before it entered service, Rolls-Royce test pilot Ronald Harker had been invited to fly AG422. While impressed with the Mk.I, he proposed that its performance at higher altitudes could be vastly improved with the addition of the Merlin engine.

It was calculated that by fitting a Merlin 61 the speed could be increased by 59mph to 414mph, much faster than any Merlin powered Spitfire. The similarities in size between the Allison A-1710 and the Merlin meant that the engine could be fitted in the same space. But considerable work was required for the cooling and plumbing systems, especially so the radiator position could remain unchanged. Rolls-Royce informed North American of its intentions, North American responded by fitting a Packard built

## NORTH AMERICAN MUSTANG MK.III KH500 HBW BENTWATERS WING

Having had a colourful career including being shot down by Adolf Galland, Wg Cdr Harold Bird-Wilson became commander of Bentwaters Wing and flew KH500. Having flown with 17 Sqn during the Battle of Britain he had the squadron gauntlet painted on the tail of his Mustang.

## NORTH AMERICAN MUSTANG MK.III KH427 GN-V 249 SQUADRON

While based in Italy, 249 Sqn converted to the Mustang and flew them in fighter and ground-attack operations over Albania and Yugoslavia. KH427 piloted by Flt Lt R F Noble was responsible for the last aerial claim by the squadron on October 31, 1944.

## NORTH AMERICAN MUSTANG MK.IV KH774 GA-S 112 SQUADRON

KH774 was flown by Lt Blanchford while 112 Sqn was based in Italy. Having already applied the Shark Mouth to their P-40s, the tradition was carried over to the Mustang where they were based in Italy. P-51D 44-11602 operated by the Norwegian Spitfire Foundation was repainted as KH774 in 2014.

## NORTH AMERICAN MUSTANG MK.IV KM305 5J-X 126 SQUADRON

With air superiority over Western Europe, Allied forces no longer wasted weight camouflaging their aircraft so later Mustangs were finished in an Aluminium lacquer, this included KH570 which was flown by the Norwegian, Maj Arne Austeen who was lost during a sweep off Denmark on May 4, 1945.

## NORTH AMERICAN MUSTANG MK.IV KM272 QV-V 19 SQUADRON

19 Sqn Mustangs were finished with white and blue chequer on the nose towards the end of the war, DooleyBird was flown by Flt Lt Arthur 'Joe' Doley, an accomplished pilot who had already flown Hurricanes and Spitfires.

IT WAS LOVED BY THE PILOTS WHO FLEW IT AND TRULY WAS THE CADILLAC OF THE SKIES

Merlin and there arose an informal competition to see who could complete the work first.

Rolls-Royce won the race when AL975 took off on October 13, 1942, with Capt R T Shepherd at the controls. The first flight did not give a true indication of the variant's potential however, as performance was hampered by the plumbing system but these issues were soon ironed out. The most noticeable change was dictated by the carburettor. The Merlin required it to be fed from underneath so the intake was repositioned, creating the chin. The Rolls-Royce nose had rather crude fairings but North American was concerned about the aerodynamic implications

and worked hard to integrate the Merlin seamlessly. Several more Mustangs were converted on both sides of the Atlantic.

It became increasingly apparent what a potent fighter the combination of the Mustang and the Merlin would produce and orders were placed by both the British and Americans for the P-51B/Mk.III. The plant at Inglewood, California was the primary supplier of the British bound Mk.IIIs. The official US designation for those built at Inglewood was the P-51B whereas those built at the Dallas plant were the P-51C, although the RAF classed them as both the Mk.III.

Deliveries began in October 1943 with the first being sent to Boscombe Down for the inevitable testing. The following

February the Merlin powered Mustangs began arriving at frontline squadrons. Their first use in combat was on February 15, 1945, when 19 and 65 Squadrons conducted a fighter sweep over Northern France.

The Mustang Mk.III was a vast improvement over other British fighters, offering a superior range, 1045 miles on only internal fuel. This could be extended to 1900 miles with drop tanks and the much higher top speed. There were still problems with the Mk.III such as leaks and non-compatible oxygen systems which required further modifications however.

The biggest issue that RAF pilots found was the lack of visibility. The obvious solution was to employ a similar sliding bubble canopy to that found on the Spitfire. These were produced by R Malcolm Ltd and not only gave greater head room for movement and improved visibility but also made access far easier than the hinged hood of the standard Mk.III. The conversion was not a simple affair as parts of the internal structure required modification and the job was found to take on average 135 hours to complete, but the benefits were invaluable to the pilots entering combat.

Initially the new Mustangs flew as fighter escort on long range missions but this role was increasingly taken over by the USAAF allowing the RAF fighters to focus on flying closer to home with most missions being over the Channel and Northern France, although on December 12, 1944, Andrews Field provided 80 Mustangs (a mix of Mk.III and Mk.IV) to escort 3 Group Lancasters on a flight to Witten, Germany.

RAF Mustangs also took an active role in the D-Day landings, the Polish wing providing cover to the gliders on the night of the 5th/6th and conducting sweeps during the day, claiming a single Fw 190 in the process.

North American felt that there was still plenty of potential in the design, which

could be combined with the lessons learnt through combat, so they commenced on the Mk.IV/P-51D. The biggest visible difference was a complete redesign of the canopy to provide an unrestricted view, the spine was lowered and the wing structure modified to improve the armament. The Mk.III was only fitted with four .50 in Brownings and had the strength to carry one 500lb bomb under each wing, the Mk.IV could carry a 1000lb bomb and was fitted with an extra Browning in each wing. This also meant it could carry an even greater fuel load adding an extra 155 miles to the range.

The USAAF had the priority on the latest mark but the RAF had still received 486 by the end of the war, although some never got as far as a squadron, despite in some cases being shipped to the Far East and having the relevant markings applied. Most of the Mk.IV were sent to existing squadrons to supplement the Mk.III so most squadrons

operated a mix of the two, the only exceptions being 154, 303, 442 and 611 Squadrons which only flew the Mk.IV.

With the end of the war and the introduction of the Meteor and Vampire the British-based Mustang squadrons soon gave up their aircraft but those which had been based in Italy during the war continued to use the Mustang for several more years while supporting the post war effort in Italy.

If the war had lasted much longer the emerging jets might have played a more prominent role and supplanted the Mustang but it was the most successful of the Allied fighters, over 15,000 were built in total with 1810 delivered to RAF. The last Mustang was retired by the Dominican Air Force in 1984, it was loved by the pilots who flew it and truly was the Cadillac of the skies. ◉

**NORTH AMERICAN MUSTANG MK.IV KH765 HG-R 154 SQUADRON**

The ace Flt Lt Norm Lee only made one claim in a Mustang on March 27, 1945, when he was flying KH765 on a bomber escort, near Lübeck he damaged a Fw 190. A few days later the squadron was disbanded.

**NORTH AMERICAN MUSTANG MK.IVA KM112 PD-D 303 SQUADRON**

303 Sqn already had a distinguished reputation when it converted to the Mustang in April 1945, KM112 was flown by the CO Sqn Ldr Boleslaw 'Gandhi' Droinski while it was based at RAF Coltishall.

**NORTH AMERICAN MUSTANG MK.IV KM132 FY-S 611 WEST LANCASHIRE SQUADRON**

KM132 was flown by the squadron CO, Sqn Ldr P C P Farnes during the final months of the war on sweeps over France and Germany until the squadron was disbanded in August before reforming the following year with Spitfires.

**NORTH AMERICAN MUSTANG MK.IV KM735**

Anticipating that the war in the Far East would continue for possibly years, resources were redirected to the area including the final batch of Mustangs received by the RAF, KM735 was one of them and they all had Far East markings applied. It did not make it to a squadron and with the cessation of hostilities it was struck off charge on April 25, 1946.

**NORTH AMERICAN MUSTANG MK.IV KM182 DRS 239 WING**

Mustang KM182 bears the initials of GP Capt Donald R Shore the OC of 239 Wing, based in Italy during the post war period leading up to its disbandment in January 1947.

| VARIANT | LENGTH | SPAN | HEIGHT | ENGINE |
|---|---|---|---|---|
| PROTOTYPE | 32FT 2.65IN / 9.82M | 37FT 0.3IN / 11.29M | 12FT 2IN / 3.71M | ALLISON V-1710-39 |
| MK.I (NA-73) | 32FT 2.65IN / 9.82M | 37FT 0.3IN / 11.29M | 12FT 2IN / 3.71M | ALLISON V-1710-39 |
| MK.II (A) | 32FT 2.88IN / 9.83M | 37FT 0.3IN / 11.29M | 13FT 8IN / 4.17M | ALLISON V-1710-81 |
| MK.III (B/C) | 32FT 3.3IN / 9.84M | 37FT 0.3IN / 11.29M | 13FT 8IN / 4.17M | PACKARD MERLIN V-1650-3/7 |
| M.IV (D) | 32FT 3.3IN / 9.84M | 37FT 0.3IN / 11.29M | 13FT 8IN / 4.17M | PACKARD MERLIN V-1650-7 |
| M.IVA (K) | 32FT 3.3IN / 9.84M | 37FT 0.3IN / 11.29M | 13FT 8IN / 4.17M | PACKARD MERLIN V-1650-7 |

# NORTH AMERICAN P-51 MUSTANG

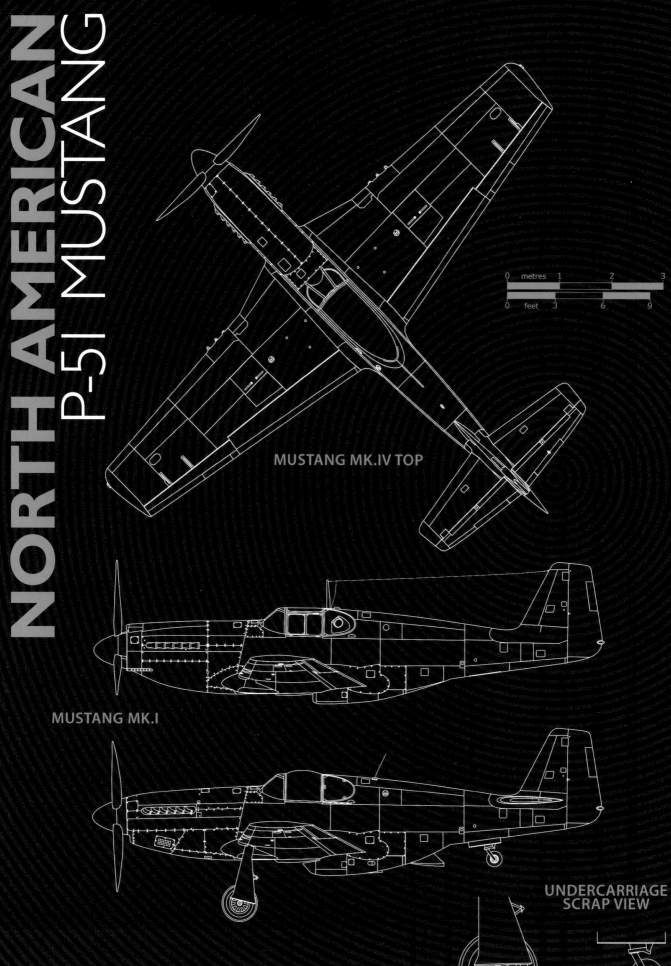

MUSTANG MK.IV TOP

MUSTANG MK.I

UNDERCARRIAGE
SCRAP VIEW

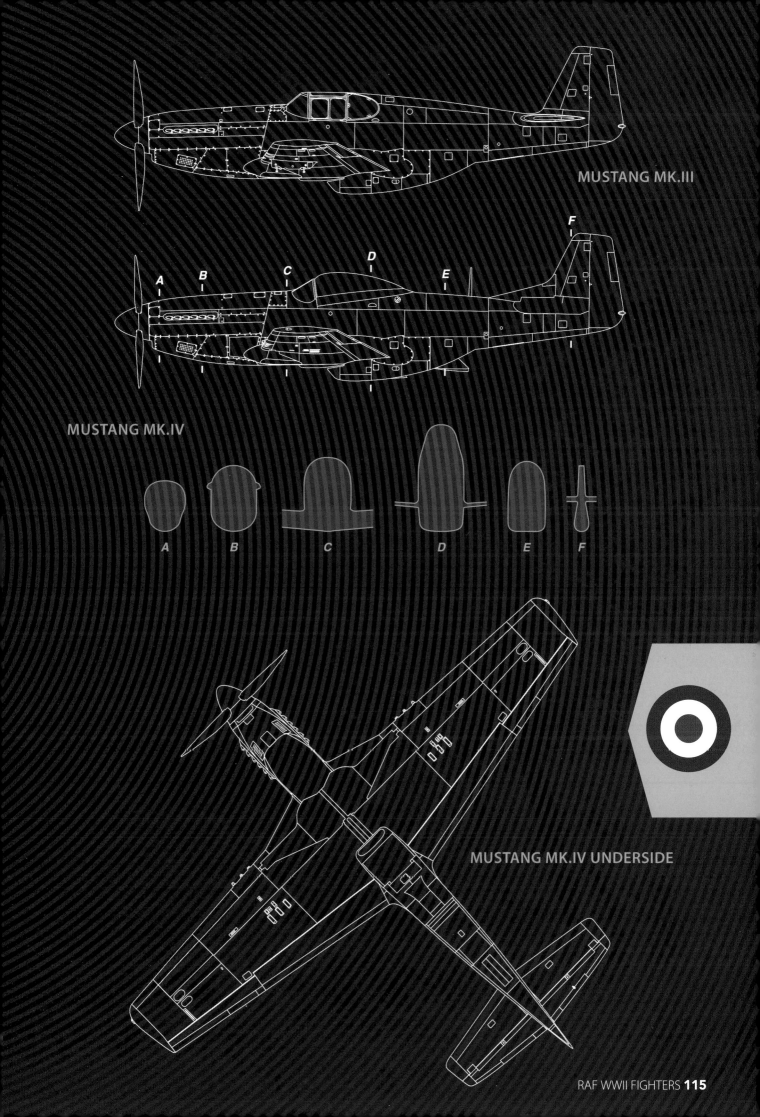

MUSTANG MK.III

MUSTANG MK.IV

A    B    C    D    E    F

MUSTANG MK.IV UNDERSIDE

The wooden wonder as the Mosquito was often called was an interesting aircraft, built primarily of wood when combat aircraft were increasingly constructed with all metal skins. The design was so good it became highly successful as both a day and night fighter – the latter into the 1950s.

# DE HAVILLAND
## MOSQUITO

**1941-1963**

**DE** Havilland was formed by aircraft designer Geoffrey de Havilland, already responsible for the Airco DH.4 and DH.9, on September 25, 1920. The company produced many reliable designs such as the DH.83 Tiger Moth and the DH.89 Rapide (with several of both types still flying in the 21st century) for the civilian market.

Although these were biplanes, the company did move on to monoplanes with the pinnacle being the DH.88 Comet racer, a compact twin-engine aeroplane intended for racing. Although only three were built for private individuals the design and construction techniques provided valuable data which heavily influenced the Mosquito.

Following the DH.88, De Havilland produced the DH.91 Albatross in response to Air Ministry Specification 36/35 for a high-speed transatlantic mail plane. Built to a similar design to the Comet but with four engines, the Albatross was primarily of wooden construction. A total of seven were built, including the two prototypes. They were first used by Imperial Airways in October 1938 but pressed into

military service as a high-speed courier until the last were retired in 1943.

As it became increasingly apparent that Germany would once again become a threat, the Air Ministry issued Specification P.13/36, which requested a long range twin engine bomber that was fitted with turrets in the nose and tail but was primarily concerned with speed and range.

Several companies submitted proposals, with Avro's resulting in the Manchester and Handley Page's eventually becoming the Halifax. De

Havilland initially looked at adapting the Albatross but this was deemed impractical, the company instead deciding to scale the fuselage down while retaining the wooden construction method and fitting two Rolls-Royce Merlin engines.

The design team also made the decision to reduce weight by sacrificing the turrets for more speed. It was hoped that the new aircraft would be capable of carrying a 6000lb bomb all the way to Berlin and return, a round trip of 1500 miles.

There were concerns about the wisdom of an unarmed bomber when fighter speeds were increasing, allowing types such as the Hampden and Battle to be easily caught. However, de Havilland was confident that the lightweight DH.98 would retain its superiority with a predicted top speed of over 400mph. The Air Ministry was keen for any bomber to have a minimum of three crew members so no individual was overworked but they were willing to concede that any photo reconnaissance aircraft could manage with two crew, therefore the initial proposal was for the PR variant. The crew were seated side by side in the cockpit, the shape of the nose and cockpit layout later being utilised in the two seat versions of the DH Vampire and Venom. An agreement on the requirements and configuration was eventually reached over Christmas 1939, resulting in an order for three prototypes, this was followed on March 1, 1940, by an order for 50 Mosquitos. The order was later amended to a mix of bomber and fighter variants. Work commenced on building the first Mosquito during early 1940 and on more than

## DH MOSQUITO FB.VI PZ471 YH-F 21 SQUADRON

Immediately after the war in Europe, squadron markings began being applied again. PZ471 had the squadron badge applied to the tail. Sky squadron code outlined in dark, possibly black colour.

one occasion the Ministry of Aircraft Production, headed by Lord Beaverbrook, considered cancelling the project. Because no official cancellation order ever reached De Havilland, work continued at a steady pace.

The fuselage of the Mosquito was built in two halves using a combination of laminated spruce for the structure, inner and outer skins with balsa wood sandwiched between, the whole structure was built up around a mahogany male pattern and then joined together. The wings used a variety of woods, the main spar was laminated spruce, stringers of Douglas fir covered in a skin of birch plywood all glued together and then reinforced with brass screws. This construction had two benefits; firstly the open fuselage allowed easy access to the cockpit and the fitting of instruments. Secondly the extensive use of wood allowed coachbuilders and furniture companies to directly contribute to the war effort, while diversifying the manufacturing meant

that it would be harder for the Luftwaffe to hinder production.

By November, work had been completed on the bomber/photo reconnaissance prototype even though at this stage the Air Ministry had still not confirmed that it would proceed with the bomber version due to ongoing reservations about an unarmed bomber. The prototype was temporarily given the serial E0234 but soon changed to W4050 and on November 3 it was transported from Salisbury Hall to the company headquarters at Hatfield.

Having undertaken a week of taxiing trials it took off on November 25, 1940, with company test pilot Geoffrey de Havilland Jnr at the controls and with John E Walker as observer. The flight lasted for half an hour but took place only 11 months after the company was officially given permission to proceed with the Mosquito.

Early trials provided a good indication of what the Mosquito was capable of and in mid-January W4050 out performed a Spitfire in level flight at 6000ft. Further speed trials by the A&AEE at Boscombe Down gave a top speed of 390mph at 22,000ft, impressive when the Bf 109 could only manage 336mph at nearly 20,000ft. W4050 eventually went on to reach 433mph at 28,500ft when the Rolls-Royce Merlin 21 engines had been upgraded to the Merlin 61. Operationally it was only the PR version that could manage this speed, fighter and bomber Mosquitos being in the region of 30-50mph slower. The only major change made to W4050 was a redesign and lengthening of the trailing edge of the engine nacelles to reduce tail buffeting.

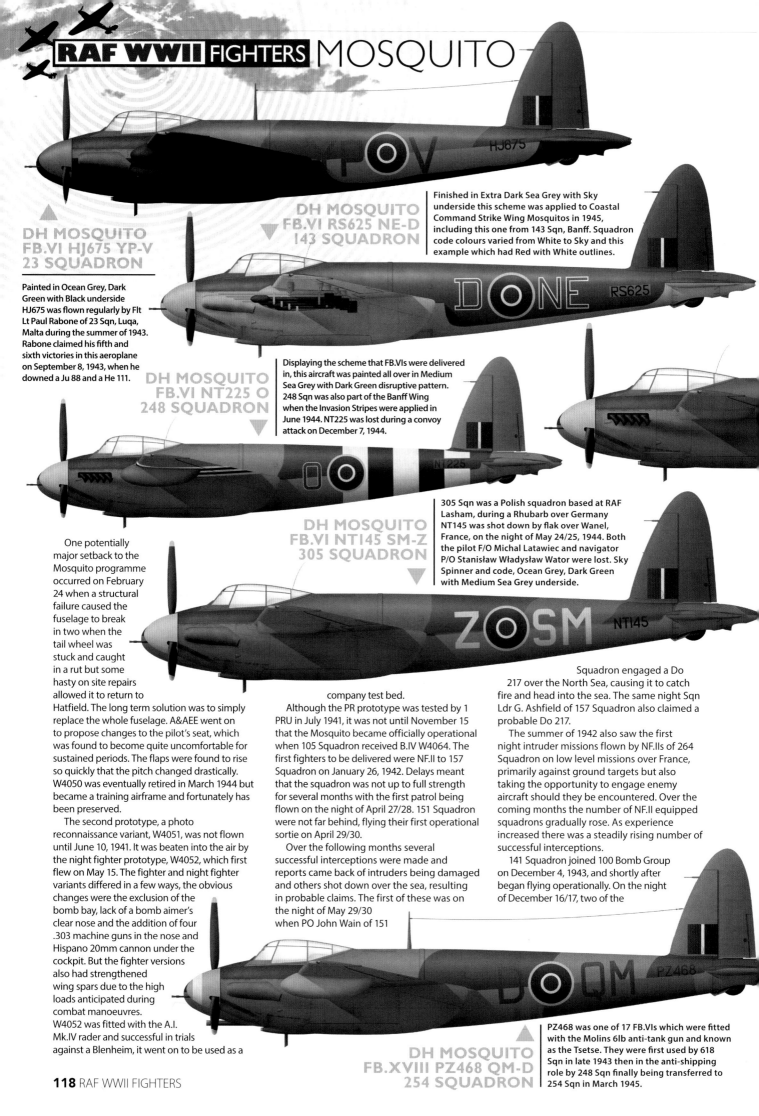

## DH MOSQUITO FB.VI HJ675 YP-V 23 SQUADRON

Painted in Ocean Grey, Dark Green with Black underside HJ675 was flown regularly by Flt Lt Paul Rabone of 23 Sqn, Luqa, Malta during the summer of 1943. Rabone claimed his fifth and sixth victories in this aeroplane on September 8, 1943, when he downed a Ju 88 and a He 111.

## DH MOSQUITO FB.VI RS625 NE-D 143 SQUADRON

Finished in Extra Dark Sea Grey with Sky underside this scheme was applied to Coastal Command Strike Wing Mosquitos in 1945, including this one from 143 Sqn, Banff. Squadron code colours varied from White to Sky and this example which had Red with White outlines.

## DH MOSQUITO FB.VI NT225 O 248 SQUADRON

Displaying the scheme that FB.VIs were delivered in, this aircraft was painted all over in Medium Sea Grey with Dark Green disruptive pattern. 248 Sqn was also part of the Banff Wing when the Invasion Stripes were applied in June 1944. NT225 was lost during a convoy attack on December 7, 1944.

## DH MOSQUITO FB.VI NT145 SM-Z 305 SQUADRON

305 Sqn was a Polish squadron based at RAF Lasham, during a Rhubarb over Germany NT145 was shot down by flak over Wanel, France, on the night of May 24/25, 1944. Both the pilot F/O Michal Latawiec and navigator P/O Stanisław Władysław Wator were lost. Sky Spinner and code, Ocean Grey, Dark Green with Medium Sea Grey underside.

One potentially major setback to the Mosquito programme occurred on February 24 when a structural failure caused the fuselage to break in two when the tail wheel was stuck and caught in a rut but some hasty on site repairs allowed it to return to Hatfield. The long term solution was to simply replace the whole fuselage. A&AEE went on to propose changes to the pilot's seat, which was found to become quite uncomfortable for sustained periods. The flaps were found to rise so quickly that the pitch changed drastically. W4050 was eventually retired in March 1944 but became a training airframe and fortunately has been preserved.

The second prototype, a photo reconnaissance variant, W4051, was not flown until June 10, 1941. It was beaten into the air by the night fighter prototype, W4052, which first flew on May 15. The fighter and night fighter variants differed in a few ways, the obvious changes were the exclusion of the bomb bay, lack of a bomb aimer's clear nose and the addition of four .303 machine guns in the nose and Hispano 20mm cannon under the cockpit. But the fighter versions also had strengthened wing spars due to the high loads anticipated during combat manoeuvres. W4052 was fitted with the A.I. Mk.IV rader and successful in trials against a Blenheim, it went on to be used as a

company test bed.

Although the PR prototype was tested by 1 PRU in July 1941, it was not until November 15 that the Mosquito became officially operational when 105 Squadron received B.IV W4064. The first fighters to be delivered were NF.II to 157 Squadron on January 26, 1942. Delays meant that the squadron was not up to full strength for several months with the first patrol being flown on the night of April 27/28. 151 Squadron were not far behind, flying their first operational sortie on April 29/30.

Over the following months several successful interceptions were made and reports came back of intruders being damaged and others shot down over the sea, resulting in probable claims. The first of these was on the night of May 29/30 when PO John Wain of 151

Squadron engaged a Do 217 over the North Sea, causing it to catch fire and head into the sea. The same night Sqn Ldr G. Ashfield of 157 Squadron also claimed a probable Do 217.

The summer of 1942 also saw the first night intruder missions flown by NF.IIs of 264 Squadron on low level missions over France, primarily against ground targets but also taking the opportunity to engage enemy aircraft should they be encountered. Over the coming months the number of NF.II equipped squadrons gradually rose. As experience increased there was a steadily rising number of successful interceptions.

141 Squadron joined 100 Bomb Group on December 4, 1943, and shortly after began flying operationally. On the night of December 16/17, two of the

## DH MOSQUITO FB.XVIII PZ468 QM-D 254 SQUADRON

PZ468 was one of 17 FB.VIs which were fitted with the Molins 6lb anti-tank gun and known as the Tsetse. They were first used by 618 Sqn in late 1943 then in the anti-shipping role by 248 Sqn finally being transferred to 254 Sqn in March 1945.

squadron's NF.IIs along with a pair of Beaufighters flew escort on a raid to Berlin. Other squadrons were allocated to 100 Bomb Group and the first successes while flying escort were on the night of January 28/29 with 141 Squadron getting a Bf 109 and 239 Squadron claiming a Bf 110. By June 1944, 10 squadrons had joined 100 Bomb Group.

Improvements in radar meant that the NF.II was replaced by the NF.XII. The inclusion of the A.I. Mk.VIII required a redesign of the nose to house it, this meant the four machine guns in the nose were removed and a new larger 'thimble'

nose introduced. The NF.XII also had the capacity to carry 50 gallon drop tanks, increasing the range considerably for the night intruders. 85 Squadron received the first production NF.XII at the end of February 1943 and made their first confirmed kills on the night of April 14/15 when two Do 217s were intercepted over Chelmsford. The squadron was able to claim four and one probable Fw 190 on the night of May 16/17. Beaufighters continued to be replaced with the NF.XII, 29 and 96 Squadrons both converting in June 1943 and a total of 10 squadrons eventually using the type.

Only 97 NF.XIIs were built before it was

superseded by the NF.XIII which saw further refinement to the nose, this new shape was known as the universal 'bull' nose and was a constant with all subsequent NF variants. A total of 270 NF.XIIIs were completed before the American built A.I. Mk.X became available. Aircraft fitted with this were designated the NF.XVII and had begun life as NF.IIs. Having been upgraded to NF.XIIs on the production line, the 99 airframes were then sent directly to Marshalls for the new radar to be fitted.

85 Squadron became the only one to utilize the high-altitude NF.XV which was based around the B.XVI with the intention of flying at altitude to intercept the Ju 86P reconnaissance aircraft. Only five of these were completed. Yet more

## DH MOSQUITO FB.VI HX913 SB-N 464 SQUADRON RAAF

Based at RAF Hundson 464 Sqn RAAF converted to the Mosquito VB.VI in July 1943 and continued to operate the type for the duration of the war. The squadron was involved in Operation Jericho, the precision attack on the prison at Amiens. HX913 has a Sky Spinner and code, Ocean Grey, Dark Green with Medium Sea Grey underside. Photographs show signs of exhaust shroud being removed due to decolourisation. ▼

## DH MOSQUITO FB.VI MM417 EG-T 487 SQUADRON RNZAFF ▲

Displaying an unusually low demarcation line, the aircraft is painted in all over Ocean Grey, Dark Green with Medium Sea Grey underside and White squadron code. Based at RAF Hunsdon during the same period as 464 Sqn RAAF.

## DH MOSQUITO FB.VI NS898 SY-Z 613 SQUADRON ◄

Wearing the typically hastily added invasion stripes, Sky spinners obscuring part of the squadron code, NS898 served with 613 City of Manchester Squadron from April 1944 until March 1945. It later served with 60 OTU and 11 Sqn where it was lost on May 27, 1949, when it stalled and spun. Painted in all over Medium Sea Grey/Dark Green with Sky spinners.

## DH MOSQUITO FB.VI RS565 3P-E 515 SQUADRON

All over Medium Sea Grey with Dark Green upper, the aircraft only carries the invasion stripes on the lower fuselage as per instructions issued on July 6, 1944. This particular FB.VI has been converted to have a radar unit fitted in the nose.

## DH MOSQUITO FB.VI NS993 N 617 SQUADRON ►

Despite being known as a Lancaster squadron 617 Sqn had a total of four Mosquitos on strength during the war including NS993. Interestingly the squadron code was never applied. The aircraft became the personal choice for 617 Sqn CO Leonard Cheshire during the spring of 1944 and continued to be flown by his successor Willie Tait. Painted in Ocean Grey, Dark Green with Medium Sea Grey underside.

## DH MOSQUITO NF.II DZ717 UP-G 605 SQUADRON ◄

The squadron converted to the Mosquito in February 1943 and continued using them until after the war. DZ717 was one of the first aircraft delivered to the squadron and retained the day fighter colours.

## DH MOSQUITO FB.VI G-AGGD BOAC

◄ Based at RAF Leuchars, nine FB.VIs were converted for use by BOAC as civilian couriers to Stockholm. G-AGGD was formerly HJ681. When received, the aircraft were painted in Dark Slate Grey, Extra Dark Sea Grey with Sky undersides. The Sky was later replaced with Black. Insignia Blue letters with Aluminium outline.

improvements to the engine resulted in the Merlin 25 which created the NF.XIX, these entered service in May 1944, going to 257 Squadron.

The final night fighter to see service during the war was the NF.30, fitted with the slightly longer two stage Merlin 72 or 76 which pushed up the operational top speed to 407mph. The NF.30 entered service with 219 Squadron in June 1944. By this stage in the war there was minimal enemy activity over Great Britain until the V-1 began being launched, many of these were accounted for by the Tempest squadrons. However, an almost equal number were brought down by the Mosquito squadrons: 638 by Tempests and 623 by Mosquitos. Over Europe the NF.30 continued the tradition of night intruder missions, flying both as escort and ranging patrols taking advantage of shooting down Luftwaffe aircraft, frequently over their own airfields.

Just after the war the final night fighter variant entered front line service; the NF.36 and NF.38 both had the Merlin 113 engine fitted, retained the same armament as previous variants, the same distinctive nose and in the case of the NF.36 the American A.I. Mk.X. The NF.38 was instead fitted with the British A.I. Mk.IX radar and these were retained into the 1950s by the auxiliary squadrons until they were replaced by Meteor night fighters.

The night fighters may have performed exceptionally in their dedicated role but while flying intruder missions there were missed opportunities to destroy many ground targets. The solution was to make use of the bomb bay while retaining the fighter element. Mosquito HJ662 began life as a standard B.IV with the serial DZ434 but was taken

out of the production line for conversion.

Although the NF.II had stronger wing spars than the B.IV due to stresses placed on it, the wing of the FB.IV was further strengthened to allow for a variety of stores including external fuel tanks, a 250lb bomb or rockets to be carried. Later improvements increased wing strength so a 500lb bomb could be loaded.

The bomb bay was modified to accommodate two 250lb bombs and it had a greater fuel capacity than the NF.II. The FB.IV was fitted with the same nose as the NF.II, four .303 machine guns in the nose and 20mm Hispano cannon below the forward fuselage.

FB.IV prototype HJ662 took the air on June 1, 1942, but

**DH MOSQUITO FB.VI RF942 KU-H 47 SQUADRON**

Following VJ day the RAF flew ground attack missions in Java against Indonesian separatists, this included 47 Squadron led by Wg Cdr George H Melville-Jackson, who had become an ace with Coastal Command. Finished in all over painted Aluminium.

**DH MOSQUITO FB.VI HR118 W-3 235 SQUADRON**

HR118 was frequently flown by the ace Flg Off Noel Russell with navigator Flg Off Tom Armstrong on anti shipping patrols, covering the Bay of Biscay following D-Day. HR118 was passed to 333 Sqn and written off during a crash landing on February 22, 1945, at RAF Lossiemouth.

**DH MOSQUITO NF.II DD750 25 SQUADRON**

25 Sqn was already a night fighter unit when it replaced the Beaufighter with the Mosquito. On March 22, 1943, three aircraft took off for a Ranger sortie but were recalled to RAF Church Fenton. DD750 was given an incorrect height while holding and crashed into high ground. Both the pilot, Sgt John Hudson, and navigator Sgt Ralph Andrews were lost in the accident.

**DH MOSQUITO NF.XIII MM571 PS 264 SQUADRON**

MM571 was flown by Flt Lt Ken Rayment who was already an ace when he joined the squadron. Having intercepted V-1s during the summer, the squadron moved to France and continued providing night cover.

| VARIANT | LENGTH | SPAN | HEIGHT | ENGINE |
|---|---|---|---|---|
| PROTOTYPE | 40FT 6IN / 12.35M | 52FT 6IN / 15.75M | 12FT 6IN / 3.75M | 2X MERLIN 21 |
| NF.II | 42FT 11IN / 13.07M | 54FT 2IN / 16.5M | 12FT 6IN / 3.75M | 2X MERLIN 21, 22, 23 |
| NF.XII/XIII | 40FT 5IN / 12.30M | 54FT 2IN / 16.5M | 12FT 6IN / 3.75M | 2X MERLIN 21, 23 |
| NF.XV | 44FT 6IN / 13.50M | 59FT / 17.97M (PRODUCTION VERSION) | 12FT 6IN / 3.75M | 2X MERLIN 72, 73 |
| NF.XVII | 40FT 6IN / 12.35M | 54FT 2IN / 16.5M | 12FT 6IN / 3.75M | 2X MERLIN 21, 23 |
| NF.XIX | 40FT 6IN / 12.35M | 54FT 2IN / 16.5M | 12FT 6IN / 3.75M | 2X MERLIN 25 |
| NF.30 | 44FT 6IN / 13.50M | 54FT 2IN / 16.5M | 12FT 6IN / 3.75M | 2X MERLIN 72, 76 |
| NF.36/38 | 44FT 6IN / 13.50M | 54FT 2IN / 16.5M | 12FT 6IN / 3.75M | 2X MERLIN 113, 114 |
| FB.IV | 41FT 2IN / 12.54M | 54FT 2IN / 16.5M | 12FT 6IN / 3.75M | 2X MERLIN 21, 22, 23, 25 |
| FB.XVIII | 41FT 2IN / 12.54M | 54FT 2IN / 16.5M | 12FT 6IN / 3.75M | 2X MERLIN 25 |

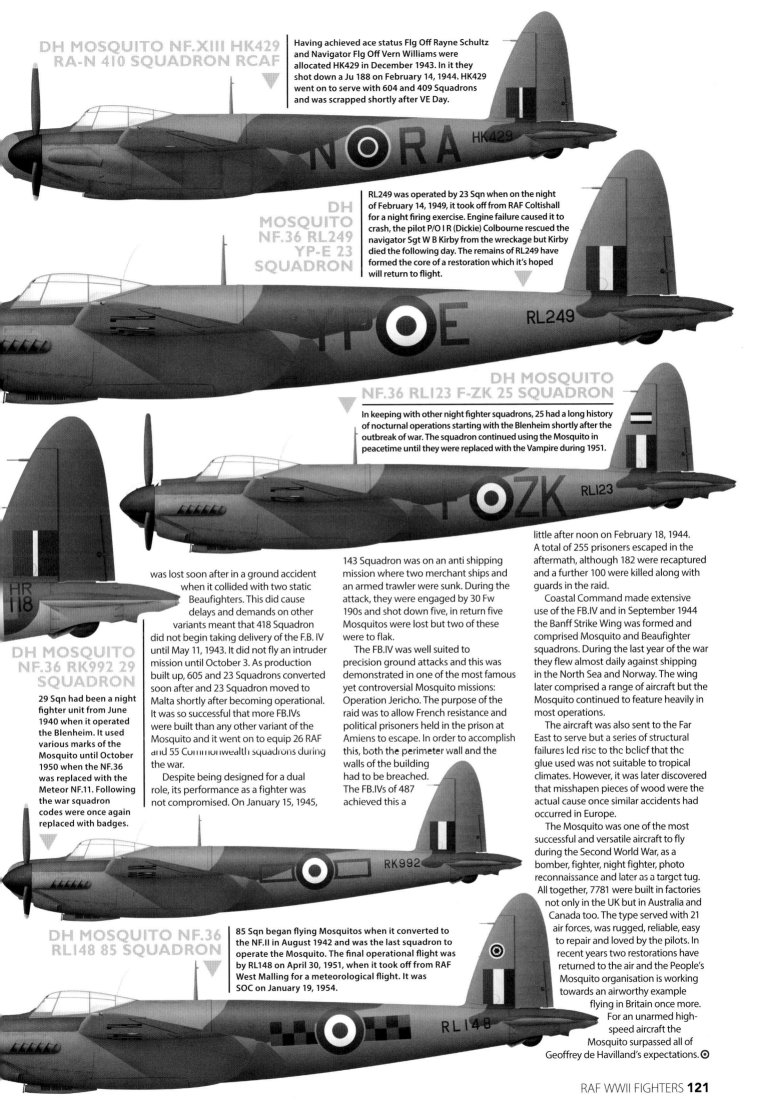

**DH MOSQUITO NF.XIII HK429 RA-N 410 SQUADRON RCAF**

Having achieved ace status Flg Off Rayne Schultz and Navigator Flg Off Vern Williams were allocated HK429 in December 1943. In it they shot down a Ju 188 on February 14, 1944. HK429 went on to serve with 604 and 409 Squadrons and was scrapped shortly after VE Day.

**DH MOSQUITO NF.36 RL249 YP-E 23 SQUADRON**

RL249 was operated by 23 Sqn when on the night of February 14, 1949, it took off from RAF Coltishall for a night firing exercise. Engine failure caused it to crash, the pilot P/O I R (Dickie) Colbourne rescued the navigator Sgt W B Kirby from the wreckage but Kirby died the following day. The remains of RL249 have formed the core of a restoration which it's hoped will return to flight.

**DH MOSQUITO NF.36 RL123 F-ZK 25 SQUADRON**

In keeping with other night fighter squadrons, 25 had a long history of nocturnal operations starting with the Blenheim shortly after the outbreak of war. The squadron continued using the Mosquito in peacetime until they were replaced with the Vampire during 1951.

**DH MOSQUITO NF.36 RK992 29 SQUADRON**

29 Sqn had been a night fighter unit from June 1940 when it operated the Blenheim. It used various marks of the Mosquito until October 1950 when the NF.36 was replaced with the Meteor NF.11. Following the war squadron codes were once again replaced with badges.

was lost soon after in a ground accident when it collided with two static Beaufighters. This did cause delays and demands on other variants meant that 418 Squadron did not begin taking delivery of the F.B. IV until May 11, 1943. It did not fly an intruder mission until October 3. As production built up, 605 and 23 Squadrons converted soon after and 23 Squadron moved to Malta shortly after becoming operational. It was so successful that more FB.IVs were built than any other variant of the Mosquito and it went on to equip 26 RAF and 55 Commonwealth squadrons during the war.

Despite being designed for a dual role, its performance as a fighter was not compromised. On January 15, 1945,

143 Squadron was on an anti shipping mission where two merchant ships and an armed trawler were sunk. During the attack, they were engaged by 30 Fw 190s and shot down five, in return five Mosquitos were lost but two of these were to flak.

The FB.IV was well suited to precision ground attacks and this was demonstrated in one of the most famous yet controversial Mosquito missions: Operation Jericho. The purpose of the raid was to allow French resistance and political prisoners held in the prison at Amiens to escape. In order to accomplish this, both the perimeter wall and the walls of the building had to be breached. The FB.IVs of 487 achieved this a

little after noon on February 18, 1944. A total of 255 prisoners escaped in the aftermath, although 182 were recaptured and a further 100 were killed along with guards in the raid.

Coastal Command made extensive use of the FB.IV and in September 1944 the Banff Strike Wing was formed and comprised Mosquito and Beaufighter squadrons. During the last year of the war they flew almost daily against shipping in the North Sea and Norway. The wing later comprised a range of aircraft but the Mosquito continued to feature heavily in most operations.

The aircraft was also sent to the Far East to serve but a series of structural failures led rise to the belief that the glue used was not suitable to tropical climates. However, it was later discovered that misshapen pieces of wood were the actual cause once similar accidents had occurred in Europe.

The Mosquito was one of the most successful and versatile aircraft to fly during the Second World War, as a bomber, fighter, night fighter, photo reconnaissance and later as a target tug. All together, 7781 were built in factories not only in the UK but in Australia and Canada too. The type served with 21 air forces, was rugged, reliable, easy to repair and loved by the pilots. In recent years two restorations have returned to the air and the People's Mosquito organisation is working towards an airworthy example flying in Britain once more. For an unarmed high-speed aircraft the Mosquito surpassed all of Geoffrey de Havilland's expectations. ◉

**DH MOSQUITO NF.36 RL148 85 SQUADRON**

85 Sqn began flying Mosquitos when it converted to the NF.II in August 1942 and was the last squadron to operate the Mosquito. The final operational flight was by RL148 on April 30, 1951, when it took off from RAF West Malling for a meteorological flight. It was SOC on January 19, 1954.

MOSQUITO NF.36

DE HAVILLAND MOSQUITO

MOSQUITO FB.VI TOP

0 metres 1 2 3

0 feet 3 6 9

MOSQUITO FB.VI TOP FRONT

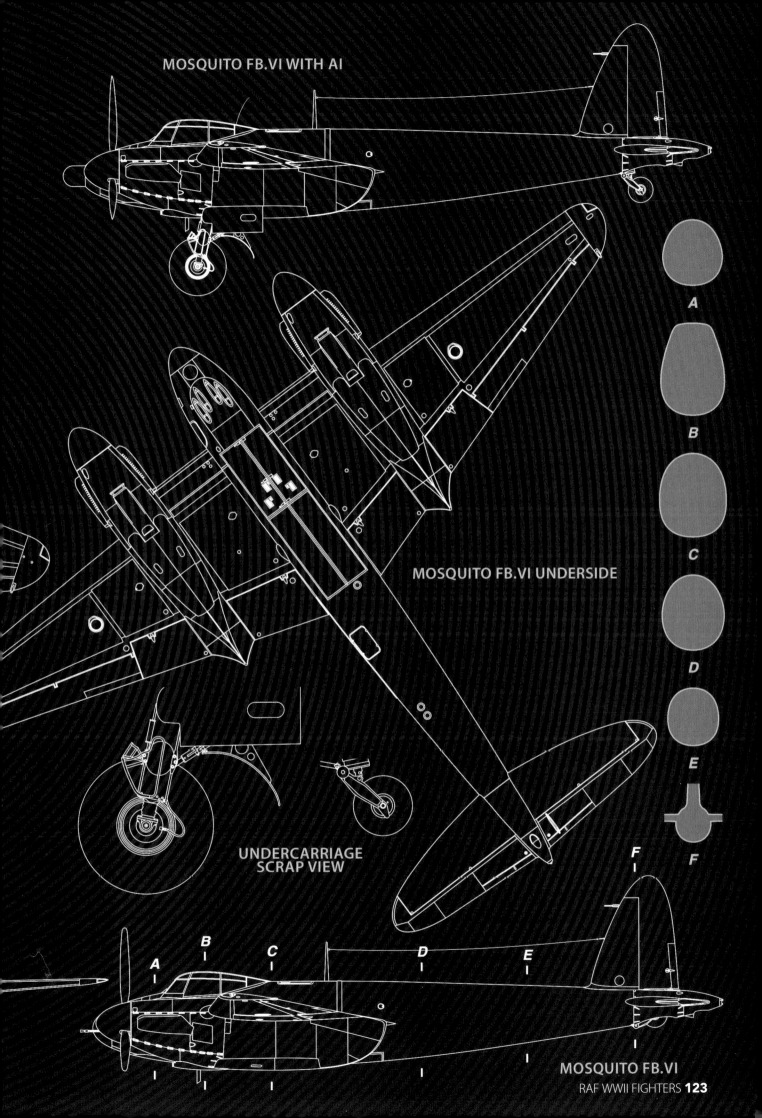

MOSQUITO FB.VI WITH AI

MOSQUITO FB.VI UNDERSIDE

A

B

C

D

E

F

UNDERCARRIAGE
SCRAP VIEW

F

F

A    B    C                D        E

MOSQUITO FB.VI

# HAWKER TEMPEST

**Hawker was known for biplanes such as the Fury and Hart during the 1930s, but less than a decade later the company was manufacturing a piston-powered monoplane capable of shooting down jet fighters – the Tempest.**

## 1944-1949

**E**ven though the Typhoon was only just entering service in mid-1941, a replacement was already being planned by the Hawker design team. Most of the original's flaws had been resolved but a redesign of the aircraft would result in an even more potent fighter. During flight-testing a number of limitations in the basic Typhoon design became apparent; most significant was the thick wing which generated a comparatively high level of drag and caused buffeting at high speeds.

Having seen the success of Mitchell's Spitfire, Hawker set about creating a totally new thin wing for the Typhoon, going so far as to emulate the Spitfire's ellipse. The firm put its proposals to the Air Ministry and specification F.10/41 was issued as a result, along with an order for two prototypes of the Typhoon II, as it was then known, in November 1941.

The new laminar flow wing too thin to accommodate both the aircraft's fuel tanks and its Hispano 20mm cannon so the tanks were relocated into the fuselage. The undercarriage were also modified but retained the wide track of the Typhoon. The initial prototype retained the Typhoon tail but in light of catastrophic failures the opportunity was taken to completely redesign the internal structure and strengthen the tail unit. Because the early Typhoons had acquired a bad reputation, Hawker did not want that to also be applied to what was actually a completely different aircraft so they called it the Tempest, in keeping with the naming tradition of Hawker fighters.

Due to the issues with the Sabre engine three power plants were chosen for the Tempest – the different variants being developed concurrently. The Mk.I would have the Napier Sabre IV, the Mk.II a Bristol Centaurus IV, the Mk.III and IV would have Rolls-Royce Griffons and the Mk.V would have a Sabre II. Continual delays to the Centaurus IV and Sabre IV along with the complexities involved in redesigning the airframe to accept the Griffon meant that the first prototype completed was based on the Mk.V.

In order to test the wing and save time the Mk.V prototype incorporated many elements of the Typhoon including the car door canopy. Production aircraft were fitted with the bubble canopy and stronger tail unit however. Construction was completed and on September 1, 1942, HM595 undertook taxi trials, the following day it flew for the first time with Philip Lucas at the controls. After an uneventful flight, Lucas began a series of trials commencing on September 3. During the second flight, the Tempest reached 300mph and 10,000ft. Over the following months trials continued along with modifications to HM595 including multiple revisions to the tail.

Work also progressed on the other prototypes, the Mk.I prototype HM599 was perhaps the most altered as the engine coolers were fitted in the inner wings, just like the Mosquito and Whirlwind in an attempt to further reduce drag. Wind tunnel tests indicated that there was a negligible difference in performance plus the chin radiators were becoming increasingly reliable. This combined with the continual delays to the Sabre IV and problems with the engine once it was fitted (under performance and excessive oil leakage) meant that the M.I was cancelled before making it to production.

The Bristol Centaurus had originally been intended for the Typhoon and despite work beginning in 1938 on the engine it was not ready for production until 1942. So it was instead mated with the Tempest fuselage and designated the Mk.II. Chief designer Sydney Camm was initially reluctant to use a radial engine but testing of a captured Fw 190 A showed what could be achieved. The Mk.II prototype LA602's maiden flight was on June 28, 1943, and the only major issue was excessive vibration caused by the rigid engine mountings. Changes to the second prototype, LA607, cured the problem and following the Mk.V it entered production.

Although it became a precursor to the Sea Fury and was renamed the Hawker Fury, the Griffon IIB engine aircraft had begun life as the Tempest Mk.III. Only three prototypes were completed and it did not fly until November 27, 1944, and was fitted with a six-bladed contra-rotating Rotol propeller. Although intended for the RAF the introduction of the Meteor and Vampire heralded the end of propeller-driven fighters. The M.IV was planned to have the Griffon 61 but was cancelled while still on the drawing board.

The first variant to make it to production and enter service was perhaps confusingly the Tempest Mk.V. The speed with which the prototype was built and tested meant that the first production aircraft flew on June 21, 1943. Early aircraft coming off the production line were retained for testing so the third production Mk.V was not delivered to A&AEE at Boscombe Down until the October where it was used for handling and performance trials.

At lower altitudes, below 20,000ft, the Tempest was faster than the Bf 109 G, Fw 190 A, Spitfire XIV and Mustang III. Above this the Tempest was slightly slower and in other aspects it was also inferior. The first batch of Mk.Vs were fitted with Hispano Mk.II 20mm cannon. Identical to those fitted in the Typhoon these were soon replaced with Hispano Mk.V 20mm cannon, which became the standard armament for Tempests.

486 Squadron RNZAF, based at RAF Tangmere, received the first Tempests on January 14, 1944, when the first three were delivered but 3 Squadron was the first to fully convert to the Tempest with 486 Squadron soon after – a flock of birds causing Category A damage to three of the aircraft and delaying the conversion programme. As the Typhoon and Tempest had sufficient similarities the conversion process was a relatively short affair. 3 Squadron commenced the process on March 6, 1944, and flew its first combat mission on April 23. The pilots soon gained confidence in the new fighter and were pleased to discover that the problems plaguing the Typhoon had been eradicated or dramatically reduced.

Production was slow, in part due to industrial action at Hawker's Langley factory delaying the deliveries to 56 Squadron until after D-Day. The three squadrons were moved to RAF Newchurch as part of 150 Wing where they provided cover for air sea rescue missions and flew some missions over France and the low countries, attacking military installations, airfields and coastal shipping.

On the night of May 8/9, Flg Off Bob Barckley of 3 Squadron encountered and shot down what he reported as a jet ship, this turned out to be the first of many V-1 flying bombs that the Tempests would destroy in the last year of the war.

The Tempest squadrons were not involved in the D-Day landings, instead they were held in reserve and would provide fighter cover over the beaches should the Luftwaffe break through the fighter cordon. As the landings took

**HAWKER TEMPEST MK.V EJ880 5R-R 33 SQUADRON**

Having been based on the continent 33 Sqn returned to the UK to replace the Spitfires with Tempests In February 1945. The Tempests still had parts of their invasion stripes in place during the conversion at RAF Predannack even though they were supposed to be removed in January.

HAVING SEEN THE SUCCESS OF MITCHELL'S SPITFIRE, HAWKER SET ABOUT CREATING A TOTALLY NEW THIN WING FOR THE TYPHOON

## HAWKER TEMPEST MK.II PR536 OQ-H 5 SQUADRON

The aircraft served with 5 Sqn just after the war when it was based at Peshwar (now Pakistan). PR536 was transferred to the Indian Air Force in 1947 where it saw action. Parts were later gifted to the RAF Museum where it formed the core of a static restoration. Currently on display at Hendon.

place without an aerial threat, 3 and 486 Squadrons went on the offensive on June 8 with Wg Cdr Beaumont leading. Near Rouen they encountered five Bf 109s. 486 Squadron provided top cover while 3 Squadron's Tempests dived down to attack and destroyed two of the Bf 109s. This was the first air-to-air combat for the Tempest.

As the Allies pushed into Northern France the Tempests continued to attack ground targets including what were labelled as ski sites. The actual purpose of these had yet to be determined but they were considered a threat. Their actual use was revealed on June 13 when the first 10 V-1s were launched at London, of these six failed to reach Britain and only one hit the actual target. As Germany increased V-1 launches, Tempest pilots along with Mustang

and Spitfire units began intercepting the flying bombs which were known as Divers. On June 16 alone the Tempests had accounted for 11.

Early attempts to destroy V-1s involved shooting them down but the ensuing explosion and debris was a threat to pilots so an interception technique was developed which involved the Tempest flying parallel to the V-1 and the pilot using the wingtip to literally tip over the flying bomb, causing it to crash. Interception was easier at night when the exhaust flame was visible for miles around. By the end of the war a total of 1954 had been destroyed, 150 Wing accounted for 638 of these.

By September 1944 the number of V1 attacks had diminished as the launch sites were destroyed or

overrun. There were still some intercepts but operations by the Tempest wings was scaled back and it was time for the Tempests to relocate to the continent, becoming part of the Second Tactical Air Force. 150 Wing moved to B60 Grimbergen, Belgium, on September 28 and were involved in combat the following day during the aftermath of Operation Market Garden.

Against the Fw 190 the Tempests were regularly getting results but the pilots began encountering a new Luftwaffe threat – the Me 262. Due to the difference in performance, the Tempests struggled to catch and engage the jet fighter. Like many aircraft though, the Me 262's Achilles heel was after a sortie when it was low on fuel and returning to base. Even with Fw 190s and Bf 109s providing cover over the airfields, several Me 262s were shot down as they tried to land.

During February 1945, 135 Wing sent the recently converted 33 and 222 Squadrons to

OQ○H    PR536

## HAWKER TEMPEST MK.II PR681 HN-R 20 SQUADRON

Displaying typical colours for Tempests just after the war of Dark Green and Ocean Grey over Medium Sea Grey with Sky spinner and band. Serial was also applied on both wings. Having served with 20 Sqn PR681 was written off when it collided with power lines in Germany on October 12, 1948, while with 26 Sqn.

HN○R    PR681

## HAWKER TEMPEST MK.II PR856 XC-K 26 SQUADRON

PR856 was delivered on New Year's Day 1947 to 26 Sqn and used by Flt Lt 'Jack' Frost, the commander of A flight. It remained on strength until the squadron converted to Vampires in April 1949. PR856 was later sold to the Indian Air Force.

XC○K    PR856

## HAWKER TEMPEST MK.II MW820 54 SQUADRON HF-T

Based at RAF Chilbolton in March 1946 MW820 wears a high visibility band on the tail and nose. The Tempests originally belonged to 183 Sqn until it was renumbered as 54 Sqn in November 1945.

HF○T    MW820

## HAWKER TEMPEST MK.V EJ750 JBW 122 WING

EJ750 was the personal Tempest of Wg Cdr John Wray and bears his personal initials. Wray replaced Beaumont as commander of 122 Wing in October 1944. While flying EJ750 he claimed a Me 262.

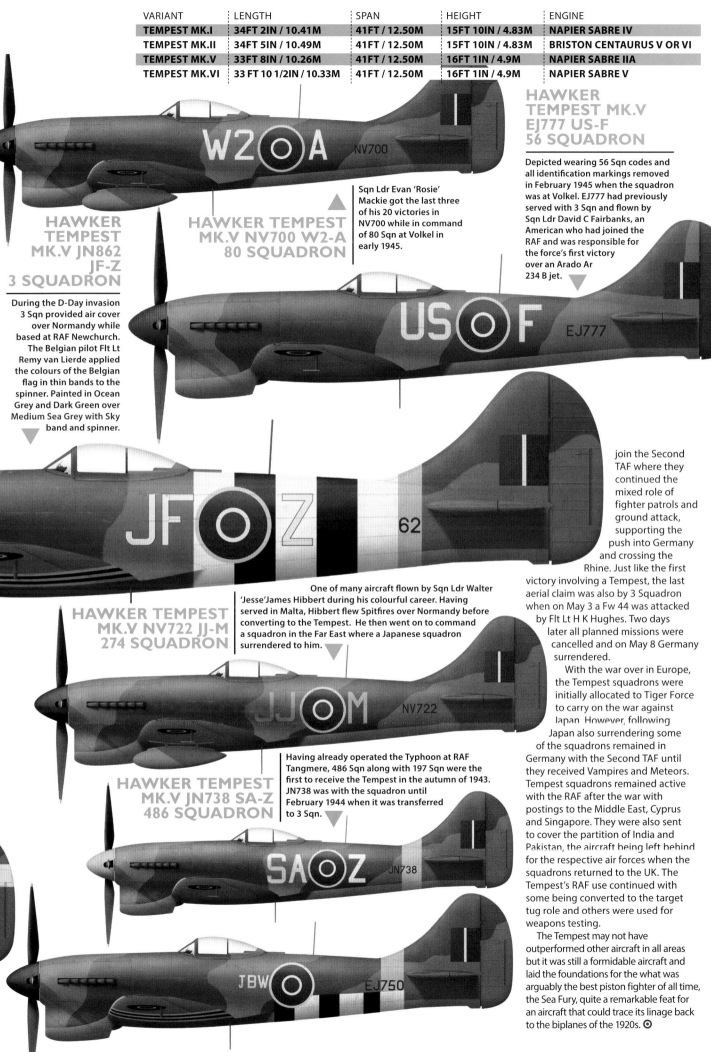

| VARIANT | LENGTH | SPAN | HEIGHT | ENGINE |
|---|---|---|---|---|
| TEMPEST MK.I | 34FT 2IN / 10.41M | 41FT / 12.50M | 15FT 10IN / 4.83M | NAPIER SABRE IV |
| TEMPEST MK.II | 34FT 5IN / 10.49M | 41FT / 12.50M | 15FT 10IN / 4.83M | BRISTON CENTAURUS V OR VI |
| TEMPEST MK.V | 33FT 8IN / 10.26M | 41FT / 12.50M | 16FT 1IN / 4.9M | NAPIER SABRE IIA |
| TEMPEST MK.VI | 33 FT 10 1/2IN / 10.33M | 41FT / 12.50M | 16FT 1IN / 4.9M | NAPIER SABRE V |

## HAWKER TEMPEST MK.V EJ777 US-F 56 SQUADRON

Depicted wearing 56 Sqn codes and all identification markings removed in February 1945 when the squadron was at Volkel. EJ777 had previously served with 3 Sqn and flown by Sqn Ldr David C Fairbanks, an American who had joined the RAF and was responsible for the force's first victory over an Arado Ar 234 B jet.

## HAWKER TEMPEST MK.V JN862 JF-Z 3 SQUADRON

During the D-Day invasion 3 Sqn provided air cover over Normandy while based at RAF Newchurch. The Belgian pilot Flt Lt Remy van Lierde applied the colours of the Belgian flag in thin bands to the spinner. Painted in Ocean Grey and Dark Green over Medium Sea Grey with Sky band and spinner.

Sqn Ldr Evan 'Rosie' Mackie got the last three of his 20 victories in NV700 while in command of 80 Sqn at Volkel in early 1945.

## HAWKER TEMPEST MK.V NV700 W2-A 80 SQUADRON

## HAWKER TEMPEST MK.V NV722 JJ-M 274 SQUADRON

One of many aircraft flown by Sqn Ldr Walter 'Jesse'James Hibbert during his colourful career. Having served in Malta, Hibbert flew Spitfires over Normandy before converting to the Tempest. He then went on to command a squadron in the Far East where a Japanese squadron surrendered to him.

## HAWKER TEMPEST MK.V JN738 SA-Z 486 SQUADRON

Having already operated the Typhoon at RAF Tangmere, 486 Sqn along with 197 Sqn were the first to receive the Tempest in the autumn of 1943. JN738 was with the squadron until February 1944 when it was transferred to 3 Sqn.

join the Second TAF where they continued the mixed role of fighter patrols and ground attack, supporting the push into Germany and crossing the Rhine. Just like the first victory involving a Tempest, the last aerial claim was also by 3 Squadron when on May 3 a Fw 44 was attacked by Flt Lt H K Hughes. Two days later all planned missions were cancelled and on May 8 Germany surrendered.

With the war over in Europe, the Tempest squadrons were initially allocated to Tiger Force to carry on the war against Japan. However, following Japan also surrendering some of the squadrons remained in Germany with the Second TAF until they received Vampires and Meteors. Tempest squadrons remained active with the RAF after the war with postings to the Middle East, Cyprus and Singapore. They were also sent to cover the partition of India and Pakistan, the aircraft being left behind for the respective air forces when the squadrons returned to the UK. The Tempest's RAF use continued with some being converted to the target tug role and others were used for weapons testing.

The Tempest may not have outperformed other aircraft in all areas but it was still a formidable aircraft and laid the foundations for the what was arguably the best piston fighter of all time, the Sea Fury, quite a remarkable feat for an aircraft that could trace its linage back to the biplanes of the 1920s. ◉

# HAWKER
# TEMPEST

TEMPEST MK.V TOP

TEMPEST MK.V

A    B         C         D                    E

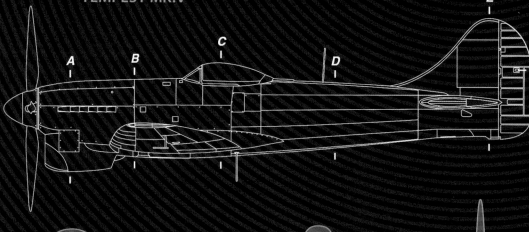

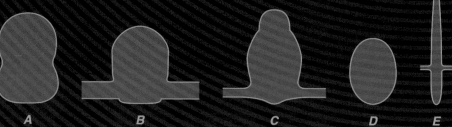

A          B          C          D     E

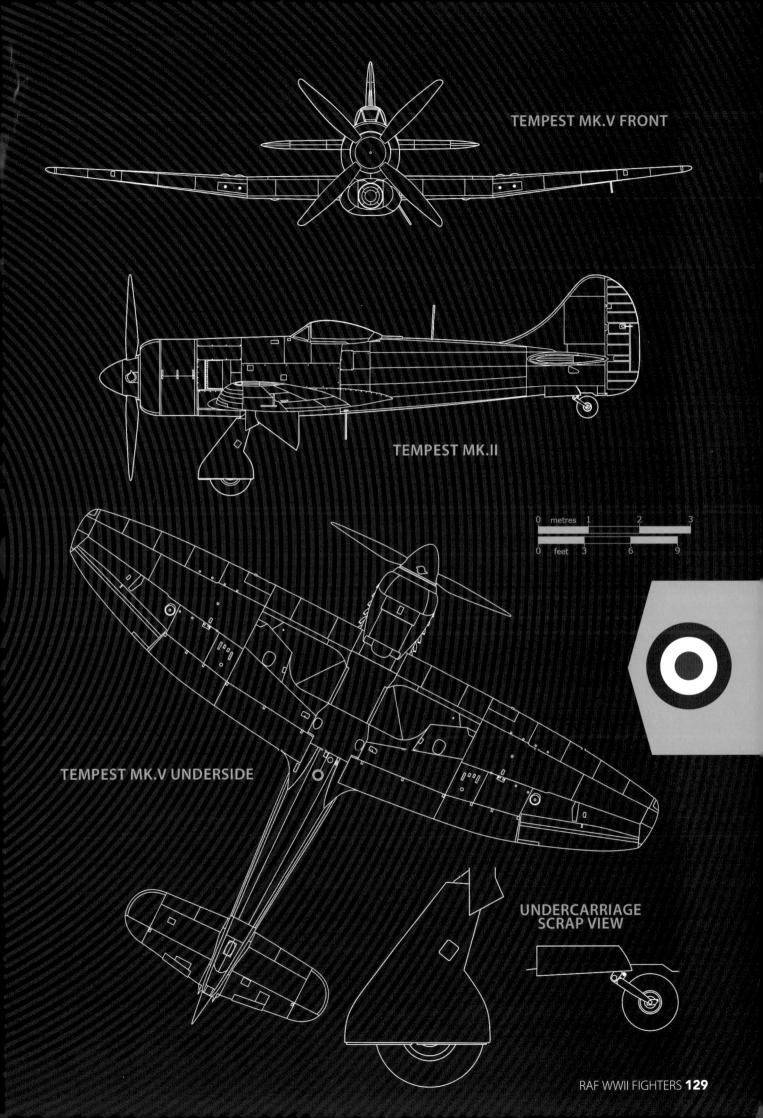

TEMPEST MK.V FRONT

TEMPEST MK.II

TEMPEST MK.V UNDERSIDE

UNDERCARRIAGE
SCRAP VIEW

0 metres 1 2 3
0 feet 3 6 9

# RAF WWII FIGHTERS — COLOUR CHART

| COLOUR | ALUMINIUM | LIGHT STONE | EXTRA DARK SEA GREY | DARK SLATE GREY | AZURE BLUE | YELLOW | WHITE | NIGHT | MEDIUM SEA GREY | MEDIUM STONE | OCEAN GREY | SKY | DARK GREEN | DARK EARTH |
|---|---|---|---|---|---|---|---|---|---|---|---|---|---|---|
| AIRACOBRA | | | | | | | | | • | | • | • | • | • |
| BEAUFIGHTER | | | • | • | | • | | • | • | • | | • | • | • |
| BLENHEIM | | | • | • | • | | • | • | | • | | | • | • |
| DEFIANT | • | | | • | | • | | • | • | • | • | • | • | • |
| GLADIATOR | • | | | | | | | | • | • | • | • | • | • |
| SPITFIRE (G) | | | | | | | | | • | | • | • | • | • |
| HURRICANE | | • | | | • | | | • | • | • | • | • | • | • |
| KITTYHAWK | | | | | • | | | • | • | | | | • | • |
| SPITFIRE (M) | • | | | | | | | • | • | | • | | • | • |
| MOSQUITO | • | | | | | | | | • | • | • | • | • | • |
| MUSTANG | • | | | | | | | | | | • | • | • | |
| TEMPEST | | | | | | | | | | | • | • | • | |
| TOMAHAWK | | | | | • | | • | • | • | • | • | • | • | • |
| TYPHOON | | | | | | | • | | | | • | • | • | |
| WHIRLWIND | • | | | | | | • | • | | | • | • | • | • |